The Politics
of Social Work

The Politics
of Social Work

Fred Powell

SAGE Publications
London • Thousand Oaks • New Delhi

© Fred Powell 2001

First published 2001

SAGE Publications Ltd
6 Bonhill Street
London EC2A 4PU

SAGE Publications Inc
2455 Teller Road
Thousand Oaks, California 91320

SAGE Publications India Pvt Ltd
32, M-Block Market
Greater Kailash - I
New Delhi 110 048

British Library Cataloguing in Publication data

A catalogue record for this book is available from
the British Library

ISBN 0-7619-6411-8
    0-7619-6412-6 (pb)

Library of Congress catalog record available

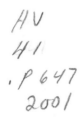

Typeset by SIVA Math Setters, Chennai, India
Printed and bound in Great Britain by
Athenaeum Press, Gateshead

Contents

Introduction

Making sense of the politics of social work is a challenging task. Very strong ideological positions have been taken up, which tend to be unduly reductionist. Much of this debate has focused on the relationship between social work and the state. Radical critics of social work view it as the victim of the totalising influence of the state (Bailey and Brake, 1975; Corrigan and Leonard, 1978; Galper, 1980; Jones, 1983, 1997, 1998). Ironically, many of these Marxist critics of state control in the United Kingdom and other Western countries share common ground with the opponents of Marxist regimes in Eastern Europe. In Eastern Europe, dissidents sought to counterpose the idea of civil society to state tyranny (Gellner, 1994; Powell, 1998). Stubbs (1999: 57) has commented on this apparent anomaly 'in a strange parallel with the UK debate, theories and practices of "civil society" tended also to essentialise the state and fail to distinguish between different kinds of state forms'.

Globalisation has widened intellectual horizons by reframing the old parochial debate about the role of social work in the nation state into an international concern with the state–civil society debate (Lorenz, 1999: 10). As Stubbs (1999: 57) puts it 'in other words, the globalisation of the state–civil society debate, in a world in which nation states and their civil societies no longer exist in a vacuum, is a key piece of the jigsaw missing from much current discussion'. We are undoubtedly part of a 'global society' but it would be naïve to underestimate the complexity, diversity and culturally specific nature of the world which we inhabit. Stubbs (1999: 58) notes in this regard: 'To address these complexities, new frameworks and approaches are needed, going beyond a simplistic treatment of the role of "external" actors on "internal" social processes'.

The social sciences during recent decades have become increasingly preoccupied with meaning and the processes of social construction (Hughes, 1998). This book seeks to investigate what social work 'symbolises' and 'stands for', how it has been represented historically and how it is represented today, its relationship with the welfare state, citizenship and civil society. This will involve a deconstruction of the policies, discourses and practices that have shaped social work. Ultimately the book argues that social work is confronted with three options: (1) marketisation; (2) radical resistance and (3) social inclusion.

It is important to define terms at the outset. The *Oxford English Dictionary* (1989: 912) defines social work as 'work of benefit to those in need of help, especially professional or voluntary service of a specialised nature concerned with community welfare and family or social problems arising mainly from poverty, mental or physical handicap, maladjustment, delinquency etc.' It defines social service as 'service to society or to one's fellow men especially exhibited in work on behalf of the poor, the underprivileged, etc.' While the language may be slightly archaic, the definitions are sound. This book is based upon the assumption that social work has professional, voluntary and community forms. The vision of social work informing the book is of an activity that goes to the core of an ethical civil society. The nationalisation of social work in the post-war welfare state complicates this vision. Moreover, in recent years the transformation of social work through the emergence of quasi-markets in the public sector, complemented by private practice in therapeutic and counselling activities, has added to this complexity.

The framing of social work within the context of the political domain links it directly to the idea of citizenship. Social work in its professional form has traditionally been formulated in the language of clientisation. Brown (1997: 102) has observed: 'Clientisation refers to processes whereby bureaucrats' claims to expertise and control over information and resources places citizens in positions of dependency and need *vis-à-vis* the state'. It is a basic contention of this book that the client, as a citizen, is an actor in making his or her own history. The term 'service user' has been preferred in the text, though it is important to acknowledge at the outset that the service user may often be a victim of social exclusion. In other words the citizenship experienced by the poor and oppressed is of a degraded variety. The political task of social work is to respond to both the reality of exclusion and the underlying injustice. This implies a politics of conscience. Vaclav Havel (1999: 54) commented, on receipt of the First Decade Prize in Poland:

> It has been our absolutely basic historical experience that, in the long run, the only thing that can be truly successful and meaningful politically must first and foremost – that is, before it has taken any political form at all – be a proper and adequate response to the fundamental moral dilemmas of the time, or an expression of respect for the imperatives of the moral order bequeathed to us by our culture. It is a very clear understanding that the only kind of politics that truly makes sense is one that is guided by conscience.

In this statement Havel links the political and the moral, arguing that the social good provides a transcendent purpose:

> I don't say this as a moralist who wishes to preach proper comportment to people and politicians, or to hold himself up to them as an equal. Not at all. I am speaking exclusively as an observer, as one who is convinced that ethical behaviour pays in the long run. To be sure, such behaviour can often lead to suffering, and can't always be expected to deliver immediate and obviously positive results. I don't need to dwell on that here, in a country in which entire generations have shown their willingness to suffer and die for freedom. Ethical behaviour pays not only for the individual, who may suffer but is inwardly free and therefore fortunate, but mainly for society, in which tens and hundreds of lives lived thus can together create what might be called a positive moral environment, a standard, or a continually revitalised moral tradition or heritage, which eventually becomes a force for the general good.

The underlying themes of social work resonate with Havel's moral imperative: concern for the poor and oppressed; the hope for social justice and an enduring belief that human action can create an inclusive society for all citizens.

The book starts out, in Chapter 1, by posing the question 'Postmodernity: the End of Social Work?' The following chapters examine both historic and contemporary paradigms of social work. Three chapters are devoted to historic paradigms. Chapter 2 reviews the Victorian origins of social work in voluntary organisations and active citizenship. Chapter 3 charts the development of reformist practice in the welfare state. Chapter 4 focuses on radical social work. The remaining three chapters examine contemporary paradigms of social work in response to social exclusion (Chapter 5), the renaissance of civil society (Chapter 6) and multiculturalism, feminism and anti-oppressive practice (Chapter 7). The conclusion (Chapter 8) examines the options facing social work in the twenty-first century and argues the case for a civic model of social work based upon the pursuit of social justice in an inclusive society.

I would like to thank the two research officers at the Social Studies Research Unit of Cork, Donal Guerin and Brendan Hennessy, who have worked with me on a series of research projects over the past five years. These projects have embraced civil society, community development and citizens' charters. My work with them has helped inform my vision of contemporary social work and where it may be going in a rapidly changing world. I would also like to thank Norma Griffin for typing the manuscript with great patience and good humour. Finally, I wish to thank my eight-year-old son, Caleb, who has been a wonderful source of inspiration and support.

1

Postmodernity: The End of Social Work?

Critics of the welfare state have identified a structural shift in postmodern society, which has brought the dirigiste Fabian model of social democracy into disfavour. The public no longer perceives social democracy to be self-evidently emancipatory in practice. As Keane (1988: 2), writing in a British context, puts it: 'formerly recognised as the main procedure for limiting the abuse of authoritarian power, democracy becomes an ally of heteronomy, and democratic socialism becomes virtually synonymous with the bureaucratisation of existence within the domains of State and society'. Marsland (1996: xvii) argues from a neo-conservative perspective that welfare reform is an urgent imperative:

> State welfare is causing grave damage in the United Kingdom, in the United States, and elsewhere throughout the free world. It is impeding the dynamism of global economic competition and thus slowing world economic growth. Through bureaucratic centralisation and the underclass dependency, which it mentally creates, it poses a serious long-term threat to liberty and to the stability of democracy.

The emergence of social movements and identity politics, based on race, gender, sexuality, disability and age, has questioned the traditional universalist assumptions of redistributionist social policy, which extolled the civic virtues that created the basis for a moral community. It has also challenged the notion of class as the basis of inequality. It postmodern society the unidimensional nature of traditional social politics has been challenged by identity politics with a particularistic or fractured definition of inequality. This has created a crisis for the welfare state that in turn has generated a crisis for social work. This opening chapter examines the postmodern debate about welfare reform in the age of globalisation and how it has impacted upon social work.

The changing politics of welfare

The post-war world sought to lay the spectres of mass unemployment, hunger and destitution, which had characterised the 1930s, to rest. Keynesianism provided the economic strategy which underpinned the welfare state. The welfare state has been described by the distinguished German social scientist, Claus Offe (1984: 147) as 'the major peace formula of advanced capitalist democracies for the period following the Second World War'. The welfare state not only guaranteed a modicum of social rights, it also offered trade unions influence over policy-making in return for a disciplined and collaborative approach to economic management. This was corporatism (associated in the inter-war years with Fascism) in new democratically acceptable clothing. While the welfare state has been widely perceived as the apotheosis of social democratic values and the realisation of the Fabian socialists' dreams, Marxists have tended to view it as a treacherous arrangement which has tied the poor into the capitalist system, leaving basic social inequalities intact. But even Marxists have had to concede that despite its limitations the welfare state has substantially improved the living standards of the majority. Electorally the reformism of the welfare state has proved highly popular, attracting conservative political parties into a broadly based political consensus which fostered the growth of the welfare state.

Until the emergence of the New Right phenomenon, advocating a return to Victorian social and economic ideas in the mid 1970s, the welfare state enjoyed widespread support across the political spectrum. The New Right in fact consists of two distinctive elements: libertarians and traditionalists. The libertarians are preoccupied with a return to the free market *laissez-faire* conditions of the nineteenth century. The traditionalists on the other hand are concerned about the growth of 'the permissive society' and advocate a return to Victorian social morality. Both are united in their support for capitalism and renunciation of the welfare state. This political viewpoint, so long on the margins of political discourse, quickly entered the mainstream and became the dominant ideological influence in the 1980s. Novak (1988: 179) has concluded that it gave rise to a 'fundamental assault on the expectations and achievements of working people'. Novak's language is perhaps overly apocalyptic. Nonetheless, it is indubitably correct that New Right commentators, such as Gilder (1981), Murray (1984) and Marsland (1995, 1996) have called for the dismantling of social rights and a return to unfettered free enterprise and the Darwinistic principle of self-help.

Ironically, the New Right critique of the welfare state was shared in a number of important respects by leading Marxist theoreticians including Gough (1979) O'Connor (1973) Offe (1984) and Habermas (1989). While there is an element of caution in their predictions, the logic of the Marxist analysis leads inexorably to the conclusion that in the long run the crisis tendencies inherent in the capitalist system (arising from conflicting expectations) will ensure the disintegration of the welfare state. For example, the influential American Marxist, O'Connor (1973), might well have been commenting from a New Right perspective when he made the following observation:

> Every economic and social class group wants government to spend more and more money on more and more things. But no one wants to pay new taxes or higher rates on old taxes. Indeed nearly everyone wants lower taxes.

But while the New Right ultimately favours the abolition of the welfare state, Marxists view it as an essential part of society. Offe has highlighted both the similarity and discontinuities between New Right and Marxist theorists. He has observed, 'the embarrassing secret of the welfare state is that while its impact upon capitalist accumulation may well become destructive (as the conservative analysis so emphatically demonstrates), its abolition would be plainly disruptive (a fact systematically ignored by the conservative critics)'. He concluded: 'the contradiction is that while capitalism cannot coexist with, neither can it exist without, the welfare state' (Offe, 1984: 153).

In reality the pessimistic predictions of the crisis theorists of both the New Right and the Marxist Left have proven premature. The welfare state remains significantly intact despite unremitting attacks by its opponents both in and out of power. A series of international and national studies demonstrated that support for the welfare state remains undiminished (Coughlin, 1980; Taylor Gooby, 1985). What does emerge from these studies is that public support is qualified for certain marginal groups such as the unemployed, recipients of means-tested bene-fits, single parents, asylum seekers, etc. But this has always been the case and points to a fundamental weakness in the welfare state apparatus. The failure of the welfare state has not been to satisfy the expectations of the majority (as the crisis theorists have suggested) but to include the minority 'underclass' in a social order which is predicated upon a fragile balance between collective responsibility and possessive individualism. The 'underclass' represent a poignant reminder that the welfare state has eliminated neither poverty nor inequality: indubitably, the 'underclass' are second class citizens. Yet the welfare state has brought relief from the stagnation and despair of the inter-war years through the promotion of social and economic development.

Nonetheless, there has been a shared consensus between parties of both Left and Right on the need for welfare reform geared towards a new and looser com-pact between the self-reliant individual and an enabling state. The parallels with Victorian social attitudes are unmistakable. In an editorial comment, the *Guardian* on 6 September 1999, observed in relation to the British Prime Minister, Mr Blair, 'Immoral means to him what it did to Octavia Hill in the 1880s: the evils of poor people fornicating'! A new moral economy is being defined in postmodern society.

Postmodernity, globalisation and the shrinking state

As the old certainties propounded by Fabians have disintegrated, new perspectives are emerging. Many of these new perspectives arise in the context of globalisation. But there is also a sense of timelessness in some of the debates about welfare that are rooted in antiquity. Concepts such as civic virtue, civil society and citizenship are all derived from classical civilisation. Yet, in postmodern civilisation classical values have re-emerged with a renewed sense of importance and vigour. This is partly due to the growing sense of fragmentation and social disintegration that postmodernity has engendered.

Globalisation is the defining paradigm of postmodernity. Albrow (1996: 4) observes: 'Fundamentally the Global Age involves the supplanting of modernity with globality and this means an overall change in the basis of action and social organisation for individuals and groups'. He cites five major ways that global-ity has impacted on human life: environment, economy, warfare, economics and reflexivity. Albrow (1996: 5) concludes that 'the total effect is of a social transformation which threatens the nation-state in a more extensive way than anything since the international working-class movement in the nineteenth century'. Similarly, Zygmunt Bauman (1992: 65) has concluded that postmodernity has undermined our conceptual understanding of the nation state. Bauman in a general comment on the transformation that is being experienced by society at the end of the twentieth century, has observed: 'Postmodernity is marked by a view of the human world as irreducibly and irrevocably pluralistic, split into a multitude of sovereign units and sites of authority, with no horizontal or vertical order' (Bauman, 1992: 32). Other commentators have pointed in particular to the impact of this fragmentation on social inequalities and the implications for increased polarisation within postmodern society (Bradley, 1996; Jordan, 1996).

Globalisation has become a major focus of public debate. Professor Anthony Giddens, Director of the London School of Economics, in his 1999 BBC Reith Lecture series, entitled 'Runaway World', made globalisation the 'main theme'. Giddens identified two schools of thought, namely 'radicals' and 'sceptics'. Radicals, according to Giddens (1999: 2), argue:

> that not only is globalisation very real, but that its consequences can be felt everywhere. The global marketplace, they say, is much more developed than two or three decades ago, and is indifferent to national borders. Nations have lost most of the sovereignty they once had, and politicians have lost most of their capability to influence events. It isn't surprising that no one respects political leaders any more, or has much interest in what they have to say. The era of the nation state is over. Nations, as the Japanese business writer Keniche Ohmae puts it, have become mere 'fictions'.

Echoing Albrow and Bauman, Giddens is asserting that a historic shift has taken place in our civilisation, wrought by globalisation.

Sceptics, on the other hand, retort that globalisation is essentially a myth. Politicians do have the power to intervene in the economy, but lack the will. They, as Giddens acknowledges, point to a powerful popular consensus for maintaining the welfare state in place (Giddens, 1999). The sceptics perceive globalisation as a process of Westernisation, or simply Americanisation. Global cosmopolitanism boils down to the icons of American popular culture: Hollywood, Coca-Cola and McDonalds.'

The distinguished French sociologist, Pierre Bourdieu, in his book, *Acts of Resistance*, published in 1998, has challenged postmodernity as one of the 'new myths of our time'. He asserts:

> I have used the word 'globalisation'. It is a myth in the strong sense of the word, a powerful discourse, and *idée force*, an idea which has social force, which obtains belief. It is the main weapon in the battles against the gains of the welfare state. European workers, we are told, must compete with the least favoured workers of the rest of the world. The workers of Europe are thus offered as a model to countries which have no minimum wage, where factory workers work twelve hours a day for a wage which is between a quarter and a fifth of European wages, where there are no trade unions, where there is child labour, and so on and it is in the name of this model that flexible working, another magic word of neo-liberalism, is imposed, meaning night work, weekend work, irregular working hours, things that have always been part of employers' dreams. In a

general way, neo-liberalism is a very smart and very modern repackaging of the oldest ideas of the oldest capitalists. (Bourdieu, 1998: 34)

Bourdieu regards globalisation as a counter-revolution or 'restoration' of pre-socialist society in which politicians have lost their moral courage and social vision, capitulating to the global capitalist order typified by the all-powerful International Monetary Fund (IMF). Globalisation, concludes Bourdieu, is nothing more than a neo-liberal myth that has elevated the economic over the social, copper-fastening inequality as an inevitable part of life. Bourdieu views the state as the bulwark against the global market tyranny and calls for a strengthened European Social State. Bourdieu's critique finds echoes in Mishra's 1999 study *Globalisation and the Welfare State*, which also argues that globalisation is a neo-liberal myth, supported by the United States, world markets, the IMF and the OECD.

Sceptics are undoubtedly right to point to the essential continuity of global capitalism. They cite the *Communist Manifesto*, published in 1848, by Karl Marx and Friedrich Engels, in support of their position (Leonard, 1997: 1). In this seminal revolutionary statement, Marx and Engels saw global capital as the enemy of equality and harmony. In the *Communist Manifesto* they wrote:

> The bourgeoisie cannot exist without constantly revolutionising the instruments of production, and thereby the relations of production, and with them the whole relations of society. Uninterrupted disturbance of all social conditions, everlasting uncertainty and agitation distinguish the bourgeois era from all other ones. All fixed, fast-frozen relations, with their train of ancient and venerable prejudices and opinions, are swept away, all new formed ones become antiquated before they can ossify. All that is solid melts into air, all that is holy is profaned. (Marx, 1994: 161–162)

This powerful piece of writing is deeply prescient of globalisation. In essence the argument running through the *Communist Manifesto* is that the economy and social structure in every historical epoch determine its historical and intellectual debates. The globalisation debate is fundamentally about the reassertion of bourgeois hegemony.

Teeple (1995: 56) argues that there has been an evolution towards a global economy that has allowed markets to expand, but while more interdependent, a system of national capitalism remains in place. He concludes: 'one of the central effects of this intenationalisation of capital has been the shift of key or core economic policies informing government practice in the industrial world from Keynesianism to Monetarism'. Keynesianism promoted the state as the dominant partner in the management of the economy. It has been displaced by a return to the *laissez-faire* economics characteristic of the nineteenth century, widely referred to as 'monetarism', but also known as Reaganomics, Thatcherism or neo-liberalism. This economic liberalisation has produced a powerful political synthesis with authoritarian conservatism, generally referred to as the New Right or neo-conservatism. The social consequences of this economic and political shift in public policy have been catastrophic for the welfare state, because it has undermined the values that underpinned its commitment to distributive justice and social citizenship.

Karl Marx is reported to have observed that 'social reforms are never carried out by the weakness of the strong but always by the strength of the weak' (cited in the *Guardian*, 9 October 1999). The twentieth century allowed organised labour to have a voice in politics. As we enter the new millennium that voice has become much weaker. Postmodernity has witnessed the decline of the organised labour movement and the collapse of the Soviet Union. That has redefined capitalism as a global force, in which humanism has an increasingly precarious position, as the anarchic and antinomian values of the market reassert themselves in every aspect of life. Through a process of delayering and downsizing the working class have become reproletarianised in a project that has dismantled societies' defences against the free market (Gray, 1998).

The global markets that dominate postmodern society evoke the *belle époque* of 1870 to 1914. Whether a similar outcome, of war and revolution, as social and economic tensions increase, is in prospect cannot be predicted. However, it is clear that the social market that supported the welfare state is being undermined by the free market, with its lower social costs. We are witnessing the phenomenon of 'the shrinking state' (Crook et al., 1992: 79–105). Leonard (1997: 1) has observed in this regard: 'throughout western countries, it now seems self-evident that the role of the state as provider of a wide range of public services rooted in the promise of dramatically evening up the life chances of individuals and populations is coming to an end'. He argues that the explanation for this profound change in the role and authority of the state cannot simply be located in the economic sphere. Rather, it is necessary to look at the structure of cultural production, the changing nature of individualism and growing value diversity. This observation raises profound epistemological issues (Leonard, 1997: 1–2).

Postmodernity and social theory

Postmodernity as an analytic construct has transformed the discourse of social science, from an analysis of social structures into a study of social meanings and the way they are represented in cultures. 'Grand Narratives' of human progress, including humanism, Christianity and Marxism, are rejected by postmodernists as foundationalist, essentialist or totalising theory. Influenced by French structuralism, notably the ideas of Derrida, Foucault and Lacan, attention has focused on discourses or social constructs. In this reconstructed world view, Marxism and Fabianism have become outmoded because of their inherent authoritarianism. According to the distinguished German sociologist, Ulrich Beck (1993: 87): 'we increasingly confront the phenomenon of capitalism without classes but with individualised social inequality and all the related social and political problems'. This analysis would appear to suggest the death of collectivism. 'All power to the workers' has been replaced by 'all power to the individual'. However, this may be an illusion. One of the basic problems with postmodern social theory is its 'deconstruction of the subject'. In the postmodernist intellectual project, individual agency is dissolved into social construction. Seligman (1998) suggests that with the decline in individual moral and social agency there is an accompanying decline in trust. Modern individualism dates from the Renaissance and is predicated upon moral self-knowledge. Seligman views waning trust as an episode in the career of the modern subject and concludes that in the postmodern social order personal and social responsibility have been delegitimised. If Seligman's analysis is correct, there is little room left for emancipatory action. Humanism has lost its civilising influence.

Leonard (1997) has rejected this perspective in his book *Postmodern Welfare*, in which he sets himself no less a task than 'reconstructing an emancipatory project'. Utilising critical theory he argues the case for a 'confederation of diversities' (Leonard, 1997: 177). However, Leonard does not underestimate the complexity of the task, in a society where civic trust is challenged by an anarchic and all-pervasive market and a shrinking state. Essentially, the case for welfare ultimately boils down to a recognition of shared human needs and the desire for greater social justice in a more virtuous society.

Traditional values, welfare reform and the workfare state

In recent years political parties, of both the Right and the Left, have begun to grapple with the issue of welfare reform. Much of the focus has been on traditional family responsibility, as opposed to dependence upon state welfare. This 'new consensus' devolves on a belief that something must be done about long-term welfare dependency. The problem for the exponents of welfare reform (as the Blair government in the UK has learned) is that the level of consensus is very limited. In reality this 'new consensus' seems to be predicated on the flimsy structure of acceptance by the Left of the neo-conservative critique of the welfare state – epitomised by the politics of the third way.

Central to the 'new consensus' thinking is the espousal of a belief that it is a mistake to provide welfare benefits without imposing on recipients the obligations that other citizens have to endeavour to become self-sufficient through education, work and responsible family behaviour. In essence, the argument is that government sets the moral climate – properly directed, it can promote a philosophy of self-reliance and moral rectitude for all the citizenry. British Chancellor Gordon Brown's claim that there are many opportunities for the unemployed, which they should take up, even though few are worth having, is a good example of this moral economy of conduct (*Guardian*, 29 February 2000).

Workfare (or welfare to work) is the centrepiece of the 'new consensus'. Governments of both Right and Left have been united in their demand that welfare recipients should be required to work (or to participate in work training placements) as a condition of receiving their welfare entitlements. Much of the attention has focused on single mothers, who were the sole beneficiaries of the main US welfare programme, Aid to Families with Dependent Children (AFDC). Moral crusaders have demanded that young mothers be required to complete their schooling and prepare themselves for the labour market; older mothers (with previous work experience) are expected to find work in rapidly expanding secondary labour markets – notably in the voluntary sector.

A conservative American social theorist, Charles Murray, has been at the centre of this debate about welfare reform. In *Losing Ground*, published in 1984, Murray argued that a new welfare-dependent underclass was being spawned by women who were having children out of wedlock. Murray held the welfare state responsible for this supposed moral decline. Politicians of the conservative Right have seized upon Murray's analysis to traduce the moral basis of the welfare state and attack single parents. There is nothing new in this attack. Two decades ago Keith Joseph, a former Tory Secretary for Social Services, remarked that women from poor backgrounds were breeding the delinquents and denizens of our Borstals of the future (*Guardian*, 9 July 1993). Recently Murray apocalyptically warned that British society is in danger of self-destruction (*Sunday Times*, 13 February 2000). Once again single parents were identified as the main culprits in this British malaise in an age-old argument that seeks to provide a moral basis for damning the poor.

In 1994 the Republicans gained control of the US Congress for the first time in forty years. They issued a ten-point programme that put welfare reform at the centre of the political agenda. It was called *Contract with America*. This manifesto pledged itself to 'end welfare as we know it' (Gingrich, 1994: 65). Welfare beneficiaries, primarily identified as single parents, were to be required to work. No state funds were to be made available to support teenage mothers. Instead, *Contract with America* declared, 'the state will use the funds for programmes to reduce out-of-wedlock pregnancies to promote adoption, to establish and operate children's group homes, to establish and operate residential group homes for unwed mothers, or for any purpose the state deems appropriate' (Gingrich, 1994: 70). These proposals clearly represented a return to the moral economy of the Poor Law.

In August 1996 the Personal Responsibility and Work Opportunity Reconciliation Act abolished Aid to Families with Dependent Children, replacing it with Temporary Assistance to Needy Families (TANF), which contained no entitlement to benefits. The control of welfare was devolved to individual states. Federal funding was to be cut, in order to ensure that welfare rolls were halved by 2002. Teenage mothers were to be prevented from receiving TANF unless they were living at home and attending school. There was little that was new in this programme of welfare reform. Workfare has been practised by a variety of states for over a decade, including California, West Virginia and Wisconsin. What was new was the federal government's decision to sweep away the New Deal at a stroke. This was 'the end of welfare as we know it'.

Britain's welfare to work programme seeks to mimic the United States' welfare reform agenda. The policy to remove benefits from asylum seekers and replace them with vouchers and demeaning pocket money is indicative of policy shift towards stigmatising and impoverishing marginalised communities (*Guardian*, 9 November 1999). Critics of workfare have detected a deep misogynistic purpose. Christine Pratt-Marston, Co-Chair of the US National Anti-Hunger Coalition, has asserted in this regard:

Workfare is a 'stick' instead of a 'carrot' and sticks tend to produce hostility, anger and passive resistance. The person or agency forced to use the stick and the poor person – usually a woman – who is hit with the stick are both in no-win situations. With carrots – education, job training, safe affordable day care and affordable health insurance – sticks would not be necessary and the situation becomes win-win. (*NASW News*, November 1984)

Lemann (1986: 34) has observed that welfare reform 'is a polite way of asking what we do about the black underclass'. The reality is that the welfare reform debate is substantially directed at the lifestyles of excluded minority groups, raising fundamental questions about the ethical basis of caring for people in need.

Ethical questions also arise for the voluntary sector from its participation in workfare programmes. The Canadian Workfare Watch group argues that workfare 'threatens the entire ethic of voluntarism' (*Workfare Watch*, 1996: 1). It explains its reasoning:

> Workfare is one of the most divisive issues ever faced by the voluntary sector. There are numerous issues that the voluntary sector has to consider in relation to workfare. We need to recognise that requiring work outside the home in exchange for social assistance represents a fundamental shift in the nature and purpose of social programs. Workfare moves assistance away from eligibility based on need, towards providing assistance only to those who prove their deservedness through work. (ibid.)

Workfare, as a crusade to promote traditional family values, would seem to challenge the ethical basis of civil society. It evokes the former tyrannies of slavery and coercive poor relief stratagems. As such, workfare is arguably the very negation of the values that it purports to advocate. It seems that postmodern society overlooks the fact that the humanism contained in the universalist principles of the welfare state was only partially accomplished and that the underlying truth it represented was a counterweight to the hollow claim that society is inherently just. Noam Chomsky, the celebrated American social critic, in his rollback theory points towards an explanation that brings together, in a very disturbing critique, both Western and Eastern dimensions of the movement by corporate propagandists to revive the Poor Law as an alternative to state welfare:

> For a long time the purpose was to resist and contain human rights and democracy and the whole welfare state framework, the social contract, that developed over the years. They [neo-conservatives] wanted to contain it and limit it. Now they feel, in the current period, that they can really roll it back. They'd go right back to satanic mills, murdering poor people, basically the social structure of the early nineteenth century. (Chomsky, 1996: 17)

Chomsky may be right: concern with the rollback of the welfare state goes to the core of contemporary *angst* about the future. It raises seminal democratic questions regarding the ethics of removing social citizenship. This is the basis of the rollback strategy that sustains the neo-conservative attack on the welfare state. On the other hand, *Contract with America* (Gingrich, 1994: 125) views the 'roll back of government' as the key to prosperity and modernisation of industry. The price is the end of welfare as entitled citizenship, with social work as a prime target for rationalisation, ideally abolition. Social work as a profession has responded by retreating from its historic mission to support the poor and oppressed rather than confronting the spectre of welfare reform – which is profoundly at odds with the notion of an inclusive democratic society.

Social work, postmodernity and uncertainty

Ife (1997: 92) in a discussion of the implications of postmodernism for social work practice concludes:

> For our present purposes it is sufficient to note that postmodernism fails to incorporate a vision of a better society, or a universal understanding of social justice and human rights. As such an understanding is fundamental to social work, it is clear that post-modernism, while it has important contributions to make to an alternative social work, is not sufficient to form a basis for practice.

Howe (1994: 158) sees social work as the product of modernity, which has shaped its purpose and character: 'in its own way social work has pursued the beautiful (aesthetics), the good (ethics) and the true (science) as it attempts to bring about a pleasing quality of life and a just society by using the insights of the social services'. Postmodernity has accordingly shattered the basis of social work, which was informed by the Fabian verities of care, control and cure, that provided its coordinates within the welfare state. Outside 'the shell institution' of the welfare state, social work has had to wrestle with the postmodern reality of uncertainty, fragmentation and polarisation. This scenario promises a very bleak future.

Specht and Courtney (1994) in *Unfaithful Angels*, suggest that social work has abandoned its historic mission to the poor and oppressed for the pursuit of thera-peutic individualism, private practice, autonomy from bureaucratic welfare agen-cies, and augmented status and income. In similar vein, Hardcastle et al. (1997: 9) observe: 'the problem is not so much that individual social workers have aban-doned the traditional mission of the profession and, in a sense, the profession, but rather that the profession itself has abandoned its historic mission, the com-munity, and the community's most needy and vulnerable citizens'. They argue that the National Association of Social Work (NASW), in the United States, has over the past two decades refocused its political lobbying away from promoting social legislation and towards professional recognition issues and state approval of payment for private practice for therapists. Many of these therapies 'lack any scientific basis; instead, social workers embrace faddish interventions resting on spiritualism and mysticism' (Hardcastle et al., 1997: 8–9). According to this cri-tique the profession is removing the 'social' from 'social work' in favour of the entrepreneurial path of therapeutic individualism. In allowing the market to deter-mine the agenda, 'social work forsakes its claim to professionalism' (Hardcastle et al., 1997: 9).

While the United States has diverged from Europe and most of the rest of the English speaking world in the minimalist nature of its welfare state, in an age of global capitalism it may be setting the trend. If social work is breaking its links with the welfare state in favour of the market this certainty represents a paradigm shift. In Britain this shift towards market values is manifesting itself in the emer-gence of consumerism and privatisation in the delivery of personal social services. Consumerism has become a key paradigm in welfare reform, reflexively restructuring the welfare state and the social work role and task in the shape of the economic rationality favoured by the market. Humanisim and democratic values have no place in this scheme of things.

For Bourdieu, the state, encompassing its social programmes and professionals (e.g. teachers, social workers, nurses), is being marginalised by government – including socialist governments. He observes:

> I think that the left hand of the state has the sense that the right hand no longer knows, or, worse, no longer really wants to know what the left hand does. In any case, it does not want to pay for it. One of the main reasons for all these people's despair is that the state has withdrawn, or is withdrawing, from a number of sectors of social life for which it was previously responsible.... All that is somewhat shocking, especially for those who are sent into the front line to perform so called 'social work' to compensate for those flagrant inadequacies of the logic of the market, without being given the means to really do their job. How could they not have the sense of being constantly undermined or betrayed? (Bourdieu, 1998: 2–3)

In Bourdieu's estimation, professionals are caught in a web of contradiction that requires them to respond to 'social suffering' without the means and without the support of the state. This makes the reality of front-line practice a painful one.

Postmodernity, society and individualism

We live in a society defined by risk, polarisation, global markets, chronic change and fragmentation. As Stokes and Knight (1997) note, 'today we seem to be plunging into a chaotic, privatised future, recapturing medieval extremes of wealth and squalor'. Postmodernism has drained the meaning from social life. It appears to celebrate the fragmentation of society. There is a flatness in its vision that promotes meaninglessness over purpose.

According to postmodern theorists, including Anthony Giddens and Ulrich Beck, our lives are no longer governed by nature or tradition. Instead there is a socio-symbolic order (what Lacan calls the 'Big Other' – a kind of superego diffused throughout society) that regulates human behaviour in the postmodern world. Reflexivity 'colonises' the everyday aspects of lifestyle (including child care, parenting, diet and leisure) which are habits to be learned and changed as the fashion of the time requires. Even the 'social' is now reflexively constructed. In vulgarised terms the postmodernist version of reflexive society is that it is 'whatever we tell ourselves it is'. This gives us a sense of 'choice' over our lifestyles and identities, since we 'are' ultimately whoever we choose to 'be' – the products of our own narrative imagination.

On the face of it, our civilisation is both atomised and fractured. Yet there is a paradox that confounds such conclusions. While the self, in the form of the independent citizen, may have become sovereign in the choice of lifestyles, solidarity is maintained by recognition-based social relations such as love, friendship, trust, empathy and compassion, charity, altruism and mutualism and the willingness to make sacrifices for others. In short, as Berking observes, 'these are cognitive, normative and emotional competencies which anything but reduce interest in the other to the mode of a merely strategic interaction' (Berking, 1996: 192).

Love and friendship clearly belong to the private sphere. Charity, altruism and mutualism exist in the space between government and market occupied by 'the voluntary or third sector', which is increasingly referred to as civil society. These virtues point towards the existence of active citizenship in the form of participation and dutiful citizenship in the form of obligation towards others. Trust, empathy and compassion are the common elements that transcend utilitarian individualism and define social solidarity. This is the essential contradiction of contemporary Western society that provides the basis for civic trust in an increasingly fragmented and polarised social order.

Berking has noted that 'the triumphant advance of utilitarian values, which now seem to oblige the individual to secure and augment his own advantage, is today described under the heading detraditionalisation and individualisation, above all the cumulative effect of the process of cultural modernisation' (Berking, 1996: 191). The assumption that the modern individual is less committed to society than his/her traditional counterpart is doubtful. Carmen argues that the reverse is the case:

> Traditional society is essentially non-participant. It deploys people by kinship into communities isolated from each other and from the centre. Modernity, on the other hand, is essentially a mode of communication and participation. What makes communication possible, the sociological pivot upon which hinges that activisation of psychic mobility, is the acquisition of literacy. An increase in literacy and therefore an increase in the capacity to empathise is the very yeast which permeates the system of self-sustaining growth and mass consumption. This is the ne plus ultra of modernity and by implication of development.... Empathy is the bridge which makes transition from the traditional to the modern way feasible. (Carmen, 1990: 4)

Other commentators who have sought to examine the nature and quality of trust and its connection with co-operation and prosperity have also discovered a positive correlation between modernisation and civil society (Fukuyama, 1995; Putnam, 1993). Fukuyama found higher levels of trust in developed societies compared with less developed societies such as Latin Catholic countries and China, which he concluded were low-trust societies. Similarly, in Italy Putnam found higher levels of civic trust in the more developed northern region, 'Padania', than in the less developed South. We must, therefore, conclude that, despite its tendencies towards fragmentation and polarisation, postmodernity has engendered social participation and more sophisticated forms of communication between people that promote empathy and trust. This is the paradox of contemporary civilisation.

On the face of it, this is a two-world theory of an economic world defined by utilitarian values and a social world defined by solidaristic values. However, Fukuyama (1995) and Putnam (1993) contend in their theses on trust and solidaristic values in the social sphere that these are positively correlated with the creation of prosperity in the economic sphere. In reality they claim to have discovered a civilisational configuration between altruism and self-interest. However, it should be noted that the three fastest growing post-war economies were Japan, France and Italy – one high-trust and two low-trust societies by Fukuyama's reckoning. A more realistic assessment of Fukuyama's and Putnam's position is that it represents a reconfiguration of 'the social' in an era when neo-conservatism and global capitalism have become dominant and 'the social' increasingly privatised. Their use of 'social capital' as a term to describe a trusting social order encapsulates their realignment of social solidarity with capitalism. This is clearly a post-socialist analysis.

For neo-conservatives there is no society, only individual enterprise and self-reliance. Hayek has contended that 'the social' is merely 'something which has developed as a practice of individual action in the course of social evolution' (Hayek, 1976: 78). For Hayek, 'the social' was an abhorrent concept that conjured up images of totalitarianism. In *The Mirage of Social Justice* (1976) he equates the pursuit of equality with tyranny. Neo-conservative social theorists have challenged the normative basis of social solidarity, which they view as creating a dependent underclass (Gilder, 1981; Murray, 1984; Marsland, 1995, 1996). Marsland (1995: 4) likened welfare to a 'cancer in the body politic' and added that 'it has also spread its contagion through more and more organs of society'. He concluded that 'only markets can provide effectively for the range and ambition of human wants and needs' (Marsland, 1996: 140).

Neo-conservative politicians have taken the debate into the public arena. They have attacked social solidarity as the embodiment of socialism. In their zealous efforts to destroy socialism, they have sought to deny the existence of 'the social'. In Margaret Thatcher's famous aphorism, 'there is no such thing as society' (*Sunday Times*, 9 November 1988). Thatcher went on to elaborate her ideas in a controversial speech to the Assembly of the Church of Scotland, in which she asserted that it was, above all, within the family that 'the nursery of civic virtue' lay. She contended that the family was the basis on which governments ought to construct their policies for 'welfare, education and care' (Thatcher, cited in Squires, 1990: 5). Neo-conservatism has, therefore, sought to write the obituary of 'the social' and looked backwards nostalgically to Tocquevillean visions of smaller units of social responsibility, notably the family and the community. The denial of 'the social' is, consequently, not a denial of social responsibility. It simply means that the social rights of the entitled citizen of the welfare state are replaced by the social obligations of the dutiful citizen in a reconstituted order where the market replaces society as the arbiter of moral values. The problem with the neo-conservative position is that the market is anarchic and antinomian (i.e. it rejects socially established morality).

Teeple (1995: 150–151) characterised the much-vaunted triumph of neo-conservatism and the global market as the coming tyranny, observing that:

> Capitalism must increasingly confront the world that it has made, the results of its own expansion: seriously degraded nature, an increasingly impoverished working class, growing political autocracy and declining legitimacy, and new forms of resistance.... Here, largely unfettered by political considerations, is a tyranny unfolding – an economic regime of unaccountable rules, a totalitarianism not of the political but of the economic.

Other commentators have taken a more optimistic view, detecting a new complexity in which a more democratic citizenship can emerge. Walzer (1983) suggested a break with the old normative idealism embodied in collectivist and universal notions of 'the social' and advocated new thinking around pluralist frameworks of complex equality that involves taking democratic rights beyond traditional conceptions of citizenship.

Behind Walzer's vision is the assumption that culture and society shape the nature of government. This is true to a degree. It is essential to the Tocquevillean vision of the crucial role of intermediate institutions as the generative force in society. However, an older tradition of thought, stretching from Aristotle through Montesquieu to Marx, suggests that fundamentally the state shapes society, not the other way round. If we accept this view we are thinking not about civil society in the all-embracing sense envisaged by De Tocqueville, but about the Roman virtue of *civitas*, i.e. public spiritedness, sacrifice for the community and, of course, active citizenship. This sounds very much like the *raison d'être* of social work. The evidence suggests that social work is striving hard to maintain its sense of *civitas* in postmodern society. However, it is being delegitimised in a manner that undermines its authority.

The end of social work?

Postmodernity has had a profound impact on social work, which has been transformed by the neo-liberal critique into a symbol of an overweening welfare state. Social work's regulatory power mechanisms have become reflexively categorised as 'authoritarian' although this perceived 'authoritarianism' emerges as an attempt to regulate behaviour considered 'illicit' by the predominant socio-symbolic order, e.g. child abuse. This reflexivity undermines the public view of the postmodern social worker, because the mode of symbolic authority, upon which the legitimacy of the profession rests, has been culturally rejected. Ironically, the postmodern social order employs similar modes of symbolic authority to regulate vast areas of human behaviour, notably restrictions on lifestyle: smoking, eating, sexuality, etc. Yet postmodern society, immersed in consumer values, celebrates 'choice' as the guiding influence over symbolic law. Social work, in this postmodern civilisational configuration, is perceived as the antithesis of 'choice', since it is part of the apparatus of the enforcement state – Lacan's 'Big Other'.

In the United States many social workers find themselves implementing workfare programmes forcing the poor to work or starve. Critics call it 'slavefare'. Social workers are involved not only in counselling, but in training and ultimately in ensuring that the poor find work. This transformed regime has turned the welfare system into a New Poor Law. It is difficult to see how social work values can accommodate to this new reality, since it turns the clock back to the Gradgrind regime of Victorian society. The four traditional cornerstones of social work – indignation, inquiry, compassion and caring – have little place in this moral landscape (Saleeby, 1990: 37).

Marsland (1996: 188) has concluded that 'in a reformed [welfare] system we would be better not to use social work as such at all'. He advocates the replacement of social workers by less trained front-line welfare workers. However, Marsland does allow for 'highly trained specialist' social workers. But, he adds, their training (as of social workers in the mainstream sector) would need to be transformed as radically as the communist systems of training for teachers in the former German Democratic Republic and Czechoslovakia. There would be a decisive shift away from the current emphasis on 'rights' to education in practical skills required to help people help themselves and to inculcation of values appropriate to a free society. (ibid.)

Marsland applauds moves towards an emphasis on 'competencies' in training as opposed to 'anti-democratic commitment to liberating ... clients from oppression', which he views as 'a major achievement of genuine welfare' (ibid.).

Brewer and Lait (1980: 188) is similar critical vein conclude: 'without major and painful changes, social work may well have to struggle not merely for funds but for its survival'. These are essentially New Right perspectives, but there is also a deep concern on the political Left.

Ife (1997: x) has observed:

Living with contradictions and having to make difficult moral choices is nothing new for social workers, but the political context of economic rationalism and the organisational context of managerialism have made the job much more difficult and have forced social workers to make reassessments of where they stand, and the nature of the social work task.

In human terms, Ife (1997: 2) pessimistically concludes,

For many, social work has ceased to be professionally rewarding and has become a simple matter of survival. Many social workers report increasing levels of stress, burn out is not uncommon and morale in many social agencies seems to be extremely low.

The *Guardian*, on 9 February 2000 reported a growing shortage of social workers in Britain:

In 1999/2000 the free fall continues while job vacancies in social work increase and there are real fears about ensuring that children are protected and the needs of an ageing population are adequately met.

Arguably, three basic factors can be identified that challenge the integrity of the social work task, leading to both professional and personal disempowerment and a sharp decline in people entering and staying in the profession because the value of public service has been undermined.

First, the crisis in the welfare state, which is being undermined by a resurgent market, makes it difficult for humanist social policies and professions to survive. Essentially, the idea of welfare is being delegitimised by market values that are deeply opposed to humanistic social values. Economic rationalism, which is epitomised by Thatcherism and Reagonomics, but accepted by Clintonism in America, New Labour in the United Kingdom and most European social democrats, insists that good public policy is policy that makes sense in market terms and that a healthy economy advantages everybody. In reality, a redistribution of wealth is going on but there seems to be a 'trickle-up' rather than a 'trickle-down' effect. Innumerable political scandals in many countries have underlined the moral consequences of unregulated markets and the political consequences for politicians that get too close to business, that is, the emergence of the sleaze factor. Public opinion is outraged; public servants (like social workers) who subscribe to a humanistic value orientation have become deeply demoralised. But the inexorable logic of free market capitalism remains unchecked and is likely to remain so while the global economy continues to boom.

Second, marketisation has led to the emergence of quasi-markets in the public sector. This has given rise to the so-called 'new managerialism', which believes that good management can solve all problems and will make the public services more efficient and effective. The 'new managerialism' has created many new positions for social workers. Undeniably, a welcome career structure has opened up for the social work profession. The downside is that the trend towards managerialism has been accompanied by a devaluation of the traditional professional role of social workers in the public sector. Some social workers are seeking alternative futures in the voluntary sector, where humanistic values find a more congenial and respectful environment. This shift to the voluntary sector is being exacerbated by constant reorganisation within the public sector as the latest 'management fix' predictably fails 'to deliver the goods'. The problem is that human beings cannot be equated with 'goods'. The consequence for social workers of constant restructuring and organisational 'development' is the creation of an environment of permanent uncertainty and insecurity. This chronic instability saps professionals' morale. The impact on clients is rarely considered since management is governed by top-down administrative rationality rather than bottom-up democratic accountability.

White (1999: 116) has noted that the 'new managerialism' is based upon three interlocking strategies of control:

1 decentralising operational units while achieving a greater degree of centralised control over strategy and policy;
2 establishing the principle of managed competition;
3 developing processes of performance management and monitoring (audits, inspections, quality assessments, reviews), largely directed towards operationally decentralised units.

In Britain these three strategic controls have impacted upon social work through the National Health Service and Community Care Act, 1990, and the Children Act, 1989, though in the case of the latter, managed competition is minimal. Nevertheless, there is an emerging debate about the privatisation of child care services.

The power of central management has been increased at the expense of professionalism through labour market flexibility that has created a 'contract culture' of temporary and part-time jobs. Mullander and Perrot (1998: 70) record that part-time employment in the general social services grew by 50 per cent between 1988 and 1992, 'with women predominating at the flexible fringe'.

The community care reforms of the 1990s, with their emphasis on 'enabling authority' and 'the mixed economy of care', also impacted on the voluntary sector, which 'in many instances is being asked to become an alternative rather than supplementary or complementary providers' (Lewis, 1996: 108). Increasingly, funding-driven agendas influence policy and practice. Moreover, some professionals in the voluntary sector find themselves being transformed from practitioners to administrators managing a contract with the state. Because of the 'professional' standards demanded by a contract, volunteers are sometimes faced with a stark choice to train as professionals or retire (Billis and Harris, 1996). In other instances, non-traditional organisations come under pressure to conform to the organisational and efficiency standards of the 'new managerialism' of the public sector. According to Mullender and Perrot (1998: 71): 'on a wider scale, voluntary agencies fear that competing for contracts to sustain their funding base will distance them from their pioneering roots and reduce their capacity for advocacy'. Essentially, the pragmatism of the managerialist ethos poses a major threat to both the humanism of professional social work and the full independence and integrity of the voluntary and community sector. It is difficult to view such developments as other than a deeply destructive fact of life that creates a hostile environment for practice.

The third factor that challenges integrity is the emphasis on economic and administrative rationality, which has resulted in a demand for a competency-led approach to training. The competency movement (as witnessed in the United Kingdom) is guided by the logic that occupational roles should be defined according to the competencies required to perform them and should embody transferable skills. Both the Manpower Services Commission and the Training Agency have sought to make the UK labour force more efficient through a drive towards competency-based training. The Central Council for Education and Training in Social Work has also adopted a competency-based approach (CCETSW, 1989, 1995).

The intention of the competency movements is to break the power of professional monopolies and promote labour market flexibility. The recruitment of social care managers represents a move towards a competency-led labour force. On the positive side a competency-led labour market opens up wider employment horizons to social workers and promotes choice and opportunity for many public servants. It also promotes professional diversity. However, it leads to a very technically based view of training and arguably a 'dumbing down' of academic standards. Social work education has always been defined as a combination of humanistic knowledge, values and skills. Moreover, a competency-based approach to training is likely to increase managerial power at the expense of professional power. At a more fundamental level, the competency movement can be perceived as a threat to the core identity and future integrity of social work as a professional activity, since it incorporates a basic objective of professional 'flexibility' in the light of labour market rationality. Flexibility means performing whatever task an employer assigns regardless of professionalism. Competence occurs in a political context, which is intended to have political consequences (Evans, 1997: 356). One such consequence would seem to be the deradicalisation of social work by the definition of its ethos in terms of pragmatism rather than humanism.

Undoubtedly in postmodern culture, the welfare crisis, burgeoning managerialism and a shift towards competency-based training are radically changing social work. There are advantages in efficiency and financial terms arising from this rationalisation of the personal social services, but, equally, rational systems have a tendency to dehumanise and be inhuman in practice: what Max Weber called the 'iron cage' of bureaucracy. Postmodernity with its market orientation seems to be weaving a seamless web of rationality, marginalising the human in favour of the pragmatic. George Ritzer has caricatured this process in *The McDonaldization of Society* (1993), which argues that we may be witnessing the McDonaldisation of the welfare state. The consequences for social work are potentially devastating. Ife (1997: 24) has commented: 'Many of the ideological and organisational foundations of social work practice, as traditionally under-stood, seem to be crumbling, and it is not clear whether what will take their place will be able to support the social work profession in anything like its present form'. Indeed it is legitimate to ask whether the social work profession can survive. And what of its clients?

The McDonaldisation of the welfare state aims to turn the client into a consumer and welfare into a product. Hughes et al. (1988: 158) view this reinvention of the public sphere as an inevitable outcome of the neo-liberal discourse on consumerism. On the positive side the client consumer theoretically is better placed to choose rather than be dictated to by bureaucrats and professionals. New representational spaces may be opened up, giving clients a right to challenge 'Daddy knows best' elitism. But on the downside the idea of consumer narrows the concept of the public sphere to individualised users of services. Clients of social work services are likely to be vulnerable people, already highly disempowered, and the symbolic 'dismantling of collective notions of the public' is likely to leave them even more vulnerable and unsupported. In reality, what has emerged is not a system characterised by choice and diversity but one dominated by rationality and hierarchy. This has wrought a transformation in social work that undermines its humanistic value base. The emphasis on competencies leads to checklist practice so that managerial imperatives are met. Ife (1997: 78–80) calls 'hierarchical practice' and concludes that it is simply a strategy to provide managers with more power and control. Does this represent the eclipse of professional social work?

Giarchi and Lankshear (1988: 25) suggest that social work is in eclipse in Europe as a professional activity:

> For the past fifty years social work has aspired to the status of a profession. In both the UK and mainland Europe that status has been questioned. Since the advent of post-modernity the identity of social workers has been eroded within a plural social care complex.

They go on to say that (with the possible exception of Denmark) across Europe voluntary and health care agencies are displacing social work in the provision of care services. Their essential argument is that the core professional task of social work is being fragmented 'by pluralism in a postmodern Europe, when deconstructive forces have altered the shape of the Europspace, social care structures and introduced a reconstructed panoply of alternative services' (1988: 26). They conclude that social work, having lacked professional definition (e.g. 'social worker' or 'social pedagogue', 'youth and/or community worker', 'specialist educator'), is fragmenting in the hostile environment of the 'contracting state' that characterises postmodern welfare.

Similar pessimism and uncertainty exists in the United States. Raffoul (1996: 293) in a review of the future of American social work concludes that it 'portends to be grim' and poses the question, 'Is there a future?' He observes that if the next President of the United States is 'a staunch conservative with limited budget for social welfare and entitlement programs, the question may be moot'. Under the presidency of George W. Bush, American social work faces the same challenges as its European counterpart.

Clarke (1996: 36–60) has cast doubt on whether there ever was 'a social work'. This is an important observation in the sense that social work compared to older professions, such as medicine, law and divinity, does not have professional roots in classical and medieval civilisation but is very much a product of the mass cultural needs of modern society. The reconceptualisation of 'the social' in postmodern society and the reconstruction of the post-war welfare settlement (which during the twentieth century gave social work both its *raison d'être* and legitimacy) have decentred social work. Raffoul (1996: 294) argues that social work must hold on to its historic commitment to social justice, equality and social change despite these changes, since it has no alternative *raison d'être*.

Monediaire (1998) writing in the context of the French experience identifies a loss of status due to an inability to define a coherent professional mission and a failure to influence the public policy process. He concludes: 'In short, through all the changes of the last twenty years, social workers have not seemed capable of defining professional strategies, making themselves heard by the decision-makers or taking general measures to expose problems or propose solutions, as their professional position would have normally destined them to' (Monediaire, 1998: 20).

Monediaire argues that both the theoretical and technical paradigms that have dominated social work discourse during the past twenty years have failed: 'The hypothesis is not exactly pleasant: considering the discrepancy between the dynamics of the global system and the means offered and held by social workers, their mission of seriously reducing contemporary poverty seems impossible (Monediaire, 1998: 20). Instead, of this 'Sisyphean task', Monediaire suggests a new paradigm: the adoption of the contemporary concept of 'sustainable development' based upon the discourse of international human rights conventions and national social rights and citizenship modalities. He sees this as a strategy of 'global social prevention'.

The implications of Monediaire's analysis are radical, involving a fundamental change in professional culture, an opening of minds towards other professional cultures and processes of reasoning, and a thoroughgoing reform of professional training and education. The rationale that informs Monediaire's critique points towards more highly trained social workers becoming involved in the policy-making process, and community development, abandoning social care 'to poorly qualified people such as "family helpers", "environmental agents", "lay brothers"' (Monediaire, 1998: 21).

Given social work's historic diversity and eclecticism, it is unlikely that Monediaire's proposition will find favour, even if it were desirable – which is doubtful. It is more likely that social work will fragment into multiple forms in postmodern society (i.e. hierarchical statutory practice, private practice focused on therapy and community practice in civil society) where the market dictates an ever changing reality and the Poor Law has made a return. Neo-liberals view the professions as self-seeking, employing restrictive practices to maintain their power and prestige. They advocate that service users and clients should be regarded as customers in quasi-markets, administered by managers. They also believe that, in some cases, professions should be abolished (Burden, 1998: 120–121). Social work is a prime candidate for professional abolition. Its close identification with the reformist Fabian tradition of the welfare state makes it anathema to the New Right in particular. Abolitionists are likely to seek to remove its statutory mandate. The emergence of competencies has already opened the way to this development. The downgrading of the professionalism of statutory social work is an inevitable concomitant of the gravitational pull towards the market. The professional challenge to social work posed by postmodernity is, therefore, a considerable one. It remains to be seen whether the profession is in eclipse or metamorphosis.

The highly respected theorist of postmodernity, Zygmunt Bauman, in a paper given at the 100th anniversary of the Amsterdam School of Social Work, commented on the future of social work. Observing that the impact of market values has transformed the social work landscape, Bauman (2000: 5) asserts:

> As social work, we are told, ought to be judged like any other human action by its cost and effects balance sheet, it does not, in its present form 'make economic sense'. It could only justify its continued existence if it made dependent people independent and made lame people walk on their own feet.

Clearly, the achievement of the miraculous is beyond the powers of social work. However, its moral purpose may be its defining rationality. As Bauman puts it: 'the uncertainty which haunts social work is nothing more nor nothing less than the uncertainty endemic to moral responsibility'. He concludes:

> The future of social work and, more generally, of the welfare state, does not depend on classifications, on procedures, nor on reducing the variety and complexity of human needs and problems. It depends, instead, on the ethical standards of the society we all inhabit. It is those ethical standards which, much more than the rationality and diligence of social workers, are today in crisis and under threat. (2000: 10–11)

Social work exists in a cold climate dominated by the resurgence of the market and the hollowing out of the welfare state. But its ethical imperative and moral purpose have become more urgent than ever. However, it is essential to acknowledge its changed circumstances and the impact of postmodernity on its historic mission. The old paradigms that defined the role and task of social work are in doubt, if not in eclipse, but new paradigms are emerging that challenge social work to adapt or perish in the face of the deconstructive forces of the market.

Conclusion

This chapter has sought to examine the impact of postmodernity on social work. Globalisation was introduced as the defining paradigm of postmodernity. Arguments posed by sceptics that globalisation is little more than the global capitalism analysed by Marx over 150 years ago were discussed and the rise of the New Right reviewed. Undoubtedly a paradigm shift is taking place, but whether it should be viewed in the positive futuristic terms that Giddens suggests is open to doubt. The welfare state, and the humanistic values that support it, are under powerful ideological attack. The institutions of the welfare state are being redesigned in the image of the market. A new managerialism has brought the rationality of corporate capitalism to bear on social services. It has created unbearable strains for social workers as their professionalism is reshaped in the form of hierarchical practice. The 'contract culture' is also percolating out to the voluntary sector, as a reinvented public sphere transforms every aspect of human life in the language of the market. In this transformed landscape, the 'client' has been turned into a consumer without regard to the vulnerability of that status. There are powerful resonances of the nineteenth century when social work emerged in Victorian society. But there are also equally powerful signs of a shift towards a more democratic open society based upon a renewed interest in citizenship, participation and empowerment. Social work's future will very much depend on how it responds to these new forces, which offer challenging new paradigms for practice. However, first we must look at the old paradigms, which constitute the foundation upon which social work was built in the nineteenth century and flourished in the twentieth.

2

Victorian Origins, Active Citizenship and Voluntarism

The origins of social work are in voluntary action in Victorian society. This was a period of burgeoning capitalism. There was a voluntary-statutory relationship in which the state provided the deterrent Poor Law for the 'undeserving' poor, who were perceived as being beyond help. On the other hand, local voluntary organisations sought to remoralise the 'deserving' poor in order to make them more self-reliant. In this moral economy of desert, Social Darwinism (i.e. the survival of the fittest) provided the guiding eugenicist inspiration: those regarded as socially and economically useless were 'undeserving' by definition. Many volunteers questioned the ethical basis of this social and moral order. This was the period when, according to Lewis (1999: 258), the first major epoch in the voluntary-statutory relationship occurred. While many voluntary organisations viewed their task as complementary to the state, social workers took a different view. They perceived the historic task of social work in terms of helping the poor and emancipating them from oppression through social reform. In this chapter, the conceptual and historical basis of social work is analysed in the context of its formation in nineteenth- and early twentieth-century civil society. It was an immensely complex period in the evolution of social policy (Harris, 1993). Here the role of both the state and civil society is explored in the context of nascent social policy and the emergence of 'manufactured risk' associated with urban life.

Historic mission: doing good versus being good

Social work represents a reaction to the prim Victorian faith in 'being good' characterised by the virtues of self-reliance and thrift. Samuel Smiles's *Self-Help*, published in 1859, epitomised the ethos of the times, enshrining the moral code of the dominant middle class in society and ensuring that firm limits were set against state intervention. Active citizenship in social work and social reform represented twin strands of civic engagement, directed against Victorian moral hypocrisy and social indifference. Beatrice Webb, the voice of British Fabian social reformism, also spoke for social work when she wrote in her diary in 1884: 'Social questions are the vital questions of to-day: they have taken the place of religion' (cited in Skidelsky, 1999: 13). Another founding figure of the Fabian

Society, the Irish playwright George Bernard Shaw, wrote in his play *You Never Can Tell* (1899) 'Let me tell you, Mr. Valentine, that a life devoted to the cause of humanity has enthusiasms and passions to offer which far transcend the selfish personal infatuations and sentimentalities' (cited in Skidelsky, 1999: 12). Social reformers and voluntary organisations shared a common commitment to active citizenship through the promotion of a vibrant civil society. However, social reformers went a step further by insisting upon the need to change the role of the state in the interests of the welfare of the population as a whole. For them, a healthy public domain involved an active state as well as active citizenship.

While the reformists sought to pursue collectivist solutions, by advocating statutory responsibility for the socially marginalised, voluntary organisations endeavoured to address the plight of individuals and families experiencing poverty. Both shared a rejection of the 'ruling ideas' of the time to the extent that they sought to counterpose 'the social question' against *laissez-faire* ideology, challenging the prevailing individualist orthodoxy of political economy. Political economists rejected the concept of 'society' and the need for state intervention outside the deterrent Poor Law system. This was the discursive challenge that both social work and social reform faced.

The emergence of active citizenship in the arena of philanthropy needs to be set in the social context of the Victorian world. The urbanisation that charac-terised the emergence of capitalism in the modern world had created a social gulf between classes in the major cities. It was believed that the traditional hierarchies and social bonds of rural life had been fundamentally undermined, creating a social crisis. There was also a profound sense of political crisis, as the spectre of social revolution haunted Europe between the 1840s and 1880s. Socialism arose to challenge the inequalities of capitalism and to demand full citizenship rights from the ruling bourgeoisie for the disenfranchised proletariat.

In this uncertain landscape dystopian images of the modern city began to take shape. The division between the prosperous West End of London and the impoverished East End provided a metaphor for the way the city was depicted and theorised in Victorian social commentary. Mooney (1998: 56) observes:

> the East–West metaphor was among a number of images used at this time, which served to 'distance' particular groups in the city, constituting them as a 'social problem'. In this imagery of the poor, deprived urban areas came to be configured in the Victorian mind as 'dark' and 'hostile' places. The poor became the 'other' of Victorian society. (Mooney, 1998: 59)

It has been argued that a form of domestic colonialism emerged in the *flânerie* of Victorian sociology and the active citizenship of philanthropists. These active citizens traversed a social terrain inhabited by the victims of rampant capitalism, which had created an outcast population that challenged the mores of Victorian society (McLintock, 1995).

The female social worker became a key figure in this discourse. She emerged as a pioneer in crossing social boundaries to 'naturalise' and 'moralise' the family lives of the poor, simultaneously altering the balance between the public and private spheres of life. Mooney (1998: 83) concludes that

Victorian domestic ideology was not as pervasive as we are often led to believe. The separation of public spheres was not always distinct and indeed the boundary between public and private shifted considerably during the period in question.

The male leadership reacted to what they believed was the contamination of the female volunteers, whose idealism was leading them to become over-involved with the working class (Jones, 1983: 96). One key male figure in Victorian social work, Bernard Basanquet, opined that such social workers had become 'victims of their senses', 'indulging themselves' by 'being carried away by the first impression of reasoned pity' (cited in Jones, 1983: 96). There was a growing sense amongst social workers that there needed to be a fundamental reform of the existing political order, and this posed a major challenge to the Social Darwinism advocated by the leadership of emerging Victorian civil society. Moreover, it threatened the comfortable relationship between the *laissez-faire* state and the voluntary sector, based upon a shared contempt for the marginalised poor. Politics was, therefore, in evidence in social work from its infancy and shaped its historic mission into a concern for the poor and oppressed.

Civil society and political thought

Part of the problem in interpreting social work politically has been the failure to set it within a meaningful historical paradigm. Recently several social work commentators, seeking to define social work within the emerging context of Eastern Europe, have identified it with the idea of civil society (Zavirsek, 1999; Stubbs, 1999). Civil society as a concept gives coherence to the diversity of social work as an activity within the social world, differentiating it from both market and government: civil society occupies a space – the third space – between them in the social order. But this must be described as a 'public space' shared with the state, with which it has simultaneously a symbiotic and a conflictual relationship. The origins of social work are deeply rooted in the emergence of civil society in modern civilisation, which has created a public space that can be referred to as 'the social'. The idea of civil society is based upon citizen participation in the community and a culture that promotes civic engagement in public welfare. In interpreting civil society all of the key terms – civil/civic, society, politics, community – originate in the ancient world. For our purposes, however, the debate in the modern world is traceable to the concept of civil rights that emerged in the writings of John Locke and Thomas Hobbes. The explicit use of the term is first evident in a treatise by the Scottish Enlightenment thinker, Adam Ferguson, who published *An Essay on the History of Civil Society* in 1767. In this work Ferguson explores the tensions and paradoxes inherent in the concept of civil society to the present day.

Similarly the German philosopher, Hegel, explored the concept of civil society in the definitive version of his monumental system of political and social philosophy, as it appeared in the 1821 edition of *Philosophy of Right*. For Hegel, civil society incorporates the spheres of economic relations and class formation as well as welfare and religious institutions and the judicial and administrative structure of the state. He does not include pre-state relations, such as the family and community.

The debate about civil society in modern social and political thought started in the Old World, but quickly crossed the Atlantic to the American Colonies. Essential to the widening of the debate was Thomas Paine, raconteur, polemicist and commoner, who dominated progressive political thought in Britain, France and America during the age of revolutionary struggle against absolutist tyranny in the last quarter of the eighteenth century. In his highly influential pamphlet, *Common Sense*, published in 1776, Paine introduced the term 'civilised society' as a natural and potentially self-regulating form of association, counterposed to 'government', which was in his view, at best a necessary and artificial evil. However, Paine was vague about what precisely he meant by civil society.

The French aristocrat, Alexis De Tocqueville, who visited the United States in the 1830s, was a great deal more precise. Liberal by political persuasion, De Tocqueville is sometimes regarded as having depoliticised the term 'civil society', celebrating any form of associational activity for its own sake in his study *Democracy in America*, first published in 1835. In fact, De Tocqueville laid considerable stress on participation in local democracy as the best method for ensuring that civil association reinforced and protected democratic politics against tyranny. However, the core of his conception of civil society was the health of intermediate institutions, usually the family, the community and churches. As De Tocqueville (1956: 202) put it:

> Amongst the laws which rule human societies, there is one which seems to be more precise and clear than all others. If men are to remain civilised, or to become so, the art of associating together must grow and improve in the same ratio in which the equality of conditions is increased.

While De Tocqueville was commenting from the perspective of liberal individualism other contemporary thinkers addressed the concept of civil society from a very different ideological standpoint. Utopian socialists, including Saint-Simon, Owen, Fourier and Cabet, saw the great sources of evil in society as cut-throat competition, deceit, greed and inhumanity, and the great remedy as association and co-operation to restore harmony to human life. Fourierist communities, based on the ideals of association and co-operation, were established in New Jersey, Wisconsin and Massachusetts. Robert Owen established a utopian socialist community at New Lanark in Scotland, during the early nineteenth century.

On the other hand, Karl Marx, who along with a group of fellow German refugees in Paris during the 1830s established the League of the Just (later the Communist League) as a bulwark against capitalism, rejected civil society. Marx regarded 'civil society as an illusion that needs to be unmasked' (Hann and Dunne, 1996: 4). According to Marx, modern bourgeois society was unique in a separation of the political and the civil which was not present in feudal society. Bourgeois society and civil society were one and the same thing for Marx and it is notable that they share a common linguistic meaning in German.

Marx's critique of civil society is important because he argues that it is a 'historical form rather than a universal condition' (Tonkiss, 1998: 255). However, his analysis is arguably unduly reductive in equating the social with the economic. Because of this, Marxist theory has tended to underestimate the importance of

unemployment and idleness, a new ethic of work, and also the dream of a city, where moral obligation was joined to civil law, within the authoritarian forms of constraint'. It was evident in the English Poor Law reform debate, which flourished following the decline after 1815 of the threat posed by the French Revolution to the political stability of the United Kingdom. The Old English Poor Law introduced in 1601, according to Piven and Cloward (1971: 130), 'was based on several key principles: that relief should be a local responsibility; that relief allowances should be less remunerative than wages (the principle of "less eligibility"), and that "settlement" in the local community should be a prerequisite for aid'. By the late eighteenth century the political climate had altered. In response to the challenge from the spread of revolutionary ideology and popular unrest, a more liberal administration of the Old English Poor Law had developed on the basis of local initiatives in the mid-1790s. This was known as the Speenhamland system. It permitted large-scale outdoor relief to the able-bodied poor financed by the imposition of a labour rate. Bicheno (1830: 232) observed in reference to the rationale underpinning the Speenhamland system in England that 'this principle, of relieving all who are in distress, was acted upon most comprehensively, towards the end of the last century, when the country was placed on the brink of civil war, by the revolutionary contagion introduced from the neighbouring nation'. He was referring to the impact of the French Revolution on British society.

The Speenhamland system was in essence a stop-gap response to a temporary political threat to the hegemony of the ruling order. It conferred on the poor a basic right to a subsistence living in the community. In the long term it did not provide a viable scheme for capital, because it was necessary to alter the mercantilist emphasis on settlement, if the growing demand for urban industrial labour was to be met. A Poor Law system designed to curtail the mobility of labour had become increasingly anomalous in the age of the Industrial Revolution. Moreover, the Speenhamland system was believed to encourage population growth. This was anathema to the political economists of the time, who advocated a prudential check on population and opposed statutory support for the poor, i.e. the right to poor relief. Even before the political challenge posed by the French Revolution had receded a debate about the fundamental principles upon which the English Poor Law rested had commenced. In this debate the pessimistic theory of Malthus (1796) that the multiplication of population always outstrips food production was to the fore. Malthus's pessimism was complemented by Adam Smith's (1776) theory of a 'wages fund' which asserted that there was a fixed percentage of the national income available for wages. It was also supported by Ricardo's (1819) 'Iron Law of Wages' which contended that wage payments above the market level in the long term operated to the detriment of the poor since higher wages would encourage excessive population growth, leading to greater misery.

While Malthus and Ricardo envisaged abolition as the ultimate goal of Poor Law reform, another exponent of classical economic theory, Jeremy Bentham, believed that the ideological position of this group could be reconciled with the concept of relief. He advocated in his *Pauper Management Improved*, first published in 1797, a plan whereby England's 250 houses of industry would be brought under a system of centralised control and subject to rational administrative principles. These proposed penitentiaries for the poor were to prove decisive in shaping the government's response to the Poor Law reform debate in England.

The government reacted to demands for the reform of the Poor Law by establishing the English Poor Law Commission in 1832 in which political economists, notably Chadwick and Senior, played a key role. It delivered its report in 1834. The Commission roundly condemned existing poor relief provision, citing the Speenhamland system as contrary to the spirit of the Elizabethan Poor Law:

> It is now our painful duty to report, that in the greater part of the districts which we have been able to examine, the fund, which the 43rd of Elizabeth directed to be employed in setting to work children and persons capable of labour but using no daily trade, and in the necessary relief of the impotent, is applied to purposes opposed to the letter, and still more to the spirit of that Law, and destructive to the morals of the most numerous class, and to the welfare of all. (Poor Law Report, 1834: 8)

They recommended a thoroughgoing reform of the English Poor Law which swept away the restraints on the mobility of labour. The New Poor Law (as it came to be called), which the English Poor Law Commission designed, was based on the concept of deterrence. This objective was to be achieved through the rigorous application of the doctrine of 'less eligibility', i.e. recipients of poor relief were to be exposed to conditions inferior to those of the lowliest labourer engaged in gainful employment. The able-bodied poor in England were henceforth only to receive relief in the carceral environment of the workhouse. The administration of poor relief was to be placed under the control of a Central Board with power 'to frame and enforce regulations for the Government of workhouses' (Poor Law Report, 1834: 167).

The debt to Bentham was evident in both the carceral ethos of the workhouse and the centralised control of the system. The discrepancy between the *laissez-faire* ideology which informed economic policy and the centralised control which underpinned social policy in England after 1834 exposed a fundamental paradox: that the economic freedom of the entrepreneurial class and the regulation of the poor by the state were complementary. The poor had been reduced to the status of paupers, an excluded class without rights.

As the nineteenth century unfolded, social policy in general and attitudes towards poverty in particular underwent change. Layburn (1995: 148) concludes:

> By the 1880s the concern about pauperism, which had developed in the 1830s, had given way to the concern about poverty. By the early twentieth century the concern about national efficiency had raised the issue of poverty to a new level and was forcing a compromise between the role of the state and philanthropy.

The pluralistic nature of social policy during the nineteenth and early twentieth centuries in Britain was cemented by the common theme of poverty.

The English Poor Law became the model for the rest of the English speaking world. Friedlander and Apte (1980: 62) have commented in relation to the United States:

The spirit of the English Poor Law dominated most of the colonial laws, whether or not they used degrading terminology in speaking of paupers. The public, with few exceptions, maintained its resentment against the poor tax burden and its contempt for people unable to take care of themselves in a society that identified economic prosperity and success with efficiency and virtue. Some of the most cruel forms of treatment of the poor were gradually abandoned, but there remained the spirit of unwillingness to recognise aid for the poor as socially necessary and justified.

Voluntary aid to the poor was considered sufficient.

Civil society, voluntarism and social reform

Social work emerged as a voluntary activity in response to the social transformation which accompanied the Industrial Revolution. Civil society is frequently defined as representing 'society' as opposed to the political realm of the 'state'. In social work terms, civil society is constituted by the voluntary and community sectors that provide an alternative focus to the bureaucratic apparatus of the state. In the eighteenth and nineteenth centuries there was a minimalist state, which made civil society an important force. In understanding the nature and extent of the voluntary mode of provision it is necessary to appreciate that the concept of civil society has varied throughout history. While, as Woodroofe (1962: 18) has noted, the general aim of civil society to relieve social distress has remained constant, 'the objects, scope, methods and content of philanthropic action change as the social context changes'.

In this climate of voluntary endeavour, which accompanied incipient industrialisation, charitable organisations expanded in number and variety, requiring new techniques in organisation and administration. The Prussian Elberfeld system was one of the earliest attempts in adapting philanthropy to the new social conditions. Elberfeld, a town with a population of 100,000, developed a system of relief in 1852 using almoners in twenty-six districts of the town to visit applicants for charitable relief and report on their cases to regular meetings of the district almoners for decision. Although the almoners were unpaid, their service was compulsory for a three-year term. In Britain and Ireland there were several attempts to organise charitable relief in the first half of the nineteenth century, notably the foundation of the Edinburgh Mendicity Society in 1812 and the London and Dublin Mendicity Societies in 1818. However, it was not until the Charity Organisation Society was founded in London in 1869 that substantial progress was made.

The London Charity Organisation Society and the remoralisation of the poor

The London Charity Organisation Society, or COS as it came to be called, is widely regarded as synonymous with the foundation of social work in the English speaking world. The achievement of the COS had been aptly summarised by the Australian historian Kathleen Woodroofe:

It was within the framework of this society, more than any other, that social casework was evolved, to become the first and most highly developed of the three methods of social work. Not only did the Society hammer out a philosophy and a technique to guide its own friendly visitors and social workers in their daily task, but through the early establishment of a Training School, later to become the Department of Social Science and Administration at the London School of Economics, the Society had a tremendous influence on the development of social work. (1962: 24)

The London COS, under its zealous leadership, quickly reached maturity, ideologically dominating the voluntary sector in Britain for nearly half a century, despite being an essentially locally based organisation. The COS was formed to remoralise the poor and to manage poor relief in partnership with the state. Layburn (1995: 139) asserts that the COS 'was concerned at the moral decay and unscrupulous misuse of charities by some of the working-classes, but was more concerned with bringing about co-operation between the charities and the Poor Law, and amongst charities'. He concludes: 'these aims were almost religiously applied and advertised by [its leaders] Charles and Helen Bosanquet, Edward Denison, Octavia Hill and C.S. Loch' (ibid.).

The COS prototype organisation plan was outlined in 1870 as part of the report to the first annual meeting held in London, which was presided over by Lord Derby, emphasising a hierarchical approach that was to be cultivated at both national and local levels. The plan recommended the establishment of a local charity office under the management of a local committee in each Poor Law division. Local committees were to be presided over by a chairman, secretary and treasurer and to consist of a membership drawn from the property-owning classes. For administrative purposes many localities established a sub-committee structure which reflected various functional divisions (e.g. finance). A charity agent was to be appointed to each local office, charged with responsibility for liaison with the Poor Law relieving officer and the local clergy, as well as all the charitable organisations within the area. The agent was to keep a register of all cases receiving charitable relief. He was also 'to inquire into and investigate' applications for help from those who were outside the orbit of existing agencies, and 'in the last resort' to assist them subject to the permission of the local committee.

The local COS office was, therefore, to be the 'recognised centre of charitable organisation' in the locality. Printed tickets were distributed to be given to beggars rather than alms. These tickets were to be presented by the recipients at the local COS office. The organisation plan was quickly put into operation, and by 1872 there were thirty-six district offices. The day-to-day work in local offices was partly carried out by volunteers – usually women – who assisted the agent. In some local offices the agent was also assisted by one or two paid employees called collectors, inquirers or inquiry agents, usually drawn from the working class.

In practice it soon emerged that voluntary organisation, particularly in deprived areas, was not an entirely realistic proposition. Consequently, assistance in individual cases instead of being offered 'in the last resort' by the COS became its main function, turning it into a casework agency. The Council of the COS published guidelines and various documents such as registers and forms for the direction of local committees. The publication in 1890 of 'Charity Organisation and Relief, A Paper of Suggestions for Charity Organisation Societies', established a number of principles for the administration of relief: each case must be treated individually, the welfare of the entire family must be considered; full enquiry must be made as to the causes of distress, needs, resources and character. Temporary help was to be given only if it was likely to produce permanent benefit, not merely because the applicants were honest and 'deserving'. Thrift was to be encouraged and repayment of help required, if possible. The assistance of kinship and neighbourhood networks was to be elicited and promoted.

Documentation, investigation and visitation were central to the COS methodology. It was essentially positivist in world view, believing that charity would be converted into a science. The Council recommended that applications should be taken down on a 'Visiting Form' and personal details entered as well as a reference number in the 'Record Book'. After investigation the case was to be entered in the 'Decision Book'. A register of charitable relief in each locality was also required to be kept. Innumerable other forms, lists, etc. existed for multifarious purposes. Visitation to applicants was stressed as the essence of the investigatory process. COS records bear witness to the virtuous perseverance of its workers in this task.

In assessing the significance of the contribution of the COS to the relief of poverty the large number of applicants who were not assisted, about one-third in 1871, is as important as those who were helped by advice or material aid. This category of 'undeserving' cases was the source of a continuing controversy, which greatly embarrassed the COS. It believed that voluntary provision was intended to act as a complement rather than a supplement to the Poor Law, which it perceived as providing for 'the idle, the improvident and the incorrigible', as well as the chronically dependent. Despite attempts by the COS to circumvent the issue by semantic means the fact remained, as Mowat (1961: 37) has noted, 'that the "unassisted" might be those who most needed help but least deserved it, while those helped, the respectable and provident, ought least to have needed help'. This contradiction in COS policy was due to its leadership's firm adherence to the principles of Social Darwinism. Their function, as they saw it, was to make relief more efficient in the interim through co-ordination and scientific method, and in the long term by the promotion of self-reliance through individual reform. Only the strongest and the most self-reliant amongst the poor would survive – the rest would perish. The unyielding emphasis on Social Darwinism in the discourse of the COS leadership, embodied in the person of C.S. Loch, not only isolated it from others interested in the relief of poverty but made the COS anathema to the burgeoning labour movement, to which it was equally bitterly opposed. It also began to cause internal rifts, which became public as the result of a clash between Canon Barnett of the Toynbee Hall Settlement and Loch at a meeting of the Council of the COS on 15 July 1895. Essentially, this was a clash between positivism and humanism, between those who advocated science and those who promoted social reform as an appropriate response to poverty.

Barnett (1895: 338) presented a paper to the meeting entitled 'A Friendly Criticism of the Charity Organisation Society' which argued that the COS was out of step with the times: 'Charity is as disorganised and poverty as prevalent as in the year of the funding of our society'. He was convinced that action by the state was indispensable, if the problems of umemployment and the aged poor were to be effectively dealt with. Loch was unmoved and strongly adhered to the COS Social Darwinistic principles, which he brought to bear on the Royal Commission on the Poor Law (1905–9), ensuring that the Majority Report recommended the continuation of the Poor Law (at least in spirit) and the maintenance of the voluntary sector in the teeth of Fabian opposition led by Beatrice Webb, who had started her career as a visitor with the COS (Friedlander and Apte, 1980: 35).

Although Loch's personal hegemony over the COS survived Barnett's admonitions, two divergent approaches to addressing the problem of poverty had begun to emerge. While the individualistic casework of the COS visitors continued 'they began to advocate changes within the existing framework of society which would produce less devastating effects upon the individual' (Woodroofe, 1962: 60). Through these embryonic attempts at social reform the COS became involved in organising community resources to improve housing conditions, inspired by Octavia Hill, a prominent member of the COS Council. This involvement with housing extended to other social issues, including sanitation, immigration and handicap. Similarly, Elizabeth Fry became a pioneer of prison reform, largely motivated by Christian concern. The struggle to define social work within the realms of humanism as opposed to positivism, which has waxed and waned throughout its history, had begun.

Social work in the nineteenth century, as espoused by the COS hierarchy, was a complement to the New English Poor Law of 1834 with its concept of 'least eligibility' formulated by the classical economists which denied the existence of poverty and admitted only to the problem of pauperism. The COS did not share this pessimistic view of a homogeneous dependent class. They believed that many could ultimately share in the prosperity of industrialisation with a modicum of charitable assistance to the 'deserving' able-bodied poor temporarily in need. By implication the 'undeserving' poor should be left to 'their just desserts' and the disabled looked after by their own families, obviating the need for statutory provision. Natural law would take care of the rest, in keeping with the Darwinistic thinking of the times. Octavia Hill (1901: 309) expressed the COS position laconically in a paper on 'The Relations between Rich and Poor as Bearing on Pauperism' which she delivered to the Annual Conference of Charity Organisation Societies at Cambridge in May 1901:

> I wish I could convey to those who are here any of the deep conviction I feel that the working man and woman of our day is not the poor, helpless, dependent creature our stupid doles or wide socialistic theories assume. He has thought, resource, power, capacity for commanding fair wages and common sense to expend them, if we would only let him alone to try.

The new philanthropy and civic engagement in Britain

Hill's comment encapsulates the essential philosophy of 'the old philanthropy', which was being replaced by 'the new philanthropy'. While 'the old philanthropy' was dominated by positivist and hierarchical discourses, 'the new philanthropy' sought to be more communitarian and democratic. Just as the London Charity Organisation Society symbolised the old philanthropy, the Guild of Help rooted in the North of England embodied the spirit of the new philanthropy. Layburn (1995: 155) remarks that in this context 'the COS viewed poverty as personal failure and not as a failing of society. ... In contrast, the Guild of Help was far more concerned with recognising some of the failings of British society'. The news organ of the Bradford Guild of Help summarised the distinction as follows:

> The Guild of Help is the practical expression of the civic consciousness and the embodiment of the new philanthropy. The old was clearly associated with charity in the narrow sense, and between those who gave and those who received was a great gulf fixed; 'the lady bountiful' attitude has received its death blow, the Guild worker does not go in as a visitant from another world but as a fellow creature to be helpful. (cited in Layburn, 1995: 155)

Ultimately, the new philanthropy was no more successful than the old in tackling poverty. Layburn (1995: 158–159) detects three fundamental problems that undermined the Guild of Help:

1 Local civic consciousness was riddled with dissent and tensions.
2 There was a lack of broadly based support in the community at large.
3 The Guild of Help was never able to establish its relationship with the state in an effective manner.

Socialists dismissed it as 'Gilded Help' that had no hope of abolishing poverty 'in a billion years'. The problems of the Guild of Help are characteristic of voluntary organisations throughout the twentieth century: a lack of resources and influence to tackle poverty effectively on their own. Voluntarism had no future without a partnership with the state. For the state the benefits of a civil society/state nexus were far from clear, given community rivalries, sectarianism and political divisions and the lack of civic consciousness. Yet the new philanthropy represented an important step along the road to collective social responsibility in Britain to the extent that it manifested a more positive attitude towards the poor. These developments were echoed in the United States.

Charity and social work in the New World

S. Humphreys Gurteen, who had visited London and become acquainted with the COS, established America's first charity organisation society at Buffalo, New York, in 1877. The wealthy funders of the society enthusiastically adopted the Social Darwinist philosophy of their British counterpart: 'They hoped that by giving friendly advice, by helping in procuring employment or, sometimes, by giving a loan, they could strengthen the moral fibre of the indigent and encourage them to become self-supporting' (Friedlander and Apte, 1980: 74).

While these values were endorsed by the bankers and merchants that formed the committee, as the visitors became more intimately acquainted with 'their families', they found that there were other factors that caused destitution, including living in unhealthy neighbourhoods, poor housing conditions and low wages.

This practical experience 'revealed that the concept of individual fault did not stand the test of honest analysis'. The visitors 'began to ask for measures which would fundamentally change those social conditions and became the advocates of social reform' (Friedlander and Apte, 1980: 74–75).

This realisation amongst its staff that poverty was not reducible to individual fault led the COS in the United States to promote social legislation, improvements in housing and slum clearance, the regulation of child labour, penal reform and the tackling of the scourge of tuberculosis. In some cases, local charity organisation societies established employment bureaux, loan societies, lumberyards, dispensaries, shelters and legal aid bureaux, emphasising a commitment to tackling poverty (Friedlander and Apte, 1980: 75).

Education and training in social work

Before concluding this discussion of the charity organisation movement it is necessary to look at one of its most enduring achievements – the establishment of training for social workers. Training was the logical outcome of the attempt by the COS to apply the 'scientific' method of observation and experiment, reasoning and verification, to the task of relieving the poor. It is interesting to note that the development of training commenced in the United States and Europe almost simultaneously. The New York COS organised a six-week seminar training course in 1898, which became an annual event. In 1904 a one-year training course was established at the New York School of Philanthropy (later the New York School of Social Work). By 1908 the Chicago School of Civics and Philanthropy had been founded – subsequently to be absorbed into the University in 1920. Europe's first school of social work was established at Amsterdam in 1899 (Midgley, 1997). In London the School of Sociology under the tutorship of E.J. Urwick was established in 1903 by the COS as an independent body. It was later incorporated in 1912 into the London School of Economics, representing a 'historic compromise' with Fabianism (Lorenz, 1994: 43). Training schemes soon followed in Manchester, Bristol, Birmingham, Leeds, Liverpool, Edinburgh and Glasgow, all of which were subsequently absorbed into the universities. Undoubtedly the culmination of these endeavours to create a knowledge base for social work as a professional activity was the publication of Mary Richmond's *Social Diagnosis* in 1917, which attempted to collate casework method and present it in the form of a scientific discipline. The achievement in terms of laying educational and scientific foundations of social work was considerable. But, as Friedlander and Apte (1980: 485) observe: 'Social work did not begin to be recognised as a profession until the end of World War I'.

Jones (1983: 98) has questioned the political motives of the leaders of the charity organisation movement in establishing social work education and training, which he saw as an attempt to address political contamination:

The main source of contamination for the COS was the evident attraction of large-scale social reform sponsored by the state which promised more dramatic improvement than did casework.... A common thread of that programme was the theme that the state was totally incapable of identifying and providing the personalised remoralisation which the 'deserving' working class poor were deemed to require, and, moreover, that it was potentially more dangerous than indiscriminate almsgiving in that it would not only weaken self-help and self-reliance among the working class, but that it would also create expectations among the poor which could not be fulfilled within the existing social framework.

The charity organisation movement was keenly aware of the challenge posed by socialism and radical liberalism. Their objective was to mould, according to their Darwinian principles, the minds of the young idealistic people who entered social work imbued with the hope of improving the lot of humanity. A combination of practical 'on the job' training through the provision of fieldwork placements was combined with theoretical training geared towards the promotion of personalised solutions to social problems. This was an inherently problematic task since the university tradition of humanist education is not easily compatible with practical training based upon the assimilationist principle of the apprenticeship model of training. Social science, which was intended to provide the epistemological underpinning to social work training is riven by disputes between positivists and humanists. Even if it were desirable (and the COS clearly thought it was) to shield students against critical social theory, it could be quite impossible in a university environment. Clearly, such an approach to education would amount to little more than propaganda. Nonetheless, this has not stopped professional accreditation bodies from seeking to set the agenda for social work training within a person-alised context that denies the structural reality of poverty and the need for a politi-cal response.

Moreover, professional education from the outset has been closely connected with the task of identity formation. Parallels are drawn with the detachment and 'objectivity' of the older professions, notably medicine. Students have been selected on the basis of their supposed professional 'suitability'. Professionalisa-tion consequently has provided a screening and personal development process that has very successfully served to deradicalise social work. In this regard the charity organisation movement was highly successful. Whether in the long term it has served the best interests of social work must be in doubt.

The settlement movement and social reform

Probably because of the dominance of casework method in contemporary social work, the COS is perceived as its progenitor. However, the origins of social work are more complex. We have already discussed the 'new philanthropy' in Britain. Also of significance in the formation of social work has been the settlement movement which, at least in the United States, has survived relatively intact, unlike the COS which, ironically, has been replaced by its old enemy, the state. Still, the COS legacy, as noted above, continues to be a powerful influence on the nature of social work.

The first settlement in Britain was Toynbee Hall. Established in 1884 in the deprived East End of London by Canon Barnett, it was quickly followed by several other settlements in the same part of London, notably Oxford House in Bethnal Green, and many more within the metropolis and outside. The settlement movement had a pronounced Christian socialist ethos, sharing with the COS the purpose of promoting social harmony through active citizenship, what Octavia Hill called 'a solemn sense of relationship' between rich and poor. This objective was to be achieved by the educated drawn from the universities living amongst the poor and assisting them through education and example and the promotion of social reform on their behalf. The essential difference between the settlement movement and the COS was a basic difference in world view. While the COS was rigorously positivist, the settlement movement was fundamentally humanist. The latter dismissed the comfortable belief in the inevitability of progress adhered to by mainstream COS opinion. In Barnett's (1898: 12) words, the settlement workers 'were conscious of something wrong underneath modern progress'. They optimistically believed in an appeal to humanity.

The first settlement in the New World was opened in New York in 1887 by Stanton Coit and Charles B. Stover. Two years later America's most famous settlement, Hull House, opened in Chicago under the patronage of Jane Addams, who has been described as 'more nearly a world figure than any other woman of her day' (Morrison et al., 1969: 280). Hull House, which became the prototype of American settlements, provided a day nursery, boys' club, a gymnasium, music and drama, art schools, handicraft shops and many other activities. Although the early settlements in the United States were influenced by their British antecedents, they soon diverged.

While American social work shared the fundamental belief of its British counterpart, neatly encapsulated by Jane Addams's belief that social classes are interdependent and have reciprocal obligations, it was more radical. This ideological divergence may, in part at least, be explicable in terms of the relative weakness of the American Labour Movement and the bipolarity of American liberalism. The radical element of the latter achieved separate political identity in the Progressive Movement, with which Addams and her colleagues had close links.

The American settlement movement, therefore, made its active citizenship directly felt not only in the slums, with their immigrant masses, through the establishment of over 400 settlements by 1910, but also in the legislative chambers. In the latter field 'social workers, regarded by politicians and businessmen as misguided zealots, came to be recognised as the most effective reformers of their generation' (Morrisson et al., 1969: 280). Jane Addams and her associates not only campaigned for the abolition of child labour and the promotion of better conditions and shorter working hours for women, but also helped organise trade unions. Many American settlement workers enthusiastically supported strikes, frequently experiencing arrest on the picket line. Addams herself became a strike mediator because of the confidence the workers felt in her and the overt support Hull House gave them, including the use of their premises by strike committees. This was in marked contrast to their British counterparts, who cautiously demonstrated their sympathy for the London Dock Strike of 1889 by allowing the strike leader, Ben Tillet, to visit the settlement and put his case. The American settlement movement also campaigned for reform on a variety of social issues including factory conditions, housing, health and education. One of the greatest achievements of Hull House was the enactment of the Illinois Factory Inspection Law in 1893. The resident most closely identified with the campaign was subsequently appointed Inspector of Factories in the state of Illinois. A number of settlement activists entered politics as candidates to further the cause of reform. Many of the campaigns initiated at local level became national campaigns in the twentieth century and were closely associated with Theodore Roosevelt's Progressive platform in the 1912 presidential election, which marked the high point of the American settlement movement's political influence.

While the settlement movements in Britain and America were markedly different in their interpretation of the 'citizen's duty in the neighbourhood' they shared, in common with the Charity Organisation Society in both countries, a commitment to the promotion of social harmony through active citizenship. However, they basically differed from the Charity Organisation Society. The settlement movement was humanist and reformist. Its supporters dismissed the comfortable belief in the inevitability of progress adhered to by mainstream Charity Organisation Society opinion. They believed in an appeal to humanity and reason: public knowledge of the social conditions of the poor coupled with political agitation would lead to an acceptance of the need for social change. The divergence of approach between the Charity Organisation Society and the settlement movement must be at least partly explicable by their social composition. The leadership of the COS essentially represented the propertied upper classes, who evinced an inbred condescension towards the poor. The settlement movement was the product of the social commitment of middle-class intellectuals. They understood the role of the environment in the causation of poverty through low pay, unemployment, illness, insanitary and overcrowded housing. This was translated, in America at least, into social and sometimes political action. This developing consciousness of the complexity of poverty and the need for the amelioration of social conditions involved an incipient recognition of social inequality.

The child saving movement and the emergence of risk

Child welfare and protection became a major concern of social workers during this period, giving birth to the child saving movement. In Britain this led to the foundation of the National Society for the Prevention of Cruelty to Children (NSPCC), the National Children's Home and Dr Barnardo's Homes. The NSPCC was founded during the 1880s and amalgamated into a national association in 1889, coinciding with the first child protection legislation. This legislation 'expressed the public desire to try to prevent cruelty to any child before it actually occurred and to prevent excessive suffering and overwork, which still existed in many kinds of employment open to children and not regulated by the Factory Acts' (Heywood, 1978: 102). The NSPCC expanded rapidly and by 1914 nearly 55,000 cases were being investigated annually. In total, nearly one million cases were dealt with by the NSPCC between 1884 and 1914, and of these, 13,613 children died. The NSPCC did not view this as a sign of failure; on the contrary, it 'used the statistics on child deaths to assert the value of its work' (Ferguson, 1996: 207). From the perspective of early child protection workers there was an inevitability about child mortalities that only gradually began to change as social work professionalised. Ferguson (1996: 208) has sought to explain this phenomenon:

> The conception of risk to children which held in professional ideology and practice prior to the 1900s was simply not sufficient to make children predictable subjects for preventative intervention. The deaths of children were generally placed in a context of meaning and explanation in which they were associated with concepts like sin, natural wastage and seasonal rhythm and assimilated into natural processes of decay. But as these children were becoming 'cases' a new conception of risk and optimistic professional belief began to be constituted, which held [that] these deaths could be prevented and reformation of deviant parenting effected through social intervention.

The association of early child welfare initiatives with Christianity was close. Both Dr Thomas Barnardo, founder of Barnardo's Homes, and Thomas Stephenson, founder of the National Children's Homes, were inspired by Christian virtue. Their organisations were concerned with the rescue of homeless children from the risks of urban poverty and exploitation. Risk had become a key feature of social work. Ferguson (1996: 210) concludes:

> A new concept of risk had entered social practice, the meaning of which was no longer derived externally from nature and the concepts of sin, but from expertise and science. It was a form of 'manufactured risk' that was based fundamentally on the use of reflexively organised knowledge and decisions made by expert systems. The conditions of possibility were laid which made child survival a technical issue for social intervention. Its corollary was a new tempo to practice, which facilitated and reflected the concept of 'emergency' in child protection. An increased faith in the effectiveness and 'reach' of child protection had its roots in forms of disciplinary power which are central to the emphasis in modernity on surveillance and control. The PCC [Prevention of Cruelty to Children] Acts and the 1908 Children Act gave to practitioners increased legal powers to intervene in family life. Of equal significance, moreover, was the process of cultural translation through which such administrative powers were turned into practice. This was heavily influenced by developments in science and technology which were transforming cultural practice generally.

Child protection and risk detection placed social work firmly on a trajectory towards professionalisation in Britain.

In the United States the child saving movement was instrumental in inventing the idea of the juvenile court in Illinois at the close of the nineteenth century. Platt (1969) attributes the emergence of the child saving movement to the emerging role of female social workers in the public realm that was redefining popular views of morality. He perceives the 'child savers' as discontented idealists committed to social reform. The idealism of these social workers coincided with the emergence of the positivist school of criminology, which enabled them to argue that a child's deeds could not be differentiated from its needs. Children were victims, not criminals. In 1908 this view was accepted in the UK in the 'Children's Charter'.

The child saving movement was also instrumental in the United States in exposing child abuse. In 1875 the Mary Ellen case confronted the New York courts with a stark case of cruelty. Because there was no child protection legislation, Mary Ellen had to be brought before the courts as an abused animal. A landmark decision followed that outlawed child abuse and brought the state firmly into the family sphere, by establishing the legal principle of *parens patriae* i.e. the state is the higher or ultimate parent of the child. Children's rights had come of age.

Social work, class and subordination

The nineteenth century represents the formative period of social work, when its influence rivalled that of politics and religion. Seed (1973: 39–40) in attempting to summarise the achievement of social work during this period concluded:

> As a social movement, social work sought to distinguish itself from political movements on the one hand, and from religious movements on the other hand. Social work was differentiated from politics in so far as it was less interested in the distribution of power than in the resolution of social conflict. Its goal was a social ideal, not a political system. As such, it was seen by its exponents as something better than purely political activity – in Barnett's words 'a sort of progress whose means would justify the end'. The differentiation of social work from religious movements was not always clear. In the Settlements, in particular, the social gospel was sometimes entangled with the religious gospel. The Charity Organisation Society solved this problem by seeing itself as an alternative to religious evangelism. Charity was the fruit of true religious faith, and as Loch (1904) put it 'in fervency it is religious'.

In this comment Seed captures the moral and social basis of social work in Victorian society. It was very much an idealistic movement that laid the foundations for professional social work. Jones (1997: 120) comments: 'This idealistic perspective which awards primacy to character and morality rather than material circumstances has been a decisive influence on the development of British social work, both in its practice and in its understanding of poverty and the poor'.

Mooney views the mission of philanthropy in Victorian Britain as one of 'remoralising' the poor. He observes that it was founded upon a particular class and race perspective that viewed the poor as an inferior population:

> What is important here is that this language is a language of subordination which acts to distance particular groups of people, defining (and segrating) them, while simultaneously serving to legitimate their reformation or 'civilising'. The slum-dwelling poor were regarded as an 'inferior lot', morally, spiritually and physically. The language used served to establish certain ways of seeing and acting toward the particular groups and people spoken about in these ways. This was the product of a middle-class project and world view. (Mooney, 1998: 59)

The theme of one group subordinating another in the interests of a social ideal has been reflected by other commentators. For example, Jordan (1984: 33) has observed:

> Charity was also of ideological importance. It enabled the new middle classes to justify their privileges, and to insist that capital accumulation and private property need not lead to an increasing gulf between rich and poor. The examples of the best of the early

social workers – even though they were a tiny unrepresentative group – were held up as emblems of class altruism and compassion. They also allowed a new kind of middle-class identity and sensibility, embodying many of the ideals which had been taking shape in emerging bourgeois consciousness, and influencing every later generation of young idealists motivated by 'social conscience'. The experience in the United States largely reflected that of Britain. In both societies new class formations, arising out of industrialisation and urbanisation, spawned an active and diverse civil society, which reflected the structure of feeling of the times amongst the enlightened middle-classes.

The limits of the combined efforts of voluntarism and the minimalist state were starkly exposed by the publication of the results of several poverty surveys. Charles Booth, with the assistance of Beatrice Webb, carried out a series of surveys of poverty in London between 1886 and 1902. These surveys revealed that up to one third of the population of London were living in poverty. Seebohm Rowntree, a merchant like Booth, undertook a similar survey in York which concluded that 28 per cent of its inhabitants were living in poverty. It was evident that poverty was a major social reality in Victorian urban life that remained relatively untouched by the Poor Law and philanthropy.

Socialists and evangelists also published a series of books and pamphlets vigorously putting the case of the poor. In 1845 Engels had published his celebrated study of industrial England's 'dark satanic mills', entitled *The Condition of the Working Class in England*. Another major contribution to the debate on poverty came from William Booth, founder of the Salvation Army, who published *In Darkest England and the Way Out*, in 1890. The language was particularly evocative (in both cases) of 'a world apart', largely out of sight and therefore out of mind.

The Poor Law Reform Commission (1905–9) further exposed how out of touch the COS had become. Its opposition to the progressive minority view (led by Beatrice Webb) that the deterrent Poor Law should be abolished, put it firmly in the reactionary camp. The Liberal landslide election victory in 1906, coupled with the emergence of the Labour Party, underlined the need for change and the emergence of more progressive thinking in social policy-making. The Liberal reforms followed, including the introduction of pensions (1908) a national insurance system (1911) the Children Act (1908) and free school meals legislation. The welfare state was conceived in embryo, although the Poor Law was to remain intact until 1948.

Conclusion

In understanding the nature and extent of social work at this time it is necessary to appreciate that civil society has varied throughout history. The French structuralist philosopher, Donzelot (1979: 55) noted in reference to the nature of civil society in the burgeoning capitalist societies of the nineteenth century:

> Philanthropy in this case is not to be understood as a naively apolitical term signifying a private intervention in the sphere of so-called social problems, but must be considered as a deliberately depoliticising strategy for establishing public services and facilities at a sensitive point midway between private initiative and the state.

Donzelot's strictures, as we shall see, are pertinent to one aspect of nineteenth-century civil society – the old philanthropy. However, because he attributes a homogeneous character to civil society, he fails to make allowance for its humanistic and reforming quality. One of the positive achievements of social work, as active citizenship, in the nineteenth and early twentieth centuries was to create a public domain through the development of a flourishing civil society – though it must be said it was dominated by a wealthy minority and its membership confined to the middle and upper classes. While the propertied interests that controlled the committee of the COS vehemently resisted change, middle-class female social workers extended the public domain into issues as diverse as child welfare, housing, sanitation and slum clearance, penal reform and the overarching issue of poverty.

The 'social' was reconfigured as the responsibility of the public domain. As Dahrendorf (1995: 27) states, 'in the twentieth century, the public domain was further enlarged to embrace health care and insurance against sickness, unemployment and old age, so as to guarantee social, as well as political and citizenship rights'. In the nineteenth century social workers through their active citizenship contributed to civilising social expectations and laying the foundations for social reform in the twentieth century.

Social work had developed rapidly. Its progress was rudely interrupted by the outbreak of the First World War, which shattered the faith of humanity in progress and decency. The pioneering age of social work, when it rivalled politics and religion as a moral force, was over. Gradually, the role of social work changed, as the welfare state emerged out of the ashes of war and conflict, defining a new public domain and a new arena for social work. We will now turn to consideration of the relationship between social work, Fabian reformism and the welfare state.

3

Fabianism, the Welfare State
and Reformist Practice

The Australian social work commentator, Professor Jim Ife (1997: 68) has observed
that 'social work has its foundations in the Fabian Welfare State ideal, and has
defined itself within that context'. Ife's observation underlines the role of the
welfare state as the dominant paradigm in twentieth-century public policy. Only
in the last quarter of the century has its dominance been challenged by a resurgent
market. This chapter addresses the profound influence of Fabianism on social
work, as an arm of the welfare state. However, as the chapter will show, the relationship between social work and the state was not always a comfortable one.
Social work emerged late in the development of the welfare state, due to an ambi-
guity in the Fabians' attitude towards social work and the marginalised poor.
Moreover, social work values were very much shaped in the context of human
rights, bringing an element of individualisation that was not in harmony with
Fabian collectivism. The formative influence of the COS in shaping casework
methodology, as the core paradigm of social work practice, remained. However,
the site of power had moved from the voluntary sector to the state.

The Fabians, social obligation and social work

The Fabian tradition, which has informed welfare discourse from the begin-
ning, represents the modernist exposition of the ideals of classical civic virtue.
Fabianism, which began in 1884, had a number of distinctive qualities that have
shaped the idea of welfare at a fundamental level. First, it was the product of the
English and Irish socially minded intellectuals, notably Sidney and Beatrice
Webb, H.G. Wells and George Bernard Shaw. Shaw, one of the founders of the
Fabian Society, defined its objectives as 'the collection and publication of
authentic and impartial statistical tracts' in order to make 'the public conscious
of the evil condition of society under the present system' (Shaw, 1896: 7). The
Fabians rejected the dominant influence of Marxist socialism in Europe; they
were connected to evolutionary socialism rather than the revolutionary strategy
favoured by Marxists. Named after the Roman general Fabius Cunctator (the
delayer), whose patience in avoiding pitched battles secured ultimate victory over
the Carthaginian general Hannibal, Fabians favoured a gradualist approach

to political change based upon the ideal social reform. Fabians differentiated themselves from social liberalism by emphasising collectivism over individualism.

Mutualism had a powerful influence over Fabian thought. This ideal of social obligation is usually associated with the Scottish scholar, Thomas Davidson, who spent a considerable part of his life in the United States. While both Owenite and Ruskinite utopianism were clearly also present in Davidson's mutualism, he attributed his views to an unorthodox Catholic thinker, Antonio Rosmini-Serbati, who had founded the Brethren of Charity. In harmony with Rosminian thought, Davidson advocated a reformation of mankind, replacing individualism with the civic virtues of co-operation and brotherhood. The ideal of social obligation was an ideological cornerstone of the Fabian movement.

The preoccupation of the founders of Fabianism with the concept of social obligation became the guiding philosophical inspiration of the reformist tradition in social policy. Titmuss, in his classic study *The Gift Relationship* (1970), lays down the philosophical roots of the discipline. This study, which takes the blood transfusion service as a microcosm of the British welfare state, devolves on the key role of altruism in society. Titmuss argues that 'the ways in which society organises and structures its social institutions – particularly its health and welfare systems – can encourage or discourage the altruistic in man' (Titmuss, 1970: 225).

The Fabians advocated the idea of 'parallel bars' between the state and the voluntary sector. They regarded the state as the moral community that would provide against adversity, supplementing voluntary action. The organisational basis that had defined social work in the nineteenth century under the aegis of the COS, as an essential aspect of civil society, was challenged by Fabianism. But social work was not out of sympathy with Fabianism. It showed a common commitment to the idea of social obligation and the need to build a moral community through social reform. Clement Attlee, Labour Prime Minister between 1945 and 1951, who presided over the establishment of the welfare state, had spent a year between 1909 and 1910 at Toynbee Hall Settlement in London. The essential difference between Fabianism and social work was that the former belonged to the political domain and the latter the social domain. Because of its belief in the state as the vehicle for social reform, Fabianism presented social work with a dilemma. The evidence is that social workers were aware of this dilemma and viewed it as providing 'the ideological climate for the more liberal and humane welfare theories and practices to be extended to the unorganised and impoverished dependent poor' (Jones, 1983: 39). However, social work involved an essentially individualised response based upon humanistic values rather than structural change. This is sometimes perceived as 'the triumph of the therapeutic'.

Social work and rehabilitation: the triumph of the therapeutic

In examining the contribution of social work towards the tackling of poverty and unemployment in the economically depressed inter-war years, it would be quite inappropriate to assume that it was homogeneous. Clearly the influence of psychoanalytic theory, the brainchild of Sigmund Freud, who died in 1939, did cause energy and interest to continue to be directed towards the examination and treatment of social problems in the context of individualisation and rehabilitation (Woodroofe, 1962: 118–119; Payne, 1997: 77–78). However, the extent of Freudian influence was not as great as is commonly supposed. Serious concern with the role of the environment in the causation of poverty and social problems was evident in social workers' discussion. Mary Richmond, doyen of social work theory, in her two books on social casework, *Social Diagnosis* (1917) and *What Is Casework?* (1922) 'built her concept of social diagnosis on a foundation uncompromisingly sociological' (Woodroofe, 1962: 106). The 1929 Milford Conference on Social Work in the USA also stressed social context. Jordan (1984: 51) argued that there was a split in social work practice, with the voluntary sector adopting Freudian approaches and the service-orientated public sector remaining largely immune to this influence. This is a helpful distinction. Freud had a pervasive influence on the popular imagination but very little on public policy. Therapists were drawn to his archaeology of the mind, which percolated into social work practice and many other humanistic disciplines. Scull (1998: 9) has remarked upon Freud's enduring capacity 'to attract admirers from a host of humanistic and social scientific disciplines', adding that among non-medically trained therapists his 'ideas and techniques retain some of their seductive appeal and lustre, albeit in sometimes barely recognisable form'. Freud was viewed by his disciples (some of whom were social workers) as the Copernicus or Darwin of the mind. However, social work was preoccupied, at least in the public services, with the alleviation of poverty rather than with the interiority of human suffering. Its terrain was 'the social' and its target the marginalised poor, who were neglected in the conflict between capital and labour.

Where Freudianism proved influential in social work was in shaping a humanistic response to the residuum of poor that Victorians viewed as beyond help. Jones (1983: 38) notes: 'Given that social work was changing significantly during the inter-war period and, under the growing influence of Freudian ideas, was coming to believe that positive rehabilitative work was possible with the residuum, the need to reduce the dominance of earlier negative and repressive attitudes was critical to the possibility of social work's development as a major welfare strategy'. Jones also underlined the significance of this rehabilitative ideal:

> Indeed, the very idea that the residuum had emotions or feelings worthy of respect and consideration was anathema to many past social reformers. Similarly, the idea that they could be restored to active citizenship through a caring strategy of casework and re-education would have been considered outrageous. (1983: 39)

However, Jones adds: 'These important qualifications should not detract from the crucial role played by the working-class in pushing the state towards more liberal and extensive welfare policies'. In reality, social reform dominated the agenda shaping social work responses within the larger context of political reform.

Social reform, poverty and social work

Lees (1970) has attempted to demonstrate in his reappraisal of the development of social work during the inter-war years (1918–39) that a broadly based concern with poverty as a social rather than a psychological construct remained the central preoccupation of social workers. The proceedings of three international conferences on social work held during these years attest to an enduring concern with the perennial problem of poverty (which was exacerbated by the Great Depression), and a continuing commitment to social reform. The first International Conference of Social Work was held in Paris in 1928, and was attended by 2,481 delegates drawn from forty-two countries.

The definition of social work established by the conference organiser stated that the term 'social work' encompassed all efforts to relieve distress caused by poverty, to assist individuals and families to achieve a reasonable standard of living, to prevent social scourges and to improve the living conditions of the community as a whole, through social casework, working with groups, community involvement in legislation and administration and social research. A British delegate, Percy Alden (1928: 599) contrasted the attitudes of twentieth-century social workers with their nineteenth-century counterparts, in relation to the problem of poverty:

> Our social philosophy which was then in a rudimentary condition has changed with the growth of knowledge and of economic causes. At that time we had few accurate statistics and this ignorance was the cause of the prevalent misconception of the evils we deplored. It was generally supposed that the weaker classes of society were responsible for their own suffering and that the distress resulting from poverty was due to personal misdemeanours or failure on the part of the sufferers. It is now generally admitted that while there are many people who are in distress as a result of their own ill-doing, there is a vast amount of want and misery which derives from general social causes for which the individual is only remotely responsible.

Alden (1928: 602–603) went on to attempt to delimit the scope of social work:

> If I may be allowed to use Great Britain as an illustration, I should say that social work in this country consists today (1) in relieving or preventing poverty; (2) in the cure and prevention of disease, which would of course include those who are disabled for any reason; (3) in the treatment and reform of the criminal and the problem of juvenile crime; (4) in the removal of all conditions which hinder progress in our industrial and economic life.... In other countries very much the same divisions of work are indicated as can easily be seen in America by studying the reports of the National Conference of Social Work.

Lest the delegates should get carried away by the apparent omnicompetence of social work implied in some of the speakers' statements, Dr Paolina Tarugi from Milan added a caveat:

> I think, for my part, that a distinction should be drawn between 'social work' and the 'social function' of the state and public departments. Social work has its own task, vast indeed but circumscribed, which is to restore individuals and families to a normal state. When private social action – for instance, relief to poor families or child welfare, becomes collective relief action regulated by statute and carried on by public welfare institutions, we have passed out of the sphere of 'social work' into that of the 'social function' of the state. (Tarugi, 1928: 631–632)

Tarugi was making a distinction between the individualist orientation of social work and the structural orientation of the state. The second International Social Work Conference, held in Frankfurt in 1932, addressed itself to the theme, 'The Family and Social Work'. The delegates were clearly conscious of the impact of the Great Depression on family life. In a special session on the effect of unemployment on family life, health and public morals, they rejected social insurance, public welfare and public charity as mere palliatives. The remedy was to be found, they believed, only in a complete reorganisation of the international economic order.

The Third International Conference of Social Work was held in London in 1936. The theme was 'Social Work and the Community'. This conference was directly concerned with the influence of environmental considerations on the poor and with making suggestions for social reform which were intended to acknowledge the growing recognition by governments of social rights – though not at the expense of civil and political rights. In a keynote address at the opening of the conference, Katherine Lenroot, Chief of the US Children's Bureau, reflected on the dilemma of social work in an increasingly polarised society:

> Social Work is concerned with social justice, social security, and consideration of individual needs and rights. These aims cannot be reconciled with denial of political, civil, and religious liberties; suppression of public criticism; encouragement of racial and national prejudice, or complete subordination of the individual to the larger social group. Social work, therefore, must be subject to growing tension if, as seems inevitable, economic and political struggles are to grow more acute. It will probably become increasingly realistic in its perception of the limitations on freedom under the institutions of democracy as well as under those of dictatorship, and in its appreciation of the growing necessity of collective action in many areas of life. In positive terms, if it is to justify its survival as a profession social work will strive for progression toward, not regression from, ideals of the individual's right to access to the means of securing an adequate livelihood for himself and his family; collective bargaining in labour relations; universal health protection, educational opportunities, and social assistance when needed; and full opportunity for voluntary association for cultural, recreational, and religious purposes. (Lenroot, 1936: 22)

This concern of the international confraternity of social workers is powerful evidence of a notable appreciation of environmental factors in the causation of poverty and inequality. The tendency to oversimplification inherent in the argument that social work was completely overwhelmed by 'the Freudian deluge' during this period is illustrated by one prominent social work educator and doyen of psycho-dynamic theory, Charlotte Towle. Towle (1939: 27) who was subsequently persecuted by Senator Joe McCarthy's Un-American Activities Committee, was careful to circumscribe the effectiveness of casework in an article in which she asserted, 'it is unable to modify many adverse social circumstances which are destroying people such as unemployment, inadequate educational opportunity, poor housing, lack of medical care, and the like. It can never serve as a substitute for social action but it can serve as an instrument of the people revealing widespread needs calling for action'.

Radical social work and New Deal liberalism in the United States

Radical social work was an active force in the United States during the inter-war years (Galper, 1980: 201). Bertha Reynolds, an American Marxist social worker, teacher and activist in the 1930s and 1940s, contended that political radicalism and good social work practice were synonymous (Wagner, 1990). She did not see any conflict between radical social work and the humanistic ethical base of the profession (Mullaly, 1997: 106). Radical social work sought to move social work from a position of 'neutrality' into an open alliance with the burgeoning socialist movement, which was pledged to overthrow capitalism. The radical community organiser, Saul Alinsky, during the 1930s built power-ful coalitions of churches, fraternal organisations and other groups in Chicago, around winnable issues designed to empower ordinary citizens (Wievel and Gills, 1995: 128).

The rank and file movement became the voice of radical social work in the United States during the 1930s and 1940s. It dominated the newly formed social service unions and 'found an influential place in theory development in social work, within the ranks of academia, and within social services adminis-tration' (Wagner, 1990: 6). Subsequently, members of the Rank and File move-ment, including Bertha Reynolds, 'suffered severe repression and were purged from their jobs' (Wagner, 1990: 6). But they left a legacy that was to re-emerge during the 1960s. Ultimately, the Rank and File movement stood for social justice, maintaining a link with the radicals of the settlement movement earlier in the century.

There is further evidence of this ongoing concern with poverty in the essential support which American social workers gave to the administration of the New Deal relief programmes in the United States of the Great Depression of the 1930s. The economic recession which was sparked off by the collapse of the Wall Street Stock Exchange in October 1929 marked a watershed in the development of American social work and social welfare. The Great Depression which followed exposed the ineffectiveness of voluntarism as a mechanism for wealth redistribution and, more importantly, the bankruptcy of *laissez-faire* eco-nomic doctrine. With the election of Franklin D. Roosevelt as US President, in November 1932, new Keynesian economics, founded upon high public expendi-ture, were introduced with the aim of tackling unemployment, which had peaked in 1932 in excess of 15 million. Social workers were drawn into the administra-tion of public relief programmes – the hub of the New Deal strategy. The most notable was Harry L. Hopkins, who took responsibility for the Federal Emergency Relief Administration (FERA) and subsequent emergency relief programmes. At the time of its dissolution in 1936, $3,088,670,625 had been dispensed by FERA. The enactment of the Social Security Act 1935 was the corner-stone of the New Deal that constituted America's welfare settlement. The New Deal institutionalised American social workers' involvement in the adminis-tration of public relief and allied them with the social concern of American liberalism.

Beveridge and the British welfare state

The British Federation of Social Workers, formed in 1935 to promote co-operation between social workers from different settings, considered the advocacy of social rights through public education and pressure for legislative reform a key aspect of its function. A series of Conservative governments in Britain postponed the introduction of social reform until after the Second World War. Ironically, it was the Attlee government (led by a man who had close personal associations with social work) which introduced the British welfare state in 1945. His government assigned social workers to a relatively peripheral role. Fabianism had finally replaced voluntarism with the welfare state. Social work was incorporated into the state and child welfare became a major focus in the new order that sought to realise social citizenship as the ultimate goal of democracy (Marshall, 1950).

It is largely uncontested that a 'classic' welfare state emerged in Britain during the 1940s. Fraser (1973: 222) in his influential history of the welfare state contested that 'the British Welfare State was not born – it had evolved'. In the sense that the welfare state represented the realisation of Fabian ambitions, it was an evolutionary process. But there were particular factors that influenced its development.

The decisive victory of the Labour Party in the 1945 General Election provided the political mandate for Fabianism. More importantly, the war had created a change in attitudes to poverty and related social issues. Studies had exposed the extent of poverty in British urban society and wartime evacuation of large numbers of children from the towns and cities to foster homes brought home the stark realities of social deprivation. The sense of solidarity generated by the war changed social attitudes. As Layburn (1995: 211) puts it: 'the poor social and health conditions of many children became apparent to the whole nation and it was recognised that something had to be done'.

The blueprint was provided by the Beveridge Report published in 1942. The report, entitled *Social Insurance and Allied Services*, set itself the far from revolutionary objective of establishing a 'national minimum' standard of living. (Novak, 1988: 151–152; Layburn, 1995: 214). This objective was to be achieved through a unified, comprehensive and adequate social insurance system. The Beveridge Report did establish the important principle of the state's responsibility for the financial maintenance of children through family allowances (later renamed child benefit). While there were clearly pronatalist reasons behind this development, arising from the impact of war on the population, it was also an important initiative in the fight against child poverty. As Beveridge (1942: para. 412) put it:

> The gap between income during earning and during interruption of earning should be as large as possible for every man. It cannot be kept large for men with large families, except either by making their benefit in unemployment and disability inadequate, or by giving allowances for children in time of earning and not earning alike.

The Fabians' Anglocentrism subsequently led to the mistaken belief that the institution of the welfare state was uniquely British. It assumed a national superiority in terms of social progress that belied the facts. Both New Zealand and Sweden had created welfare states, informed by similar social democratic principles, before Britain. In the case of Sweden a more elaborate welfare system had been achieved. In reality, Fabianism is a national variant of the European social democratic model, and this made it a pioneer in the field of social policy until the 1970s (EU, 1996: 30).

Because the Fabians had equated the concepts of welfare collectivism and social obligation, the benign nature of the state has been assumed. Evidence to the contrary has largely been ignored. Mishra (1997: 10) has observed that 'the social and political significance of Bismarck's Welfare State and later Hitler's concept of a people's community in Nazi Germany, has not featured to any great extent on the curriculum of social policy studies in Britain'. Moreover, the historiography of the welfare state is presented in terms of a progression from barbarism to enlightenment (see Bruce, 1968; Fraser, 1973). This idealist view of history attributes all reform to a combination of altruism and religious sentiment, which, it is argued, incrementally improve the human condition. More recent welfare historians have questioned this idealist view of social policy (Novak, 1988; Squires, 1990; Layburn, 1995). Citizenship defines the link between the individual and the state. The welfare state invented social citizenship expanding the concept beyond the realms of the civil and political.

Welfare, citizenship and the personal social services

Citizenship can be defined in T.H. Marshall's classic formulation as 'a three legged stool'. First, there are fundamental civil rights such as freedom of speech, thought and religious toleration; equality before the law, the due process of the justice system, the right to conclude contracts as equals – the rule of law in its broadest sense. Second, there are basic political rights including the right to vote, form political parties and contest elections – democratic pluralism, in essence. Third, there are basic social rights: 'the whole range from the right to a modicum of economic welfare and security to the right to share to the full the social heritage and to live the life of a civilised being according to the standards of the prevailing society' (Marshall, 1973: 72).

The development of social citizenship rights, according to the Marshallian thesis, is the product of class struggle incrementally promoting an increasingly egalitarian society for the majority. The erosion of traditional social inequalities has served to compress income differentials for the working population at both ends of the spectrum, to create a more popular and universalistic culture and to establish firm links between education and occupation based upon the meritocratic ideal. A universal status of social citizenship has emerged in democratic pluralist societies encompassing the majority of the working population.

In this regard, the Scandinavian social scientist, Esping-Andersen (1990: 21), in the tradition of T.H. Marshall, shares the view that 'Social citizenship constitutes the core idea of the welfare state.... But the concept of social citizenship also involves social stratification: one's status as a citizen will compete with, or even replace, one's class position'. Esping-Andersen is essentially endorsing the view that social rights have led to a breaking down of social class inequalities based on labour market positions. According to his decommodification theory, when social rights are added to civil and political rights, society moves away from treating people as commodities (or things) to a consideration of their essential humanity. Esping-Andersen (1990: 11) has thus reopened an old debate: 'the central question, not only for Marxism but for the entire contemporary debate on the Welfare State, is whether, and under what conditions, the class divisions and social inequalities produced by capitalism can be undone by parliamentary democracy'.

Paradoxically, the emergence of social citizenship as the direct product of class struggle has led to a decline of the latter. As the working class secured direct influence over the state, transforming it into the welfare state, working-class allegiance to its institutions was ensured. Struggle for control over the economy (in socialist parlance the 'means of production') has abated and the working class have become clients of the welfare state. Social citizenship conferred upon the working class a new status within the welfare state.

The significance of social citizenship is that democratic rights are based on the citizen's relationship not with the means of production but with the means of distribution – the welfare state rather than the market economy. This is, as already suggested, basically a clientelist relationship. The social citizen is essentially cast in a passive role. Within such an arrangement political parties vie with each other for the citizen's electoral support. In this political order the welfare state achieved hegemony through regulating the relationship between labour and business and the redistributive systems involving taxation and social welfare benefits.

The term 'status' has been widely interpreted, in this context, as meaning a set of legal entitlements from the state for minimum social and economic standards. Minimum standards are understood in the late twentieth century in terms of lifestyle and social consumption rather than working conditions – the traditional priority of the labour movement. There is widespread agreement that contemporary Western developed societies have conferred on the majority of the population access to complex status items in both the public and private spheres. In the public sphere these include above all the right to home ownership but also state-guaranteed pension rights, high-quality state-subsidised health care and increasing access to education. In the private sphere, access to privatised transportation, foreign holidays, electronically mediated mass entertainment and technologised leisure equipment are considered basic necessities of a normal lifestyle. However, these gains in the quality of life for some individuals have been achieved at considerable cost to the social. Traditional social rights (e.g. to education and training, health care, work and fair conditions of work and pay, a minimum income in the event of unemployment, a retirement pension) have been eroded by privatisation and public expenditure cuts and a lowering of public service standards. A new generation of social rights (e.g. to environmental protection, sustainable use of resources, choice of work and social inclusion) have been neglected.

Gail Lewis (1998b: 109) has asserted that 'social citizenship, and its direct link to welfare institutions, was a feature of twentieth century democratic society and made citizenship a profoundly relational concept, which constructed a particular version of the relation between the state and its citizens'. However, the democratic culture envisaged by social citizenship consigned some citizens to second class status. Marshall drew a sharp distinction between universal rights, such as health and education, and the second-order rights associated with personal social services (the arena of social work):

> The case of the welfare services, in the technical administrative sense (that is personal social services) is different. It cannot be said that society needs happy old people in the same way that it needs a healthy and educated population, nor would it suffer grave loss if the mentally handicapped were not assisted (at considerable cost in time and money) to make the most of their limited capacities. The motive that inspires the services rendered to these people is compassion rather than interest. And though compassion ... may create a right, having almost the force of law, to minimal subsistence, it cannot establish the same kind of right to the benefit of services which are continually striving to extend the limits of the possible, and to replace the minimum by the optimum. So this particular right to welfare is bound to be more dependent than the others for its driving and sustaining force on the fact that it is a moral right.... Furthermore, those in need of these welfare services are minority groups set apart from the general body of normal citizens by their disabilities. The principle of universality which is a characteristic feature of the modern rights of citizenship does not apply, and the right cannot be reinforced, as in the case of education and health, by a corresponding duty to exercise it. The most that one can say is that the handicapped have a moral duty to try to overcome their misfortunes as far as in them lies. (cited in Hughes, 1998: 115)

Marshall had made it clear that social citizenship rights largely did not apply to the recipients of personal social services. They were to be reduced to the status of welfare subjects in this differentiated categorisation of citizenship that left them largely outsiders in the post-war welfare settlement (Lewis, 1998b: 116). For this group citizenship as a cultural achievement or 'gift from history' remained as elusive under the welfare state as it did under the Poor Law. They were not to be encouraged to avail of social citizenship but rather to become as self-reliant as their capabilities permitted. For the user of personal social services it was client status rather than social citizenship.

Social work, poverty and problematisation

The achievement of a welfare state in post-war Britain, and its uncontested political formation between 1945 and 1975, represented the fruition of Fabian aspirations. However, the limitations of the British welfare state were exposed by Brian Abel-Smith and Peter Townsend in their classic 1960s survey, *The Poor and the Poorest*. It mirrored Michael Harrington's parallel study in the United States, *The Other America* (1962), which revealed that what has come to be called an 'underclass' was largely untouched by state welfare. Poverty remained endemic despite the best efforts of the state to engineer social reform. Critics began to view the welfare state as an instrument of social control rather than working-class emancipation (Piven and Cloward, 1971).

The problematisation of some variants of family and community behaviour and the pathologisation of poverty lends credence to the social control critique. Spicker (1993: 74) observes that these pathological explanations of poverty have individualistic, familial and subcultural dimensions. Social work was at the centre of this process. The problematising orientation of post-war social work embodied in the concept of 'the problem family' was justified by the widely shared, if ephemeral, belief that structural poverty had been eliminated – in Galbraith's phrase, 'the myth of the affluent society'. The fallacious assumption that poverty would be eliminated by economic growth dominated post-war policy-making. Haveman and Schwabish (1999: 1) have observed that: 'For much of the 1950s and 1960s, this faith in the anti-poverty effectiveness of economic growth seemed well grounded'.

In the United States the identification of a marginalised category called 'the multi-problem family' has been widely attributed to the Community Research Associates (CRA), who were responsible for a community-wide study in St Paul, Minnesota, of the interrelatedness of four social need factors: dependency, ill-health, maladjustment and recreational need. The CRA concluded that in every community there is a similar group of families whose needs absorbed a large part of time, service and money expended on assistance, health and adjustment agencies.

In Britain agreement concerning the origin of the concept of 'the problem family' is more equivocal. Titmuss (1962: v) claimed that there was a 'long though discontinuous tradition ... of concern about a segment of families in the population supposedly characterised by similar traits, and thought to represent a closed psychological entity – in Leadbetter's phrase 'a race of subnormals!''. There is a substance for his opinion in Charles Booth's 'submerged tenth' identified in his 1904 London survey; in the 'social problem group' of the *Report of the Joint Committee on Mental Deficiency* (Wood, 1929), and in the 'economic residuum' of the *Report of the Committee on Sterilisation* (Brock, 1934).

All of these explanations are strongly infused with eugenicist thought. While eugenics is generally associated with extreme right-wing ideology, typified by the Nazis, there is evidence that Fabians were also influenced by this socio-biological philosophy. Novak (1988: 106) notes the influence of eugenicist thought on the Fabians, 'that was to continue to be and is currently echoed in a number of areas of social policy the very poor were branded with an ideology that saw them as diseased and contagious, requiring at best drastic social engineering, and at times elimination'. Spicker (1993: 69) has commented: 'after the Second World War much of this philosophy was discredited – not least because of the association of eugenics with fascism – although the idea of degeneracy did survive in the concept of the problem family'. Not all commentators associated the concept of 'the problem family' with eugenics.

Another British school of thought argued that 'problem families' were 'discovered' during the evacuation from the cities caused by the Second World War blitz. Penelope Hall (1952: 159), for example, has observed, 'for the first time, middle and working-class people living in the country and suburbs were brought into close contact with ... a number of problem families'. Tonge (1973: 3) and his associates attribute this development to the wartime Pacifist (now Family) Service Units (FSUs) which 'personalised the social problem group into problem families', because the individualisation of the problem into pathological family systems was essential to their approach.

Ferguson (1996: 209) views the problem family as socially constructed:

Here we have the social construction of the 'dirty', 'dysfunctional', 'neglectful', problem family as the marginalised, dangerous 'other' and a category of 'case' that would dominate much of twentieth century child protection.

This emphasis highlights the process by which poverty is recognised as a social issue, and the impact of political and ideological influences on determining its meaning, at a particular moment in time. Ultimately, the social construction-ists argue that the understanding of poverty is based on convention. (Spicker, 1993: 68)

Spicker (1993: 76) notes that during the 1950s a paradigm shift took place in social work in which vulnerable families were constructed as sites of social pathology. Social work researchers studied various aspects of 'problem family' life with a view to understanding and effective intervention. Costin (1979: 197) identified two major characteristics emerging from these studies. First, a failure of 'problem families' to attain certain generally accepted social standards, which is manifested in low levels of social functioning in the following areas:

1 general disorder in family life style with failure to perform essential tasks satisfactorily, e.g. financial management, health care, fertility control, hygiene;
2 infantile parental needs which inhibit the development of satisfactory child care practices;
3 lack of a family unit e.g. marital disharmony, absence of affectional bonds or trust, continuous family dissension;
4 isolated or anomic relationships with kinship and neighbourhood networks as well as formal organisations e.g. schools, police, etc.;
5 behaviour disorders amongst the children e.g. hyperactivity, impulsivity, withdrawal, low levels of self-esteem etc.

The second major characteristic identified by Costin was a failure by 'problem families' to benefit from social work intervention: 'their chronic need is aggra-vated by inconsistent responses and hostility, and by the accumulating discour-agement with the agency personnel who approach them' (ibid.). This realisation that clients did not want their assistance presented social workers with a basic ethical dilemma. Why force help on unwilling clients? This was to become a major issue after the Seebohm reforms in the 1970s sought to establish social work as 'the Fifth Social Service'.

The association of poverty with family pathology is clearly linked with the concept of the 'cycle of deprivation' or 'transmitted deprivation'. Spicker (1993: 76) observes: 'There is at least a good argument to be made that poor parenting leads to disadvantage in development, but the "cycle of deprivation" goes further: poor parenting, it is held, generates a cycle of inadequate development and fur-ther poor parenting.' Conservative politicians seized upon this argument. Keith Joseph, a former Secretary of State for Social Services and New Right social theo-rist, declared: 'parents who were themselves deprived in one or more ways in childhood become in turn the parent of another generation of deprived children' (cited in Spicker, 1993: 76). However, a working party established by Joseph reported, after ten years' investigation, that there was no evidence to support the concept of 'transmitted deprivation' (Spicker, 1993: 77).

The influence of family-based explanations of poverty had proved to be a power-ful source of inspiration to policy-makers during the 1960s. Bowlby's (1952) World Health Organisation report, *Maternal Care and Mental Health*, was a land-mark study in promoting parenting and parental responsibility. A White Paper produced by the Longford Committee and published in Britain in 1965, *The Child, the Family and the Young Offender*, resulted in the Children and Young Persons Act, 1969. This statute dissolved the distinction between the young offender and the child in need of care and protection. The 'welfare approach' achieved an even more radical form in Scotland, when the Social Work Act (Scotland) 1968 aboli-shed the children's courts, replacing them with children's panels. The quality of parenting and the needs of the child took precedence in the panels' deliberations over the child's deeds.

The emergence of the welfare approach in juvenile justice built upon the Children Act 1908, which recognised the distinctive relationship children have with the law. They do not have a right to liberty. In reality it is impossible to distinguish between children in need and those who transgress the law. It quickly became evident that the welfare approach worked well in Scotland (Martin, 1981). However, south of the border reform was less easy. In England and Wales the full implementation of the Children and Young Persons Act, 1969, was frus-trated. Social work was seen as too powerful and permissive in its approach to the treatment of the young offender. The departure of the Labour Party from govern-ment in 1970 ensured that the momentum towards reform was lost.

The 'rediscovery of poverty' during the 1960s began to refocus attention on communities where, it was believed, problem families were clustered. Hughes and Mooney (1998: 59) assert in reference to this development: 'From this period the language of community became firmly established as a means of legitimising state intervention and regulation and, in the process, community was constructed as a site of intervention'. The establishment of community as a site of state inter-vention took two forms: community development and community care.

Welfare rights, community development and the war on poverty

The emergence of welfare rights and community development as an anti-poverty strategy during the 1960s led to what Hughes and Mooney (1998: 59) have called 'a prolonged assault on a number of deviant communities'. However, it would be inaccurate to view the poverty programmes and community development in terms of state regulation. They had a remarkable empowering dimension that defined them as radical social action. To Knight (1993: 50), 'community development is a method that involves the formation of organisations of ordinary people in geo-graphical areas so that their collective identity gives them a greater say in the forces that affect their lives.'

The poverty programmes represent a rejection of pathology-based models of social intervention in favour of controlled inclusion. These programmes, which were established in the 1960s in response to the 'rediscovery of poverty', rejected the individualisation of poverty in terms of family pathology. Their liberal and social democratic sponsors predicated them on the assumption that poverty was largely a localised problem confined to decaying inner city areas and remote rural communities, where racial violence and social isolation had become endemic. Optimistically it was believed that these problems could be overcome by targeted social intervention. The history of the poverty programmes is one of progression from a consensus to a radical model of social change both in the United States and in Britain, and consequent disillusion on the part of the state. In the United States, the Community Action Programmes (CAPs) were part of the 'War on Poverty' established as a result of the Economic Opportunities Act 1964, the cornerstone of President Johnson's 'Great Society' policy. The 'War on Poverty' had originated from the action-research-orientated Ford Foundation's Grey Area Projects and the similarly conceived President's Committee on Juvenile Delinquency.

In practice the war on poverty was based upon a welfare rights strategy that was intended to empower the poor of inner city communities, particularly the Black poor. It was very much a locally based initiative with up to 1,000 projects. Piven and Cloward (1971: 288) state that the type of welfare rights service that became most prevalent in the 1960s was 'the storefront centre, staffed by social workers, lawyers, churchmen, students and slum-dwellers themselves'. These agencies were highly effective in empowering poor people to apply for welfare, in some cases increasing local welfare rolls by more than a third in one year. Such success was likely to produce a powerful reaction from neo-conservatives deeply opposed to welfare. Wadden (1997: 71) concludes:

> Despite these tales of success, however, by the mid-1980s it had become not only the political chant of the New Right but almost the conventional wisdom to reflect on the failure of the War on Poverty. Most immediately it might be supposed that this was because the poverty rate had not been reduced in the aftermath of the 1960s. Yet perhaps the starkest evidence in justification of the specific attempt to tackle poverty came with an examination of the official poverty rate. In 1960, 39.9 million citizens, constituting 22.2 per cent of the population, lived below the official poverty line. By 1979 these numbers had fallen to 26.1 million and 11.7 per cent, respectively.

In retrospect, the War on Poverty was the product of Great Society optimism. It was in many respects the apogee of American liberalism. From the start it attracted vitriolic criticism from the New Right. Piven and Cloward (1971: 256) note that local programmes 'were charged with fiscal mismanagement and embezzlement and with encouraging demonstrations, protest and even riots'. Charles Murray (1984: 145), in his book *Losing Ground*, which became the touchstone of New Right social policy, declared apocalyptically: 'the War on Poverty had become a domestic Vietnam'. In the face of this there was a loss of liberal nerve, which ultimately paved the way for welfare reform. The redistribution of wealth achieved in the 1960s and 1970s in the United States was to be reversed during the 1980s and 1990s by both Republican and Democrat administrations.

The War on Poverty represents reformist social work at its zenith in a Western context. Social work and New Deal liberalism had forged a powerful consensus around the promotion of welfare rights and the empowerment of the poor. The connection with the civil rights movement of the 1960s, committed to desegregation, was a close one. But as Martin Luther King was assassinated in 1968 and was replaced by the Black Panthers and Malcom X, a hardening of attitudes towards equality began. Class, gender and race issues coalesced in a resurgent New Right determined to destroy New Deal liberalism, which they regarded as anathema.

A similar, if decidedly more modest, poverty programme in Britain, initiated by the Children's Department in the Home Office, was that of the Community Development Projects (CDPs). The CDPs were directly modelled on the American War on Poverty (Knight, 1993: 50) and commenced operations in 1969 with a 'remarkable brief' (Spicker, 1993: 86). The target population were those who 'through ill-fortune or personal inadequacy suffer from a multitude of inter-related problems and deprivations which cannot be resolved by uncoordinated support from a series of separately organised services' (Loney, 1980: 92). By 1971 the CDP was operating in twelve designated localities, and was described by the Home Office as a 'national action research project' to increase understanding of social needs of the poor and to devise methods for tackling them. CDPs initially adopted a consensus model of society and based their operations on a 'dialogue' approach attempting to create greater responsiveness and sensitivity on the part of government at all levels to the needs of the disadvantaged through involving them in the decision-making process, and through better co-ordination of existing social services. They asserted that the central idea of the programme was to involve the residents living in an area in community schemes arising from their own perceptions of need, which were translated into action with local participation, and subjected to research evaluation.

The National Community Development Project Forward Plan 1975–76 reflected the views of nine local projects, indicating how far the CDPs had moved from their initial strategy, which was deemed as being capable of only marginal impact on the problems of the poor because of its failure to tackle the economic and political forces pushing the target communities into decline. The Forward Plan recommended a new strategy based on an investigation of how conditions in deprived areas were determined by economic forces, such as industries moving away leaving workers 'on the scrap heap' or the migration of younger skilled workers to newer factories built in the outer suburbs, leaving an ageing, low-income population. The CDPs produced a series of reports, which overwhelmingly linked poverty to the social and economic structure. They argued the case for a radical initiative aimed at redistributing wealth and power.

As in the American 'War on Poverty', this redistributive strategy, with its welfare rights and community action orientation, came to be interpreted as inimical to government interests, resulting in the termination of the CDPs. Sainsbury (1977: 104) suggested that

> the failure of the CDPs was inevitable. By their nature, they constituted a lively local criticism of the established practices of existing services, yet they lacked the resources to demonstrate an effective and viable alternative method of provision. Their geographical

boundaries did not match the boundaries of other services. Their loyalties had somehow to reconcile the policies of the central Home Office team and the concerns of small rival groups within neighbourhoods. They were expected to achieve both the detachment of research and the involvement of community action.

Spicker (1993: 86) similarly views the CDPs as essentially victims of their own radical analysis and powerlessness. Knight (1993: 51) dismisses the poverty programme as 'false hope'. These criticisms are, in my view, a little harsh. Like the War on Poverty, the CDPs confronted society with the solution to poverty. The problem was that an increasingly conservative social and political order did not want to hear that the solution to poverty was greater equality.

The issue of poverty, despite varying interpretations of its causes, has as we have seen remained at the centre of social work in the developed world in the second half of the twentieth century. It has been noted that many social workers in Western industrialised societies had come to equate poverty with inequalities in the distribution of power and resources. Others saw the solution to poverty in more rehabilitative terms.

Knight (1993: 51) sees the legacy of community development as follows:

> Community development did make some gains in its short but unfulfilled history. Much of the language of community development survived (e.g. empowerment).... Much community development was transmogrified into work on equal opportunities and anti-racism, and institutionalized in local authority units pursuing the interests of minorities. Work with the working-class white poor on the estates virtually ended as the focus became discrimination and not deprivation.

Community development also represents a critique of traditional social work. It stands apart from professionalisation (although there is an accrediting body, the UK National Youth Agency), preferring to draw its legitimacy from the community it serves. Deprofessionalisation is a defining characteristic of contemporary community development. This is the product of the radical legacy of the poverty programmes.

Social work and family welfare and holistic practice

Under the aegis of the welfare state progressive social work was also evident. Jones (1983: 48) observes:

> Progressive features include the possibility within social work for understanding the problems and circumstances of clients in a more holistic fashion than [is] possible in other state welfare activities; it also includes more humane consideration of clients which is often at odds with much prevailing opinion concerning significant sections of the client population such as problem families and delinquents, where primitive and stigmatising ideology and theory are still rife.

This concept of holistic practice emphasised social work's capacity for progressive practice. It was possible for social workers to draw upon strategies that lifted state responses to the most marginalised above the level of instrumental relations. The fundamental humanity of communities was recognised by progressive social work practitioners commited to social reform through holistic practice. Jones (1983) concludes that however 'deformed' the relationships with service users and the tensions between individual social workers and state agencies, holistic practice offers a progressive agenda.

In the United Kingdom the impetus towards a more holistic approach to family welfare came initially from the voluntary sector. During the 1960s the voluntary sector was experiencing something of a renaissance in Britain with the dawning realisation that the welfare state could not solve all the problems of society. The voluntary sector became the cradle of innovative social work practice. At the forefront of this development in Britain were the National Children's Bureau and the Family Service Units (Leissner, 1967, 1971; Twelvetrees, 1973).

Aryeh Leissner in a series of reports from the National Children's Bureau began to pioneer more holistic thinking in relation to social work with families (Leissner, 1967, 1971). Alan Twelvetrees (1973) produced a report on an FSU project in Leicester known as the North Brainstone Neighbourhood Project.

The distinguishing features of the holistic approach are, first, the broadening of the social work focus beyond individualised treatment i.e. casework. Lagey and Ayres (1962) identified this aspect of the approach as emphasising (a) co-ordination of local services to combat social need in a neighbourhood context and (b) the utilisation of various combinations of casework, groupwork and community development. The second distinctive feature has been succinctly summarised by an FSU authority as a movement away from imposing methods of social work intervention to deriving the methods and strategies from the practice context (Laxton, 1976).

The basic principles informing holistic social work practice can be identified as follows:

1 The factors which cause and perpetuate social distress in the family must be isolated and combated in their social context, i.e. the family, the peer group or the neighbourhood.
2 A commitment to the 'deprofessionalisation' of the relationship between service users and social workers is a core principle.
3 A pronounced emphasis on social action strategies and welfare rights is central.
4 The service seeks to become geographically and psychologically accessible and to fit the social ambience of the neighbourhood.
5 Specific operational objectives can be set only by mapping needs, resources and relationships in the neighbourhood and this can only be achieved through consumer participation.
6 The fostering of community development rather than individualised casework is an explicit goal.
7 The conventional social work methodology is fused and articulated with the activities of youth workers and play-leaders, who become closely involved in the multidisciplinary professional team.

The statutory sector also became involved with a holistic approach to family welfare in Britain. *The Report of the Committee on Local Authority and Allied Personal Social Services* (Seebohm Report) was published in 1968. It declared:

> We recommend a new local authority department, providing a community-based and
> family-orientated service, which will be available to all. This new department will, we
> believe, reach far beyond the discovery and rescue of social casualties; it will enable the
> greatest possible number of individuals to act reciprocally, giving and receiving service
> for the well-being of the community. (Seebohm, 1968: para. 2)

Harris (1999: 919) observes: the universalist tone of the Seebohm Report was
complemented by a stress on the comprehensiveness of citizens' entitlements to
social work services. The Seebohm Report was followed by the Local Authority
Social Services Act, 1970 which enacted its main recommendations. In Scotland
a similar development took place. The Kilbrandon Report (1964) was followed
by the Social Work (Scotland) Act 1968. As a result of these legislative initiatives, social services departments emerged in England and Wales and social work
departments in Scotland. The 'Fifth Social Service' of the welfare state was
consequently created. Fabianism and social work had finally converged.

The emergence of a holistic approach in Britain was not unique. Similar developments were taking place in other countries. In the United States, Geismar and
Kriesberg (1969) in what has been described as 'an early skirmish in the War of
Poverty' attempted to evaluate the outcome of this approach in the Newhaven
Neighbourhood Improvement Project (NIP) which was located in a neighbourhood called Farnham Court. Although NIP relied heavily on family casework
which was utilised in concert with groupwork and community work, it is difficult
to identify discrete methodologies, since they were subordinated to the holistic
focus.

The NIP research evaluation attempted to measure the effects of the holistic
approach. Significant rehabilitative change was found in the residents of Farnham
Court, when compared with the control group in all areas of social functioning,
particularly in health conditions and practices, relationship to social worker, use
of community resources and family relationships and unity. The holistic approach
manifestly changed the dynamic between the social worker and the service user
from passive client to activist in solving their problems.

An Australian project established in 1972, the Melbourne Family Centre Project,
represents another example of the approach. The project involved sixty 'multi-
deficit' families. There was a emphasis on deprofessionalisation in client–worker
transactions, a multidisciplinary approach and, perhaps most interestingly, the
project offered all the families a modest income supplement as of right. Using structural criteria (income, housing, employment, education, etc.), the project attempted
to evaluate its impact on the families' welfare after three years. It was found that
sustained improvement had been achieved in the socio-economic position of the
families, especially those with male heads (Liffman, 1978).

In Canada, the Vancouver Area Development Project (ADP), which was
reported in 1969 by Bell and Wilder, is another example of the holistic approach.
ADP provided a co-ordinated programme of casework, groupwork and community work to ninety-two 'multi-problem families' in the City of Vancouver.
Outcome evaluation demonstrated that the holistic approach generally proved
more efficacious than the usual agency casework.

The holistic approach to family social work became widespread in Britain due to the growth of family centres, which were recognised in the Children's Act 1989. By the mid-1990s it was estimated that there were 750 family centres in the United Kingdom, many of them involving voluntary participation (Pithouse, 2000: 127). The high level of voluntary sector provision of family centres undoubtedly reflects a more positive commitment to humanistic values based upon democratic practice. Pithouse (2000: 127) has identified four types of family centre:

1 A local *neighbourhood model* that offers open access services to parents and children and, by this and other means, seeks to invigorate family and community solidarities.
2 A *community development model* that encourages families to initiate and run their own services in the belief that collective action will lead to improvements in social and environmental factors influencing family life.
3 A *client orientated model* offering assessment and therapeutic services, and sometimes described as a specialist referred family centre, restricted mainly to families referred by welfare professionals, often where aspects of child protection or welfare are paramount.
4 What might be described as a *bureau family centre* is usually local authority run, combines open access as well as more therapeutic/assessment facilities and also houses statutory social work staff who operate in the community. The centre may also provide a venue for other welfare and health professionals whom families may wish to visit. Such centres are likely to contain administrative staff and facilities required to progress statutory child care practice.

The Barclay Report (1982) sought to decentralise social service departments' work with service users. Barclay advocated a community-based approach to social work that substantially reflected the holistic approach. Barclay (1982: 13.23–13.25) defined community social work as follows:

> Community social work is concerned both with responding to the existing social care needs of individuals and families and with reducing the number of such problems which arise in the future. Its actual form will vary greatly from place to place and time to time, but its underlying rationale is more enduring....
>
> This recognition leads to a widening of the focus of social work attention. The individual or family with problems will of course remain the primary concern of social services agencies.... But the focus will be upon individuals in the communities or network of which they are part.

Jones (1983: 44) commented in relation to the significance of the Barclay Report in terms of holistic practice:

> Thus although social work practice too often fails to be holistic, the potential remains. It continues to be an avowed principle of social work practice and theory (and was confirmed by the Barclay committee) which can be exploited with immediate effect to clients' benefit and with wider political consequences in the construction of more convincing and accurate accounts of the multiplicity of pressures that affect clients.

The Barclay Report (1982) was unfortunate in its timing. Its publication took place during the early years of the Thatcher administration in the United Kingdom. There was little official support for its approach, although the idea of community self-reliance would not have been at odds with government thinking. However, in the tide of change that was overtaking the public sector the philosophy of holistic social work was lost.

But clear lessons can be learned from holistic approaches. For example it humanises social work. According to Hardcastle et al. (1997: 5–6):

> The profession's often reviewed 'cause and function' strain between social action, social change, and reform, on the one hand, and individual treatment and change, on the other hand, poses a suspicious dilemma. It is a dilemma only when wrongly framed as an either–or choice between two mutually exclusive activities rather than as two inter-related and complementary social work components.

While it is correct to argue that social work defined its methodology and approach in terms of liberal individualism, its mission was firmly located in the context of a human service ethos directed at the poor and oppressed. Community care was another manifestation of a reformist practice.

Human rights and community care

Community care became an important concept in the post-war world. The implications of the unspeakable crimes perpetrated in concentration camps during the war against minority groups (including Jews, gypsies, communists, blacks, gays and many others) gradually impacted on public opinion. After the Second World War Primo Levi, who devoted his life to bearing witness to these atrocities, published his monumental account of Auschwitz, *If this is a Man* (Levi, 1996). While it received respectful reviews, its sales were initially modest, because of lack of public interest in the issues. The post-war world was slowly coming to grips with the implications of the Holocaust, which questioned the basis of popular conceptions of progress towards a more civilised and just social and political order. Reports from the Soviet Union, popularised in the writings of Alexander Solzhenitsyn, exposed the existence of gulags, where non-conformists and political dissidents were incarcerated in horrific conditions, and the practice of mass extermination against enemies of the state. Gradually the public became engaged with the terrifying implications of these atrocities. The Universal Declaration of Human Rights in 1948 sought to outlaw such tyrannical behaviour in the future. In its thirty articles the original declaration sought to lay down a structure for universal human rights. While politicians have selectively interpreted its articles, the concept of human rights contained in the document related to the totality of human existence: spiritual, intellectual, political, social and economic freedom. These were viewed as indivisible parts of the whole.

In the post-war climate, the paradox of enshrining human rights at a historical moment, when the idea of moral universalism was deeply compromised, was evident. Hannah Arendt argued in her influential book, *Origins of Totalitarianism*, published in 1958, that stripped of civic and political rights human beings lose their essential humanity. The significance of the Universal Declaration of Human Rights, which has now survived for over half a century, has been summarised by Ignatieff (1999: 58): 'Human Rights has become the major article of faith of a secular culture that fears it believes in nothing else ... the drafters put their hopes in the idea that by declaring rights as moral universals, they could foster a global rights consciousness among those they called "the common people".'

The promotion of human rights has largely been carried out by the United Nations and a variety of voluntary or non-governmental organisations (NGOs). Amnesty International, Human Rights Watch, the Anti-Slavery Society and others have revitalised voluntary endeavour. It is possible to dismiss non-governmental organisations, dedicated to promoting human rights in the age of economic globalisation, as simply representing the interests of a new global middle class, liberal-minded and committed to doing good globally. But there are more pro-found issues at stake. Ignatieff (1999: 60) has captured the elemental importance of human rights:

> A secular defence of human rights depends on the ideal of moral reciprocity: that we cannot conceive of any circumstances in which we or anyone we know would wish to be abused in mind or body. That we are capable of this thought experiment – i.e., that we possess the faculty of imagining the pain and degradation done to other human beings as if it were our own – is simply a fact for us as a species. Being capable of such empathy, we all possess a conscience, and because we do, we wish to be free to make up our own minds and express our own justifications for our views. The fact that there are many human beings who remain indifferent to the pain of others does not imply they cannot imagine it or prove that they did not possess a conscience, only that this conscience is free to do both good and evil. Such natural facts about human beings provide the grounds for an entitlement to protection from physical and mental abuse and to the right to freedom of thought and speech.

In Italy, the home of Primo Levi, the first realisation of the social, moral and politi-cal implications of institutionalising vulnerable population groups (i.e. children, the sick, aged and infirm) became evident in the heightened consciousness of the post-war era. It led to a policy of deinstitutionalisation that became popular in the English-speaking world during the 1960s and 1970s. Deinstitutionalisation has been dismissed by social control theorists as simply a policy shift that moves the site of regulation from the institution to the community (Foucault, 1967; Scull, 1984; Cohen, 1985).

But the social control theorists' view of the world, which proved very influen-tial during the 1980s, is open to criticism for being too reductionist and betraying a lack of appreciation for the enlightenment tradition of rights. The reasons for the emergence of community care are complex but ultimately the policy shift derives from a public desire for a more humane approach to treating vulnerable population groups. It also marks an important recognition of the human rights of all citizens, regardless of their circumstances.

The politicisation of community care was brought about by social reformers and human rights activists who sought to put the politics of conscience on the public agenda. In the increasingly liberal climate of the 1960s and early 1970s this humanitarianism resonated with the public mood of confidence and optimism about the future. But there was also a powerful element of economic realism. Politicians and administrators perceived an opportunity to marry conscience and convenience by closing expensive institutions, using as justification the rhetoric of community care. Few initially expected that the cost of community care would be substantially borne by the family, and specifically women carers, such was the flush of enthusiasm for community care (Dalley, 1996: 7). In retrospect, this enthusiasm is easy to understand.

During wartime Britain vulnerable groups were pushed back into the workhouses in order to make way for 'potential effectives'. Little changed in the immediate aftermath of the war, when reconstruction and the welfare of the able-bodied became the dominant policy concern. However, the benign nature of the welfare state increasingly came to be questioned because of its treatment of vulnerable groups. Evidence of abuse perpetrated against defenceless people in institutional care began to grow. The abuse of the rights of those in care situations through physical abuse, psychosurgery, electroconvulsive therapy (ECT), neglect and isolation, shocked public opinion. It became apparent that even in democratic societies 'the vulnerable' are liable to cruelty and inhumanity. Institutionalisation was identified as the culprit, making prevention and community care key policy goals. The 'rediscovery' of child abuse during the 1960s also pushed the state towards taking a more active role in protecting the rights of vulnerable populations in the community, redefining the role and task of social work in the protective language of advanced liberalism.

A series of inquiries into poor standards of care in mental health institutions in Britain moved the government in the direction of community care. For example, the Farleigh Hospital Committee of Inquiry reported on a disturbing reality of violence, neglect and isolation (National Health Service, 1971: 24–25). Two White Papers followed, *Better Services for the Mentally Handicapped* (1971) and *Better Services for the Mentally Ill* (1975), proposing a policy of deinstitutionalisation 'relocating' mental health treatment to the community. Many of those relocated to the community from institutions posed a challenge to the tolerance of a local population conditioned to stigmatise recipients of mental health services as 'abnormal'. Nonetheless, 'the major focus of those supporting the transition was not on the development of the community itself, but on the individuals moving into it' (Barnes, 1998: 89). This was to prove a major weakness in community care in the long term, prescribing individualist treatment in a policy context that demanded a community response.

Within the community care context 'community social work' emerged. It was different to community development in its emphasis on individualising its clients. Instead, community social work sought to mobilise the collective resources of the community as part of a social care strategy. This brought social work back into the arena of civil society by promoting contacts with churches, voluntary organisations, user and community groups. However, there was little in social work training, largely based on individualised service delivery, to prepare practitioners for this task. The language of management rather than community informs the practice of community social work, e.g. social care planning. This is at odds with the humanist principles of social work.

Humanism and social work values

Ife (1997: 115) has observed: 'social work, whether it likes it or not, is inevitably bound to a humanist vision, given its value base, historical origins and political location'. Humanism promotes the philosophy that 'the proper study of humankind is humanity itself and its moral universe'. Historically, humanism originates in the 5th century in Athens – the cradle of Western civilisation. Medieval Christianity and feudalism undermined classical humanism. However it re-emerged in the 15th century during the Renaissance, when classical values were rediscovered.

Modern humanism developed during the eighteenth, nineteenth and twentieth centuries. Its development was closely linked to Enlightenment rationalism and the scientific revolution that undermined traditional Christian beliefs. Humanists view the human condition in progressive terms as a striving, evolving process towards higher states of being. They believe that human beings are endowed with the creative potentialities to solve problems confronting individuals, communities and governments. Humanists promote international co-operation, human rights and the protection of the planet from the destructive forces of war and modernity. The humanist ethic is based upon a commitment to the realisation of both individual and social possibilities within the context of mutual responsibility.

The professionalisation of social work through associations such as the British Association of Social Workers (BASW), the National Association of Social Workers (NASW) in the United States, the Australian Association of Social Workers (AASW), the Irish Association of Social Workers (IASW) and similar bodies in other countries is heavily influenced by the humanist values in these associations' codes of ethics. Ife (1997: 56) concludes: 'this is the discourse in which traditional social work has been most comfortable, with its emphasis on professional expertise, individualised service, and its combination of humanist and top-down intervention'. Yet he also locates radical social work within the humanist tradition: 'it seeks to combine the bottom-up or anarchist approach with a commitment to human values and a rejection of the certainties of positivism'. Humanism arguably provides the ethical foundation and shared purpose of social work, whether of the traditional or the radical persuasion.

Mullaly (1997: 29), writing from a radical social work perspective, asserts that 'humanism and social equality must form the twin pillars of an ideal social work society'. The emphasis on equality links social work to the socialist tradition. Mullally (1997: 35) also perceives community as one of social work's core values, identifying its links with the communitarian tradition of social intervention and the ideal of co-operative endeavour favoured by humanists. Here Fabianism and humanism coincide in framing social work values.

Mullaly (1997: 30) suggests a distinction between the fundamental values and what he calls 'secondary or instrumental values' contained in the codes of ethics of various professional associations. This does not seem to be a valid distinction since the professional values of social work (respect for persons, self-determination and acceptance) are deeply rooted in humanist discourse. Ultimately, social work's value system is located in the classical humanist notion of a virtuous society, based upon a commitment to humanity, equality and social justice, rather than the vagaries of fortune that define market capitalism. This value orientation enabled social work to root itself comfortably within the orbit of Fabian social philosophy and adapt to the welfare state during the twentieth century, placing it on the political Left.

What makes social work unusual in terms of a Left political perspective is that it does not regard individualism as a negative political value. Liberty has been a guiding principle in Western civilisation since the Enlightenment, and the emphasis on individualisation in social work clearly connects its value base to the ideal of liberty. This is essential, since human rights derive from the notion of liberty that represents a break with the Aristotelian model based on an organic concept of the state (Bobbio, 1996: xv). Social work views liberty essentially in terms of social rather than libertarian rights, maintaining its philosophical links with Fabianism. The political link with the Left explains much of the hostility of the Right towards social work. Humanism offers a profound challenge to the methodological individualism of Right, favoured by intellectuals (e.g. Hayek) and politicians (e.g. Margaret Thatcher). In an era when social reform is being abandoned by politicians of both Left and Right, social work's humanism strikes a politically discordant note.

Conclusion

The twentieth century witnessed the emergence of social work as a profession. The values social work defined itself by were rooted in humanist discourse. Social work became part of the welfare state apparatus. The state and social work were compatible, since the former remained committed to the ideals of social reform and human progress. But as the twentieth century moved to its close the contradictions of the welfare state became increasingly exposed. The emergence of neo-conservatism and economic fundamentalism basically altered the nature of the state and its mission to create a better society. In the new social order dominated by market values and the pursuit of individualism a crisis relationship between the state and social work began to develop. Radical social work contributed to this crisis by sowing the seeds of radical doubt in the social work project.

4

Radical Social Work and Radical Doubt

Radical social work developed in the 1960s and 1970s out of a sense of disillusion with the reformist agenda of the welfare state. It was the product of a movement within social work that has sought to reconceptualise the historical mission of social work to the poor and oppressed in terms of emancipatory politics, casting radical doubt upon reformist social work. Its critics dubbed it 'Revolution on the rates' (Brewer and Lait, 1980: 106). There is little doubt that the radical social work discourse is deeply rooted in Marxist social theory. But equally it is the product of a vibrant humanism, seeking to confront the stark reality that capitalism brutalises the poor and social reform can only ameliorate its worst excesses. Yet radical social work is not simply a brave and idealistic attempt to be true to the historic mission of social work: it provides an important social critique of the economic realities of an unequal society and the inadequacies of social work responses. What is singular about radical social work is that it embraces an emancipatory politics. Ife (1997: 57) writes in reference to radical social workers:

> Such [radical] social workers have often been perceived as being a minority within the profession, and many indeed have discarded the label 'professional'. They have, however, exerted an important influence on social work, in that they have prevented social workers from feeling too comfortable in a 'professional' role, they have reminded social workers of the importance of the analysis of power, and they have held out a more radical alternative. This influence has been very important in preventing social work from becoming too complacent and in maintaining a 'critical edge' to social work theory and practice.

However, Ife (1997: 176) also acknowledges that 'the place of radicalism in social work has always been problematic'. It would probably be fair to add 'highly marginal'. On the other hand radical social work has exercised an influence over social work's epistemology totally out of proportion to its minority status. Its strength is that it addresses the environmental context of social problems and links it to a highly ethical position. Its weakness is its problem with connecting its critique to the predominantly individualised nature of social work intervention.

Radical social work, as it emerged in the 1960s and 1970s, was an entirely new phenomenon. Mullaly (1997: 106) observes: 'Beginning with the Settlement House Movement, social work has always had a radical element.' During the inter-war years radical social work was also an active force in promoting social change (see Chapter 3). What was new about radical social work was the context.

A welfare state had been created and social citizenship established. Radical social work contested the achievement of the welfare state and exposed its flaws.

This chapter will examine the belief amongst politically minded social workers that the failure of the welfare state had failed to match up to its humanistic ideals. The emergence of radical social work within the context of the welfare state will be examined in terms of its contribution to forging an alternative emancipatory discourse of welfare. Radical social work practice will be analysed and critiqued. It will be argued that radical social work has succeeded in casting serious doubt on reformist social work, as an exercise in deconstruction that has shaken the foundations of professional social work through a relentless critique of its moral and social purpose. Statham (1978: 4) describes radical doubt as 'an approach, an attitude characterised by the motto *de omnibus dubitatum*' (scepticism towards everything).

Social work and regulation

Social work professes to be the quintessentially humanist profession concerned with promoting dignity. The humanist ethos is premised on the belief that the welfare state represents the culmination of an unfolding history of progress from barbarism to enlightenment. Natural man was thought to have been renounced and replaced by a more collectivist society based on a caring ethic. The original critique of the welfare state came, not from the New Right, but from some structural Marxists who perceived it as a device to keep the capitalist system in place through a process of legitimisation (Habermas, 1996; Offe, 1984). Other structuralists, such as Scull (1984) and Cohen (1985), have caricatured humanistic reforms, notably community care, as simply representing a change in the style and practice of social control (see Chapter 3). For social workers in particular, and other humanistically minded people in general, these developments have been very discouraging, pointing in the direction of analytic despair and professional immobilisation. In fact, such a conclusion would be oversimplistic and unduly pessimistic. The structuralist critique of the welfare state has helped to clarify many of the issues, which are considerably more complex than the traditionally assumed and challenged complacency of the welfare state apparatus and the Fabian political project.

First, the Panglossian idealism (i.e. all is for the best in the best of all possible worlds) of the welfare state edifice has been promoting a view of reality which has often fallen far short of the ideal. For example, the use of ECT, psychosurgery, and the compulsory admission to psychiatric hospitals of unwilling patients have been indefensible practices. Abusive regimes in children's and old people's homes and the institutionalised abuse of the disabled are other examples of inhumanity in the welfare state.

The welfare state also copper-fastened women's economic dependency over many decades, through the aggregation of their tax and welfare entitlements with those of their male partners, thus revealing the patriarchal nature of the state. The cohabitation rule, which aggregates single mothers' incomes with those of male acquaintances, has been used further to reinforce women's dependency on men.

The moral policing of this system has been anything but humanistic. Racist attitudes and discriminatory practices suggest an endemic failure to acknowledge the social citizenship rights of ethnic minorities. The inverse care law highlights the inhuman and unjust treatment of the 'underclass' minority within the welfare state in a two-tier system: that is, the more citizens need state services, the more controlled access becomes.

Second, there is a growing appreciation of the contradictory nature of the welfare state: it both empowers and regulates. However, its existence has undoubtedly greatly benefited society. As two of its sternest Marxist critics, Cloward and Piven, have put it: 'in simple and human terms, the welfare state has reduced some of the hardships and insecurities generated by a continually changing economy' (Cloward and Piven, 1982: 39). Social workers have become aware that there are contradictions in their role and tasks that reflect the contradictory nature of the welfare state. They are required to undertake many duties which are essentially regulatory in character: child protection work is the obvious example. However, these contradictions can be reconciled if the humanistic values of social work inform practice. This means that, in the child protection area, social workers are challenged to resist the populist authoritarianism of the media with its primitive demands for punishment and retribution.

Third, the failure of the welfare state to eliminate poverty and inequality made it an inevitable target of criticism from the alternative Left. Radical social work emerged within a wider ambit of Left critique of the welfare state. For radical social workers the historic mission can be achieved only by politicisation of the social work role and task into an explicit alliance with poor people, poor people's movements and allies on the political Left. Marxism provided the guiding philosophical influence, but it was strongly influenced by a humanistic idealism and evolutionary approach more evocative of radical Fabianism. Much of this radical thought was the result of the growth of the social sciences in universities during the 1960s and the 1970s rooted in critical social theory, and specifically in revisionist approaches to welfare and Marxism known as critical theory.

Marxism and critical social policy

The development of a revisionist or critical school of social policy has paralleled the crisis in welfare capitalism and the emergence of a postmodern political culture. Marxist and neo-Marxist social thought has been seminal to the critical school of social policy. The relevance of Marxist social theory has been delineated by Mishra (1997: 68):

First as a comprehensive theory of society it provides an explanation of the nature of welfare and its development in bourgeois and other societies. Secondly, as a normative theory concerned with the transcendence of capitalism it offers a particular view of problems germane to welfare and their 'definitive' solution.

Undoubtedly, Marx's thought is fundamental to a socialist critique of welfare. But, since he died in 1883, the welfare state lay outside his experience. However, in recent years a large number of social policy analysts and social economists have developed a critique of the welfare state derived from the core principles of Marx's social theory.

The Marxist theory of historical materialism turned conventional wisdom on its head. It rejected idealism as the motor force in history and replaced it with materialism. The superstructure consisting of the ideological make-up of society (ideas, morality, culture, etc.) was ultimately determined by economic relations. As Lee and Raban (1988: 11) observed, 'Marxists employed a "catastrophic" theory of history'.

Welfare was, therefore, simply a reflection of class interest. Social citizenship was impossible in a society based on class conflict. History, for Marx, reflected a struggle between classes through a dialectical process, which would ultimately lead to a proletarian state. Progressively, more modern forms of society replaced older ones. Capitalism replaced the feudal social order, which in turn had replaced ancient society, the successor of Asiatic civilisation. Each civilisation was characterised by the fact that a set of property relations had been successfully challenged by a revolutionary class and had given way to a new social order. Marx predicted that the capitalist system in turn would perish as the result of its internal contradictions, leading to the emergence of a socialist society based on common ownership and equal citizenship.

The internal contradictions of capitalism are explained in the labour theory of value. According to Marx, all economic value derives from labour, which is essentially commodified by capitalist relations of production: i.e. workers are turned into commodities or objects. Capital has a purely parasitical role in the process of production, creaming off the surplus value of labour, i.e. profit. The capitalist minority, through its monopoly of wealth, forces the worker to sell his labour in return for a subsistence wage, creating an exploitative relationship analogous to that with the slave in ancient society or the serf in medieval society. The essential difference from earlier social formations is that the worker is freed from the bondage of settlement (largely because capitalism requires the mobility of labour) and the citizen worker enjoys basic human rights arising from the power of organised labour. In a constant battle to maximise profits, capitalists seek to increase productivity through deregulation, cutting wages, extending working hours, automation and redundancy, casualisation of labour or moving to Third World economies where wages are lower. Workers, through the trade union movement, seek to counteract this process and improve working conditions and pay. This leads to an ongoing class war, which crucially affects the social policies and legal decisions of the state according to the relative strengths or weakness of the organised working class at any given point in time. Ultimately, the Marxists claim, government in capitalist society seeks to protect the rights of property. The immiseration of the working class is its inevitable consequence, fomented by crises in the capitalist system.

According to Marxists, crises in capitalism occur for two reasons. First, through the over-accumulation which arises when profit and investment outrun demand, since the latter is constrained by the consumer power of the workers (O'Connor, 1973; Ginsberg, 1979; Gough, 1979). Marx argued that these crises would become increasingly severe until a terminal stage was reached. Cole and Postgate (1961: 419) observed in this context: 'Herein lies the growing contradiction of capitalism – its tendency to defeat itself by producing more than it allows society the means of consuming, and its tendency, by filling up the world with rival capitalist groups, to destroy its power to get rid abroad of surplus products which cannot be consumed at home'. The Wall Street Crash in 1929 was caused by this factor but it did not bring an end to capitalism, which was reformed by the New Deal and the welfare state.

Second, according to Marxists, crises in capitalism arise when workers succeed in achieving real wage increases and the expansion of state expenditure on social services – i.e. a measurable degree of social reform. This results in domestic inflation and disinvestment by capitalists in the national economy. As a result, a structural gap develops between revenue and expenditure, leading to economic retrenchment, unemployment and ultimately, it is hoped, to the return of capital investment.

The welfare state, Marxists posit, is based on a contradiction. It grants workers social and economic rights in order to bind them to the capitalist system and prevent the threat of revolution, which would create a workers' state. According to Offe (1984: 153), this is the ultimate contradiction in capitalism: 'while capitalism cannot coexist with, neither can it exist without, the welfare state'. In other words, Marxists believe that in order to maintain social cohesion capitalism promotes civic virtue through the extravagant and potentially ruinous mechanism of the welfare state.

Marxist critics have tended to overstate their case, viewing the welfare state essentially as doomed by inherent flaws including: (1) ineffectiveness and inefficiency, (2) its repressive nature and (3) the conditioning of a false (ideological) understanding of social and political reality within the working class (Offe, 1984: 154). As Lee and Raban (1988: 108) have put it, 'a definite and quite dramatic tension exists between Marxism as a guide to political practice and Marxism as a body of critical theory'.

Empirical research (Taylor Gooby, 1985; Pierson, 1991) has indicated broad public support for social expenditure on pensions, public health insurance, education and family/child allowances – all entitlements that benefit the majority. Much less popular is welfare expenditure on unemployment and public assistance, which is directed at the minority underclass (Pierson, 1991: 169). Nonetheless, despite the most pessimistic prediction by Marxists, the welfare state has retained popular support in liberal democratic societies, confounding the logic of their critique. The ultimate problem of the Marxist critique of the welfare state is what Lee and Raban (1988) describe as the 'theoretical excesses of fundamentalism' conditioned by economic reductionism and functionalist forms of analysis. By discounting democracy as a force for social change, Marxists ignore the crucial relationship between democracy and state welfare. Before democracy there was no state welfare. The welfare state is the product of democratic pluralism and the embodiment of modern citizenship.

However, Marxism, despite its Stalinist legacy in Eastern Europe, represents an important theoretical synthesis of naturalism and humanism – 'secular humanism'. It provides an alternative societal basis, shaping moral commitment and ethical outlook for those who reject the consumerism of the market. Marx was committed to the core ideal of feeding and clothing all citizens, which was achieved in Eastern Europe. At a deeper level his theory of alienation sought to emancipate humanity by decommodifying labour. As Erich Fromm (1961: 3) put it:

> Marx's aim was the spiritual emancipation of man, of his liberation from the chains of economic determinism, of restituting him in his human wholeness, of enabling him to find unity and harmony with his fellow man and with nature. Marx's philosophy was, in secular, non-theistic language, a new and radical step forward in the tradition of prophetic messianism; it was aimed at the full realisation of individualism, the very aim which has guided western thinking from the Renaissance and the Reformation far into the nineteenth century.

Marxism, like capitalism, was the product of the Enlightenment. It dreams of a society based upon the principle, 'from each according to his ability: to each according to his need'. This a noble vision of humanity transcending its fate. It provides the basic ethic of socialism.

Fromm, like several other radical theorists influential during the 1960s (e.g. Wilhelm Reich and Herbert Marcuse), sought to synthesise Marxism and Freudianism. This preoccupation with emancipatory discourses influenced thinking about the welfare state. The anti-psychiatry movement questioned the concept of madness (Szasz, 1962; Laing, 1965, 1969; Cooper, 1970; Sedgwick, 1972). Sociologists also began to explore the social and economic construction of deviance (Cloward and Ohlin, 1960; Goffman, 1968; Taylor et al., 1973). Social policy (or social administration as it was then called) had been primarily concerned with a descriptive and empirical approach to the analysis of the welfare state. Its normative basis had been unchallenged. The emergence of 'the critical school of social policy' (O'Connor, 1973; Gough, 1979; Ginsberg, 1979; Offe, 1984; Williams, 1989) represented an attempt to theorise welfare. The journal *Critical Social Policy* has been an important source for radical welfare thinking. All of these influences combined to lay the foundations for radical social work.

Critical theory and radical social work

In 1975 the publication of *Radical Social Work*, edited by Roy Bailey and Mike Brake, gave radical social work a core text. It was followed by a second volume in 1980, entitled *Radical Social Work and Practice*. In 1978 Daphne Statham, published *Radicals in Social Work* in which she argued that radicals in social work need to co-operate with progressive social movements. Her book was significant because it located radical social work within a critical perspective. A British news-sheet, *Case Con*, which described itself as 'a revolutionary magazine for social workers', promoted radical social work amongst practitioners. *Case Con* produced twenty-five issues between 1970 and 1977, which provided an important forum for articulating the basic themes of radical social work.

The *Case Con Manifesto* cogently stated the philosophy of the radical social work movement, advocating the replacement of the welfare state by a 'workers' state':

The idea of the state as a neutral arbiter between different sections of society who may have some minor temporary differences is wholly inadequate if we are to understand the development of the welfare state and the role of the social worker. An understanding of the state is a vital prerequisite to effective action because, far from being neutral, the state in any class society represents the interests of the *ruling* class and has at its disposal the instruments necessary to keep it in power. Thus, in Britain, the state safeguards the interests and development of British capitalism. Only on this basis can we make sense of the developments in the welfare state since the war and understand how we must organise. If the state cannot be neutral, it is important to analyse the expectations placed on social workers by the state, as our employer, and to assess, in the light of this, where and how action supporting the class struggle is most effective.

We are supposed to 'help' our 'clients' by making them 'accept responsibility' – in other words, *come to terms* as individuals with basically unacceptable situations. We must counterpose this to the possibility of *changing* their situation by collective action. We can only do this by acting collectively ourselves.

Therefore, we do not merely concentrate on democratising a few of the state's outposts (such as social service departments) for all this does is to make them more efficient. We should fight for powers of veto over any decisions which are against our best interests and the interests of the people we are supposed to serve. We should also constantly demand the provision of improved services, geared to the real needs of the community. To be in a position to do this requires a lot more than office meetings and working parties. The crux of all our actions must be to organise independently of the state and in the interests of the working class. These interests are in opposition to those of capitalism and its administrative tool – the state.

Case Con believes that the problems of our 'clients' are rooted in the society in which we live, not in supposed individual inadequacies. Until this society, based on private ownership, profit and the needs of a minority ruling class, is replaced by a workers' state, based on the interests of the vast majority of the population, the fundamental causes of social problems will remain. It is therefore our aim to join the struggle for this workers' state. (cited in Bailey and Brake, 1975: 146–147)

Radical social work and Marxist social theory were combined in this clarion call to social workers to unite on a socialist platform (Statham, 1978; Simpkin, 1979).

A variety of other fora provided fertile ground for forging the ideology of the radical social work movement. The National Deviancy Conference established an important area for the discussion of radical social ideas. The International Congress on the Dialectics of Liberation, held in London in 1967, gave voice to a unique expression of modern dissent. Its main papers were published in *The Dialectics of Liberation* (Cooper, 1968). This book contains the disparate voices of dissent: Marxists, anarchists, black activists and anti-psychiatrists articulated the radical political agenda of the 1960s. The Marxist philosopher, Herbert Marcuse, captured the optimistic mood of the Congress:

Now in what sense is all dialectic liberation? It is liberation from the repressive, from a bad, a false system – be it an organic system, be it a social system, be it a mental or intellectual system. (Marcuse, 1968: 175)

He further declared: 'the capitalist welfare state is a warfare state' (1968: 181). While carefully distancing himself from Stalinist autocracy in Eastern Europe,

Marcuse prescribed socialism (Utopian socialism) as a means to create a 'rupture' with a compromised historical past:

> If today these integral features, these truly radical features which make a socialist society a definite negation of the existing societies, if this qualitative difference today appears as utopian, as idealistic, as metaphysical, this is precisely the form in which these radical features must appear if they are really to be a definite negation of the established society; if socialism is indeed the rupture of history, the radical break, the leap into the realm of freedom – a total rupture. (1968: 177)

For Marcuse the existing social order was based on one-dimensional thought, repressive tolerance and economic exploitation. Marcuse reminds us that there are multiple political lefts. The 'official' Left is composed of formal organizations (e.g. the British Labour Party, the Trades Union Congress and the Co-operative Society). There is an alternative or cultural Left that thrives on the university campus, informed by the critical intellectual debates of the time. It is loosely intellectually connected to new social movements (feminism, ecology, black power, gay rights, disability equality awareness, etc.) that challenge traditional hierarchical forms in society, including the 'official' Left. The organisations of the 'official' Left are often viewed with suspicion by those associated with the alternative Left, because of a perception that it wishes to incorporate more radical agendas and mould them to its own purpose. Equally, the 'official' Left tends to view the alternative Left as the expression of a counterculture that electorally would mean political nemesis.

During the 1980s, the relationship between the British Labour Party and the alternative Left became closer and a public perception developed that the latter was setting the political agenda. A hostile media reacted with a vitriolic campaign that made the British Labour Party unelectable. Indubitably, the reformist politics of the 'official' Left is challenged by the radicalism and revolutionary rhetoric of the alternative Left: it is its conscience and *enfant terrible* simultaneously. Radical social work was the *enfant terrible* of its post-Seebohm professionalised form deeply rooted in the status quo of welfare state reformism.

While Marcuse's critique was addressed to the question of 'liberation from the affluent society', other critiques of capitalism came from the Third World. Ivan Illich and Paulo Friere, who were primarily concerned with the relationship between underdevelopment and education, proved to be powerful influences on critical social thought in the West. They both injected the important ingredient of critical reflection upon practice.

Illich in *Deschooling Society*, published in 1973, argued that economic development was deskilling previously self-sufficient people and making them dependent on professionals to meet their educational, health care and cultural needs. He asserted that schooling had become compulsory in order to socialise children into conformity through the 'hidden curriculum'. Illich argued for educational liberation, where the learner is empowered by having a personal choice in what to study. In an earlier study Illich et al. (1970) had coined the phrase 'the disabling professions'. They argued that professionals did not apply their knowledge and expertise in the interests of humanity but for personal profit and aggrandisement of power and prestige. Illich's critique of professionalism gave rise to the concept of 'deprofessionalisation', which imagined a more democratic relationship between service user and helper.

The *Case Con Manifesto* reflected this critique of professionalism:

> It is important to examine the 'professional approach' that has been accentuated by Seebohm and happily accepted by social service hierarchies and workers alike. 'Professionalism' firstly implies the acquisition of a specialism-knowledge and skills not possessed by untrained workers. This isolates the social worker from the population at large. Secondly, social workers come to see themselves as part of an accepted specialist group on a par with doctors and lawyers. Thirdly, it encourages the introduction of businesslike career structures, where 'correct' and 'professional' behaviour (such as 'detachment' and 'controlled emotional involvement') is rewarded with advancement. Clearly, such an approach is welcomed by the ruling class.
>
> One important tool of professional social work has been casework – a pseudo-science – that blames individual inadequacies for poverty and so mystifies and diverts attention from the real causes – slums, homelessness and economic exploitation. The casework ideology forces clients to be seen as needing to be changed to fit society. Social work has now expanded to include new (and not so new) tricks, such as community work, group work, welfare rights work, etc., which, when professionalised, end up by becoming the same sort of mechanism of control as traditional casework, often with the additional merit of being less expensive for the ruling class. Professionalism is a particularly dangerous development specifically because social workers look to it for an answer to many of the problems and contradictions of the job itself – i.e. being unable to solve the basic inadequacy of society through social work. It must be fought at every opportunity. (Bailey and Brake, 1975: 145–146)

This searing critique called into question the image of the professional social worker as an altruistic public servant, working within the caring context of the welfare state. It also highlighted the complex process of professionalisation and identity formation, questioning the compatibility of professionalisation with the historic mission of social work to help the poor and oppressed.

The Brazilian adult educator, Paulo Friere has become an iconic figure amongst social activists. In two important books *The Pedagogy of the Oppressed* (1972) and *Cultural Action for Freedom* (1973) he argued that the core task of community development is 'conscientisation' (consciousness-raising). The aim of conscientisation is the establishment of critical awareness amongst service users of the social, economic and political realities of their oppression. Friere advocated dialogical relationships based upon the democratic principle of equality between professional and service user. His ideas became very influential. Many radical social workers viewed his methods as an alternative to casework.

Peter Leonard (1975: 54), one of the key intellectual figures in the radical social work movement, has recorded that the concept of conscientisation was highly influential on Latin American schools of social work; he cites the report of a conference in Ecuador in 1971:

> Social work will be able to contribute to the transformation of the present situation only so long as it commits itself to man and society in the social change process.

Social work implies talking in terms of a reflexive, horizontal, dynamic, communication which will dialectically feed back into action.

In spite of the fact that reality conditions man, we conclude that he is capable of influencing and transforming his reality. Even under conditions of oppression, man is capable of seeking his own liberation.

Social work should place itself within an ideology of liberation. It should get its start from the deepest causes that have subjected men to oppression and underdevelopment.

The social worker will contribute to form this free man, preferably through an education function which will be enabling and conscientizing.

The potential for applying the Frierean model to the developed world was discussed by Leonard (1975: 57–59):

> While in general terms the aim of radical social work in capitalist society is both to mitigate individual suffering caused substantially by the consequences of economic production and to engage with others in the struggle to resist and overcome an oppressive social system, the key task of radical practice is an educational one. This role aims at contributing to the development in people – especially those suffering most profoundly, such as the clients of social welfare systems – of a critical consciousness of their oppression, and of their potential, with others, of combating this oppression.
>
> If the key task of radical practice is education, then the method by which it must be achieved is through the process of conscientisation by dialogue between the worker and other people. Paulo Friere has written extensively on the problems involved in developing dialogical relationships to replace the authoritarian and oppressive relationships which characterise the contacts existing between most professionals in education and social welfare and their 'clients'. While the oppressive nature of traditional educational and social-work transactions can be seen fairly clearly, we have to recognise that the cultural domination of 'banking' approaches to education and controlling approaches to social work infects also those who attempt more radical interventions. Radical change can only come from consciousness developed as a result of exchange rather than imposition.

Leonard's espousal of Friere's ideas, which were deeply rooted in Catholic liberation theology, is notable. These humanistic ideas were more connected to the campaign for democracy in Latin America in the 1960s and 1970s than to the Western Marxist tradition. Friere, himself, had been a political victim of the military in Brazil and his ideas were to attract powerful hostility from the dictatorial Pinochet regime in Chile. Leonard subsequently adopted a more orthodox Marxist perspective: within the secular value system of the West, where Enlightenment values predominate, this was not a surprising decision. Leonard edited an important series of 'critical texts in social work and the welfare state'. As part of the series Corrigan and Leonard wrote *Social Work Practice under Capitalism: A Marxist Approach*, which was published in 1978. This book claimed it was possible 'to be a Marxist social worker who relates her practice to a theory and her political activities to that theory and practice' (Corrigan and Leonard, 1978: 9). Another book in the same series, written by Chris Jones and entitled *State Social Work and the Working Class*, took a more pessimistic view. Jones (1983: 157) concluded: 'it seemed probable that state social work would continue to be used as an instrument of social control by the state'.

In the New World radical social work also found a voice. In the United States Jeffrey Galper published *The Politics of Social Services* in 1975, which was followed in 1980 by *Social Work Practice: A Radical Perspective*. Galper's work represents an important attempt to theorise social work as a revolutionary social-ist discourse. Saul Alinsky's *Rules for Radicals* (1971) also proved to be a formative influence on radical social work in the United States. Alinsky was a community activist with roots going back to the protest movements of the 1930s (see Chapter 3). Radical social work thinking in the United States was also strongly influenced by the publication of Piven and Cloward's deservedly celebrated book, *Regulating the Poor*, in 1971. While Piven and Cloward were concerned with producing an intellectual critique of social policy from a Marxist perspec-tive, their rootedness in activism gave the book a powerful moral authority. In essence, Piven and Cloward argued, in *Regulating the Poor*, that welfare provi-sion expands and contracts in response to the level of social unrest in society. It is also related to levels of unemployment and labour market shortages. As the labour market expands, welfare recipients are pushed back into the labour market. Piven and Cloward concluded that the welfare system acts as a safety valve enabling capitalism to survive the vagaries of the trade cycle. Welfare is conse-quently highly utilitarian.

Richard Cloward and Frances Fox Piven were crucial in shaping and legiti-mising radical social work. They argued, in 'Notes toward a Radical Social Work', the introduction to the American edition of Bailey and Brake's *Radical Social Work*, that the daily struggle on behalf of service users can contribute to the revolutionary socialist objective:

> If we manage to get people who are hungry a bit of bread, or to protect the weak against the assaults of the courts or the mental hospitals, then we will have gone a short way toward redressing the wrongs of a harsh society. Which of us is so arrogantly unfeeling, or so confident of the prospects for revolutionary transformation as to think these small gains are not important?
>
> In the longer run, if we fight for the interests of the people we claim are our clients, then we will also be waging a struggle against the institutions of the capitalist state. There is a kind of tautological trick inherent in some Marxist arguments, to the effect that any actual effort to deal with the contradictions created by capitalism will produce reforms that paper over the contradictions. The trick is a professionally convenient one, for it enables us to say that no action short of the final cataclysmic one ought to be taken. But revolutions are not made all at once. (quoted in Galper, 1980: 114)

This statement distances radical social work from the orthodox Marxist position that capitalism can only be overthrown by a cataclysmic revolution and replaces it by a notion of incremental struggle: evolutionary Marxism as opposed to revolu-tionary Marxism. The parallels with radical Fabianism are unmistakable. In Britain, Pritchard and Taylor (1978: 89–90) had made this argument in their analysis of the respective cases for social reform and political revolution: 'there is, indeed, a significant number of evolutionary Marxian socialists arguing for the creation of a socialist system ... through the relatively untainted and indigenous institutions of the working class; most notably the trade unions and the welfare state'.

Mullaly (1997: 93) took up this theme in a Canadian context in his book *Structural Social Work*, noting that 'evolutionary Marxists believe that the welfare state can be used as a stepping-stone towards socialism'. He seeks to move the argument on from orthodox Marxism, while continuing to maintain that social-ism provides the best model for social work, since it is most congruent with its humanist values. However, Mullaly (1997: 104) argues that his variant of radical social work, called 'structural social work', while based upon socialist ideology, is 'informed by postmodern critique as well'. He comments:

> The contribution of postmodernism to a structural analysis is to help us recognise that although oppression and exploitation may be universal phenomena, they will be experi-enced differently by different people living in different contexts.... Marxism, for example, has often overlooked other forms of oppression, such as patriarchy and racism and has often viewed the working-class as a homogeneous group whose members are equally exploited, not recognising stratification, ethnicity, gender, and other types of difference within it. (1997: 115–116)

Mullaly's contribution to radical social work theory is very significant because he has sought to forge a synthesis of the social politics of the traditional socialist Left and the identity politics of the alternative Left, embodied in the new social movements, such as feminism, anti-racism, etc. In this respect his work seeks to incorporate a multiculturalist perspective, while retaining an essentially socialist world view: 'Based on socialist ideology located within the radical social work camp, grounded in critical theory, and operating from a conflict view of society, structural social work views social problems as arising from a specific societal context – liberal/neo-conservative capitalism – rather than from the failings of individuals' (Mullaly, 1997: 133).

There has been a vibrant interest in radical social work in Australia, which gave rise to a rich body of literature during the 1990s. Jim Ife's study, *Rethinking Social Work*, was published in 1997. In *Rethinking Social Work*, Ife (1997: 92) is critical of postmodernism because 'it fails to incorporate a vision of a better society, or a universal understanding of social justice and human rights'. He believes that humanism, which has provided the traditional value base of a hierarchic discourse, needs to be democratically adapted to the more varied cultural and social mix of postmodern society (Ife, 1997: 56, 103). Ife concludes: 'social work, whether one likes it or not, is inevitably bound to a humanist vision, given its value base, historical origins and political location' (1997: 115).

But Ife's vision of humanist social work is radically different to traditional social work. Ife's thought is influenced by critical theory and incorporates Frierean perspectives into the analysis. He advocates a bottom-up rather than top-down welfare model grounded in a user participation philosophy, with the social worker as a community enabler, publicly accountable through the democratic decision-making process.

Not surprisingly, Ife is critical of professionalism, and professional codes of practice in particular. Instead, he favours a form of situational ethics designed to meet the needs of democratic dialogically based practice. Ife believes that 'if professionalism is unable to be constructed except in disempowering terms, that it has no place in a social work based on critical theory' (Ife, 1997: 114). However, he does not go so far as to recommend the abolition of the social work profession: 'rather, it is necessary to engage in the task of deconstructing professionalism and helping social workers to reconstruct a form of professionalism more consistent with critical practice that allows them to use their professionalism in a positive, creative and liberating way'.

Other Australians have made significant contributions to the radical social work tradition. In 1993 Jan Fook published *Radical Casework*, which seeks to redefine radical social work in individualist terms: 'individually orientated help which focusses on structural causes of personal problems, more specifically on the interaction between the individual and the socio-economic structure which causes problems' (1993: 41). The influence of the feminist maxim that 'the personal is the political' is clearly evident in Fook's approach. She views personal liberation from patriarchy, racism and other forms of domination as an integral part of radical social change. Her argument is incontrovertible in terms of the development of a critical social work praxis but it departs from the radical social work focus on structure and returns it to the individual. While her work is intended to bridge the divide between radical and traditional forms of social work, it is debatable whether it takes the argument for radical social work forward. It is nonetheless a challenging contribution to social work theory and practice that pushes the boundaries of casework in the direction of more inclusive practice.

Bob Pease and Jan Fook edited a study, entitled *Transforming Social Work Practice*, which was published in 1999. This series of essays seeks to demonstrate that postmodern theory offers new strategies for social workers concerned with political action and social justice.

Not all Australians view radical social work as the way forward. In 2000, Karen Healy's *Social Work Practices* criticises the radical school of social work for marginalising activist social work and for subordinating practice to theory. She asserts: 'quite simply, radical analysis can overlook the emancipatory potential in everyday social work practices by establishing standards that devalue much of the change activity in which social workers are involved' (Healy, 2000: 5). Healy concludes that critical theory points to a 'new pragmatism' based upon local, contextual and incremental proposals for change. From Healy's perspective social work is presented with multiple choices: 'a myriad set of possibilities for change' in the age of postmodernity. Her penetrating critique of radical social work strikes a powerful cautionary note for those who espouse social work as a vehicle for radical social transformation, in an era when global capitalism is once again in the ascendant.

Healy's concerns echo earlier criticisms. Rein (1970) writing from a sympathetic perspective, argued that radical social workers were erroneously conflating social work with social policy. In reality, both social work and social policy do share a common interest in the social politics of the welfare state. Once social workers divert their gaze from the therapeutic individualism of casework to the larger environmental context, they inevitably become preoccupied with the policy context – but from an activist rather than an academic perspective. This can only serve to enrich both social policy and social work by facilitating the exploration of shared normative perspectives. After all, a large number of professional social workers are social policy graduates.

Less sympathetic criticisms came from several prominent figures in the field of social work education in Britain, notably the London School of Economics (LSE), where professional training had its origins. They have been concerned to protect the professional neutrality of the social work profession. Zofia Butrym, Senior Lecturer at the LSE, accused radical social work of 'a preference for slogans over issues of substance', concluding: 'one serious result of this type of confusion is the omnipotent nature of the claims about the qualitatively different nature of current changes which are not self-evident' (Butrym, 1976: 127). Professor Robert Pinker of the LSE observed: 'it is inevitable that social workers will find numerous examples of misery and injustice in the course of their work, but that does not justify switching the focus of social work from the personal to the political' (Barclay, 1982: 241). Other social work theorists suggested that the task of social work needed to be viewed in more positivist terms of system maintenance, containment, control and support (Davies, 1981: 137–139). In a sense these critical perspectives only served to underline the highly politicised nature of social work. While critics of radical social work saw themselves as defending the historic legacy of social work, they assumed that it did not have a radical dimension with a deep moral purpose that needed to be debated and valued.

Payne (1997: 236), in *Modern Social Work Theory*, defends radical social work from its critics: 'Among the advantages of the radical perspective which negate these general criticisms is that it highlights certain aspects of life, including the importance of power, ideological hegemony, class and status, professionalism and oppression'. He welcomes the clarity Marxist theory brings to social work's understanding of power. Radical social work has played a key role in the generation of multicultural perspectives based on anti-discriminatory and anti-oppressive practice. Its emphasis on structural aspects of social work also contributes to the generation of socially inclusive approaches to practice. These new paradigms will be explored in subsequent chapters of the present book.

Radical social work literature shares a common commitment to emancipatory politics but its analyses vary over time in response to changing political conditions. The earlier literature, which is primarily committed to Marxist class analysis, has been criticised for ignoring gender and race in its social analysis. Langan and Lee (1989: 9) note: 'while radical social workers were highly perceptive of the class inequalities reinforced by the operation of the postwar welfare system, they failed to recognise the systematic denial of power to women and black people'. The explanation for this omission is that radical social work, like socialism and humanism, was primarily rooted in universalist discourses in welfare based upon a politics of equal dignity. The particularism that developed, with the rise of identity politics and the emergence of a multicultural society, was, in a sense, in conflict with the basic universalism of the socialist and welfare project. Taylor (1994: 82) notes:

> By contrast ... the development of the modern notion of identity has given rise to a politics of difference. There is, of course, a universalist basis to this as well, making for the

overlap and confusion between the two. *Everyone* should be recognised for his or her unique identity. But recognition here means something else. With the politics of equal dignity, what is established is meant to be universally the same, an identical basket of rights and immunities; with the politics of difference, what we are asked to recognise is the unique identity of this individual or group, their distinctions from everyone else. The idea is that it is precisely this distinction that has been ignored, glossed over, assimilated to the dominant majority identity.

The fall of the Berlin Wall in 1989 symbolised the collapse of the socialist project in both the East and the West. This involved a turning away from the politics of equal dignity towards a more polyvalent political tendency.

Radicalism within social work adapted to this change. More recent writing in this tradition is much more concerned with questions of race and gender than it is with class. Langan and Lee (1989: 14) describe this as 'the *prefigurative* strategy, which is heavily influenced by feminism and the slogan the personal is political'. However, the universal experience of social work service users of poverty and inequality makes the issue of class inequality a fundamental concern of any social workers wishing to embrace a radical perspective. Mullaly (1997: 107), on the basis of a close examination of the literature, enumerates the basic themes of radical social work, demonstrating that it is predominantly orientated towards a class analysis:

1   capitalism is rejected in favour of socialism;
2   liberal reformism is rejected as a way of dealing with social problems;
3   the capitalist welfare system carries out interrelated political and economic functions that prop up capitalism;
4   social welfare as a societal norm is antithetical to capitalism;
5   conventional social work perpetuates social problems;
6   the 'individual vs society' is a false dichotomy as private troubles cannot be understood or treated apart from their social or political causes;
7   the feminist perspective is an epistemological imperative for radical social work; it not only decodes sexism and patriarchy but links the personal and political better than any other theory and emphasises transformational politics;
8   classism and patriarchy are not the only oppressions concerning radical social workers; racism, ageism, heterosexism, imperialism and ableism are increasingly viewed as structurally oppressive forces;
9   professionalism distances professionals from service users and serves the former at the expense of the latter; unionisation is the preferred mode of organisation for radical social workers.

Mullaly's thematic analysis reveals that while issues of race and gender have permeated radical social work discourse, there is clearly a modernist preoccupation with class-based inequalities. This represents a severe limitation on the capacity of radical social work discourse to capture the imagination of the postmodern social worker, particularly in a profession largely composed of women.

Communicative competence and transformative change

It is notable that the radical social work debate has been essentially confined to the English speaking world. In Europe, with its social market economy and stronger sense of solidarity, the preoccupation has been with social exclusion. However, with the growing impact of globalisation and liberal market economics on the welfare states of European Union member countries, things may be set to change. The cuts in public expenditure, ushered in by the Kohl government in Germany (and adopted by his successor Chancellor Schroeder), are undermining a long established consensus. Similar attempts to downsize the Italian welfare state are likely to undermine social solidarity in that country.

Lorenz in his book *Social Work in a Changing Europe* notes that there are no 'equivalent Marxist challenges' being voiced in continental European countries. In Europe radical challenges to the traditional 'neutrality' of social work have been sporadic and fragmented. However, he records: 'Intellectually the Critical School of Sociology associated with Jürgen Habermas in Frankfurt is now beginning to provide practice paradigms for social work in a broader sense on the strength of its analysis of communication processes' (Lorenz, 1994: 85).

Habermas's theory of communicative competence has proven highly influential in theorising civil society in the English speaking world (Cohen and Arato, 1992). It has also shaped much of the critical pedagogy in adult education, achieving a level of esteem only equalled by Friere amongst its practitioners and theorists (Mezirow, 1991). Surprisingly, social work has remained largely uninterested in Habermas's work. Yet his vision constitutes a vital and coherent source of radical thought, even if Habermas has become less optimistic about the possibilities of transformative change in recent years.

Jürgen Habermas is widely regarded as the most influential living German social theorist. His scholarly range as a philosopher, sociologist, economist, expert in linguistics, political science and history make him remarkable by any standards. Habermas's intellectual roots are in the Frankfurt School of Marxism, that embraced some of the twentieth century's most radical thinkers, including Horkheimer, Adorno, Marcuse and Fromm.

During the 1980s, Habermas published his *Theory of Communicative Action* (1984). This study contends that in a society where communication is systematically distorted and manipulated in the interests of power and domination, human emancipation is conditional upon democratic dialogue, where problem-solving involves validity testing and the achievement of consensus about the truth. Habermas argues for a society where everybody is empowered to speak, explain and interpret, free from domination and manipulation, which he calls 'communicative competence'. He subscribes to the idea of achieving consensus that is based upon ethical principle rather than vested interest. Habermas suggests that 'communicative ethics' offers a path to a universal morality that can resolve the legitimation crisis of contemporary capitalist society and create in its place the cultural context for a classless society to emerge. Clearly, Habermas's concept of an idealised discourse assumes a human capacity to overcome vested interests without the violent conflict of a revolutionary struggle. This goal involves the creation of a system for developmentally advanced communication that enables its participants to achieve communicative competence.

Mezirow (1991: 77–78) has outlined the optimal conditions for rational discourse, based upon Habermas's theory of communication, in which participants will:

- Have accurate and complete information;
- Be free from coercion and distorting self-deception;
- Be able to weigh evidence and assess arguments objectively;
- Be open to alternative perspectives;
- Be able to become critically reflective upon presuppositions and their consequences;
- Have equal opportunity to participate (including the chance to challenge, question, refute, and reflect and to hear others do the same);
- Be able to accept an informed, objective, and rational consensus as a legitimate test of validity.

The communicative ethics that informs this mode of dialogue seeks to replace instrumental forms of communication by transformative communication based upon consensus and truth. This is an essentially humanistic approach to practice, based upon a radically altered mode of communication, and clearly has the potential to shape new paradigms of radical social work. It is likely that any such new paradigms will emerge within civil society rather than the state and will involve a reconstituted concept of citizenship.

Radical social work and socialist practice

Radical social work is regarded (even by some of its proponents) as a theory in search of a practice. For example, Mullaly (1997:106) has asserted that prior to the 1990s radical social work 'was long on analysis but short on practice'. This statement misunderstands the purpose of radical social work. It has two objectives. First, transforming social work into socialist practice based upon close links with the 'struggles' of traditional social movements, trade unions, claimants' rights campaigns etc. for social justice. This radical prescription for social work practice may be incompatible with professionalised forms within the state. However, it does contain powerful ingredients for the development of a transformative approach to practice, based upon a presumption of the growing immiseration of the poor in a society that is rejecting social citizenship as a basis for civilised democratic life.

Second, radical social work offers a vital critique of traditional social work practice. Cloward and Piven state the indictment of traditional casework practice with unique clarity:

We have to break with the professional doctrine that ascribes virtually all of the problems that clients experience to defects in personality development and family relationships. It must be understood that this doctrine is as much a political ideology as an explanation of human behaviour. It is an ideology that directs clients to blame themselves for their travails rather than the economic and social institutions that produce many of them.... This psychological reductionism – this pathologising of poverty and inequality – is, in other words, an ideology of oppression for it systematically conceals from people the way in which their lives are distorted by the realities of class structure. (cited in Galper, 1980: 143)

Galper (1980: 145–146) summarises the nature of radical practice:

The analysis on which a radical worker approaches a direct service situation differs from the analysis of conventional approaches in two respects. First, it locates individuals within the broad social context of their lives and analyses their particular problems in light of their personality structures, socio-psychological environment, and in terms of the nature of the society as a whole. That analysis, rooted in a socialist critique, influences each aspect of the way a worker looks at a discrete problem. Second, a radical perspective is grounded in the belief that people have the power to change their circumstances when they understand them concretely and act on them in a collective political way. Radicalism is not pessimistic about the possibilities for change, and it understands that working people, acting together as a class, are the primary shapers of history. For a given individual the implications of this view may not be clear in the short run, but a radical analysis of a particular problem situation is necessarily the first step in formulating an action strategy.

This statement by Galper throws light on the relationship between radical social work practice and the individual. It poses a classic dilemma for structural Marxism. It is concerned with societal change, based upon a class analysis, that dismisses the individual actor as simply the reflection of economic forces. However, action theories of Marxism emphasise the importance of 'struggle' and it is here that radical social work practice finds its inspiration.

While the links *forged* by radical social workers have been primarily targeted at traditional social movements, they have become increasingly open to supporting new social movements (feminism, anti-racism, disability equality awareness, etc.). But their mode of thought and organisational approach remain very much in line with that taken by the working-class movement. As Langan and Lee (1989: 12) put it: 'Radical social workers have always emphasised their identity *as workers*, as members of identity trade unions and the wider labour movement'.

The strategic significance of social movements and coalition-building has been clearly delineated by Mullaly (1997: 189): 'on a more macro-scale, social work can contribute to social transformation by forming coalitions and alliances with other groups and organisations also committed to changing the destructive social relationships and operating principles of our present society'. Social work must become part of a social movement? Coalition-building with campaigning organisations like the Child Poverty Action Group in Britain, Action Canada and the Canadian Centre for Policy Alternatives, and the National Welfare Rights Organisation in the US are strongly advocated by the exponents of radical social work (Bailey and Brake, 1975: 10; Galper, 1980: 132; Mullaly, 1997: 192). Such coalitions are vital to the process of changing the focus from the individual service user to the rights of marginalised groups within the welfare state. This political focus is fundamental to the discourse of radical social work practice.

'Micropolitics', a term first employed by Statham (1978), provides another important strategy plank for radical social work based upon the practice of welfare rights and community development at local level. This strategy for change may be a long way from overthrowing capitalist society, but it offers an authentic form of social work practice that goes back to the historic origins of social work in struggles for social justice. At a point in history when liberal market capitalism is once again resurgent, micropolitics offers a 'resistance social work' that seeks to defend the poor from the vagaries of the market.

Welfare rights as a strategy goes back to the 1930s, when claimants' unions were first inspired by Wal Harrington's National Unemployed Workers' Movement in Britain closely allied to the Communist Party. Bailey and Brake (1975: 6) record a march in Sheffield in 1935 in protest at cuts in unemployment benefit that proved successful in changing the policy of national government. During the welfare state era much of the activity of claimants' unions has concentrated on rights awareness, mutual support and social struggle against a welfare state that discriminates against the poor in an increasingly two-tier society. Tenants' rights campaigns, action by single parents' groups, disability awareness campaigns etc. all contribute to local resistance against domination and discrimination in people's everyday lives. While social workers employed in state welfare bureaucracies often find it difficult to participate in these rights campaigns as part of their professional activities, they can and do as active citizens.

Community development is quintessentially about active citizenship and its roots lie in the Settlement Movement of the Victorian era. It needs to be stated that, ideologically, community is a much disputed territory. Radical and socialist community work practice 'has traditionally been undertaken by community activists who have employed a class analysis and the rhetoric and pursuance of class struggle at local and regional level' (Popple, 1995: 35). Some of these activists have sought to find an 'oppositional space' as state-funded employees. However, the decline of socialism has posed a dilemma for advocates of a class analysis since it has lost its popular appeal and direct source of legitimacy (Popple, 1995: 36). Cloward and Piven (1990: xii) see 'some hope for a new cycle of protest' amongst 'women and minorities in the service sector that will provide its crucial social base'.

Conclusion

Premature obituary notices have been written about radical social work. Its demise is unlikely. Radical social work is an authentic part of the social work tradition. It survives because it adapts and mutates. While the reverses experienced by socialism and the fragmentation of the traditional working-class movement have undermined the concept of radical social work advocated by Marxists during the 1960s and 1970s, the new social movements have opened up alternative radical discourses and sites for progressive practice. Moreover, growing concern about social exclusion, which threatens to fragment the post-war welfare consensus, has given rise to a concern in the European Union with more inclusive social work practices. While the focus of social exclusion has moved from economic equality (which socialists argued was the basis of solidarity) to more classical republican ideas of citizenship, it offers the basis for progressive social work practice in the future. The renaissance of civil society created the potential for a wider 'space' for social work practice as the 'site' of social intervention broadened to include the state/civil society axis in a new contract between the community and voluntary sector and the state. These themes will be explored in subsequent chapters in this book as potentially new paradigms for social work practice rooted in the political culture of the times.

5

Poverty, Social Exclusion and Inclusive Practice

In postmodern society as we enter the new millennium, the paradoxes of modernisation have acquired increasingly extreme forms. Greater wealth stands in marked contrast to endemic poverty. Substantially increased diversity and choice in terms of 'lifestyle politics' have been accompanied by fragmentation and polarisation across the globe, and as rural life has declined in response to the forces of industrialisation and urbanisation, inner city ghettos characterised by poverty, drugs and crime have come to dominate the social landscape. Social and political life is no longer organised in terms of traditional identities and shared values. This is partly because contemporary inequalities of income, wealth and power do not produce the homogeneous classes, notably business and workers, that shaped the social and political geography of modern society. Instead new social movements have organised around issues as diverse as gender, environment, urban inequalities, ethnic issues, social amenities, the poll tax, animal rights and so on. Social conflicts have become more pluralistic, representing a much wider set of interests. These conflicts involve a different set of targets including the state, bureaucracies and professionals.

A generic repertoire of skills is essential to social work practice in postmodern society, where the environments of trust and risk have been reframed. Social work practice is consequently reconstituting itself in different and more challenging forms. The new complexity of modern society makes it increasingly difficult to find answers to the policy dilemmas that face social work in particular and the welfare state in general. Both society and social work are confronted with multiple choices.

The realities of postmodern society for social workers, like the rest of the population, are that the environment of trust based on kinship networks, local community ties, religious cosmologies and traditional certainties has been undermined. Traditional relationships, notably within the family and community and between professionals and service users, have been disembedded. Trust is no longer certain and cannot be taken for granted. Social exclusion has created a gap between rich and poor, that shows every sign of widening.

A new environment of risk has emerged. In premodern society, risk was defined in terms of threats and dangers emanating from nature, the violence of war, and a fall from religious grace or malicious magical influence. In postmodern society, the reflexive nature of society, which constantly revises most aspects of social relations in the light of new information, has created a world without certainties. Instead, an environment defined by the calculation of risk has emerged in which the reality of polarisation and fragmentation is all pervasive. In this changing environment, social work is challenged to respond reflexively by reacting to the growing perception that we live in a society characterised by degraded individualism. Ultimately, degraded individualism is attributed to degraded citizenship and the powerlessness of the socially excluded minority.

The purpose of this chapter is to analyse the challenges facing social work in postmodern society in terms of two key paradigms: trust and risk. Both of these paradigms will be examined within the larger context of social exclusion, fragmentation and polarisation. But first it is essential to deconstruct social exclusion and assess its relevance to the public policy debate.

Social exclusion: the Brazilianisation of the West

Economic and social trends in recent years have undermined civic trust significantly by increasing the numbers of those marginalised or excluded from the mainstream of society. This process, which has been graphically characterised as 'the Brazilianisation of the West', entails increasingly ostentatious forms of exclusion with groups of people living in severe poverty and under barely life-sustaining conditions – in the garbage of 'normal' society. Oxhorn (1995) calls this process 'coerced marginalisation'. Unemployment has broken the link for many with the external world of work. A lack of child care facilities makes it difficult for women to participate in the workforce in the first instance and militates against equality in the labour market. These problems are compounded in certain areas, such as the peripheral housing estates, where marginalised groups are concentrated and where physical isolation and the sparseness of community facilities reinforce social exclusion. Beatrix Campbell, author of *Goliath: Britain's Dangerous Places* (1993), has referred to 'the geographical other – the ghettos' – places characterised by endemic debt and 'male violence'. Minority groups, including black people, HIV/AIDS victims, drug addicts, refugees and asylum seekers experience the sharp end of exclusion in a growing climate of social tensions exacerbated by the increasing emphasis on ethnicity in defining citizenship. Social exclusion represents a qualitative change in the way people relate to each other, manifested by the ever-widening inequalities, spiralling levels of violence and a breakdown in social solidarity. It involves a crisis of civic trust because it breeds a popular lack of confidence in the social order.

Levitas (1998: 21) has located social exclusion within the discourse of the European Union, observing, 'exclusion is understood as the breakdown of the structural, cultural and moral ties which bind the individual to society, and family instability is a key concern'. In countries where social thought is strongly influenced by Catholicism, Durkheimian sociology and a concern with moral integration, the concept of social exclusion is very influential. France has been cited as an example, (Silver, 1996; Levitas, 1998: 21). Ireland, which has much in common with France in terms of its cultural tradition, has also put social exclusion at the core of its social policy agenda. Even in Eurosceptical Britain, the Blair government launched a Social Exclusion Unit in 1997. However, there are concerns that this adoption of the concept of social exclusion may be simply a policy manoeuvre by the government to detach itself from the Fabian imperative of tackling poverty and promoting distributive justice (Levitas, 1998: 147–152). Social exclusion broadens the concept of inequality beyond the traditional Fabian concern with a lack of material resources, especially low income. It is primarily concerned with degraded citizenship rather than economic inequality, although the two are closely interlinked.

What is literally meant by the term 'social exclusion'? The association of poverty with a more divided society has led to this broad concept, which refers not only to low consumption due to material deprivation, but to the inability of the poor to participate fully through exercising their social, cultural and political rights as citizens. The concept of social exclusion has become more particularly influential in European Union policy circles; for example, the 1993 *Green Paper on European Social Policy* argues that 'social exclusion ... by high-lighting the flaws in the social fabric ... suggests something more than social inequality, and, concomitantly, carries with it the risk of a dual and fragmented society' (European Union, 1993: 551). It calls for the harmonisation of social policies across Europe, emphasising the importance of workers' rights and measures to stimulate 'solidarity and integration'.

The *Report on Wealth Creation and Social Cohesion* (Dahrendorf Report) was published in 1995 and sought to establish a 'vocabulary for change'. It observed in relation to social inclusion:

> Exclusion is the greatest risk accompanying the opportunities of the new economic era. Significant numbers of people lose their hold first on the labour market then on social and political participation in their community.

This definition suggests that social exclusion is a counter-concept to citizenship. It closely associates uncontrolled economic growth with the idea of risk to the social fabric and the problem of democratic deficit. Social exclusion also leads to civic exclusion, promoting hostility and xenophobia towards minority ethnic groups, asylum seekers and refugees.

The distinguished Irish social policy commentator, liberation theologian and redoubtable poverty crusader, Father Sean Healy (1990: 35–36) graphically describes the meaning of social exclusion:

> Exclusion is experienced in many ways. If you are excluded it means your opinion is not sought and it doesn't count. In fact you are not expected to have an opinion, rather you are encouraged to trust the opinion of the shapers of society. Ultimately it is not only the feeling but the reality of powerlessness....
>
> When you are one of the excluded, politicians and policy-makers can ignore you without fear of censure or loss of position. If your rights are infringed, the avenues of redress are very few and haphazard. Since society fears excluded groups you are always suspect – guilty until proven innocent....

> Generally speaking poverty is the companion of exclusion. People on low incomes
> have a struggle even to provide the necessary food, clothing and heat. They are not
> simply 'less comfortable' than everyone else – they have shorter lives, sicker children,
> babies which are more likely to die in infancy.

In this searing analysis of the 'underclass', a minority group denied meaningful
participation in citizenship and discriminated against by the majority clearly
emerges. The cause of this profound social inequality belongs to the sphere of
political economy, since the exclusion of the underclass derives in the first
instance, as Father Healy suggests, from their poverty. Exclusion from income
and welfare is closely linked to exclusion from broader citizenship rights, such as
the right to justice and participation, suggesting that a competing cultural paradigm is emerging to challenge the traditional economic paradigm of social
inequality.

Egalitarian theorists in modern society sought to conceptualise social injustice
in purely economic terms. These theoretical frameworks include Karl Marx's
theory of capitalist exploitation, John Rawls's account of justice as fairness in the
distribution of 'primary goods', Amartya Sen's concept that justice requires that
people have equal 'capabilities to function', and Ronald Dworkin's argument that
it necessitates 'equality of resources' (Rawls, 1971; Dworkin, 1982; Sen, 1985;
Marx, 1994). Postmodernity has involved a reconceptualisation of social inequality in terms of republican values.

At the end of the twentieth century culture-blindness of a purely economic
paradigm had become increasingly obvious. The decline of social democracy and
the collapse of the Soviet Union is symptomatic of the limitations of socialism in
postmodern society, where the politics of redistribution is being challenged
by cultural politics based on class, gender, race, age, disability and sexual orientation, reflecting the fractured nature of social identity. The replacement of 'poverty'
in the vernacular of social science by the more widely encompassing concept of
'social exclusion' further illustrates the process of discursive change. Social
exclusion represents a qualitative restructuring constituting a change in the way
people relate to each other, manifested by ever widening inequalities, spiralling
levels of violence and a breakdown in social solidarity.

In this context a new paradigm of injustice has emerged, which analyses social
justice in cultural and symbolic terms. It is grounded in social patterns of representation, interpretation and communication. Fraser cites several examples of cultural and symbolic injustice:

1   Cultural domination: being subjected to patterns of interpretation and communica-
    tion that are associated with another culture and are alien and/or hostile to one's
    own;
2   Non-recognition: being rendered invisible via the authoritative representational,
    communication, and interpretative practices of one's culture;
3   Cultural disrespect: being routinely maligned or disparaged in stereotypic public
    cultural representation and/or everyday interaction. (Fraser, 1997: 14)

Manifestly, in postmodern society neither an economic nor a cultural paradigm is
in itself adequate to explain injustice. Social injustice must be pursued at both the

economic and the cultural level, simultaneously augmenting redistribution and recognition in society as paradigms for change. However, social work, which operates primarily in the cultural rather than the economic domain of society, has much to contribute in the promotion of remedies to injustice based upon cultural respect and social recognition. Arguably, in postmodern conditions social citizenship is increasingly dependent upon democratic participation based upon a generative policy strategy, i.e. one that empowers. However, this assumes a progressive political climate sensitive to the need for social inclusion.

In reality, attitudes towards poverty have greatly changed in postmodern society, redefining citizenship in terms of duties and obligations rather than the Marshallian construct of social, as well as civil and political, rights. This redefinition in terms of classical values has been associated with the political reassertion of market values. It has legitimised welfare reform and public expenditure cuts. A more lasting legacy of welfare reform is likely to be the consequent reconceptualisation of poverty in terms of desert, dividing the poor into 'deserving' and 'undeserving' groups based on a moral economy of conduct. Fiscal and moral rectitude have thus become reflexively connected in the welfare reform agenda.

In postmodern society the exclusion of the 'underclass' poses the ultimate challenge. The inclusion of a substantial section of the working class in consumer society has served to fragment its traditional solidarity. An excluded 'underclass' has emerged, defined by its prescribed status as supplicant in the welfare state. This is a potent manifestation of the importance of productive relations in determining class solidarity. The underclass is differentiated from the majority population by age, gender and ethnicity, as well as employment status. A thumbnail demography of the underclass according to a multitude of studies reveals a population on the periphery of society consisting of the unemployed, lone (usually female) parents, the disabled and elderly, as well as ethnic minorities. Beyond these exist several minority groups which experience social exclusion in its most extreme form, including gypsies, people suffering from HIV/AIDS, drug abusers, refugees and asylum seekers. The fact that they are usually excluded from poverty studies exacerbates their social exclusion. (Gans, 1996: 151) has suggested that the term 'undercaste' might more accurately describe this 'population of such low status as to be shunned by the rest of society'.

During the 1960s and 1970s, as noted in Chapter 3, the emphasis was on incorporating the marginalised through targeting problem families and communities. In the 1980s, the emphasis changed in terms of technologies of control. While the underlying thrust of public policy during the 1960s and 1970s might be described as controlled *inclusion*, since then it has changed to coerced marginalisation (Oxhorn, 1995). Hoggett (1994: 46) comments: 'the new forms of social control seem to be based much more on processes of political and spatial exclusion'. He concludes that the underclass is being subjected to a process of 'spatial apartheid', treated as an excluded 'other', beyond the pale. In this analysis the 'underclass' becomes decoupled from the rest of society, living in 'collapsing communities' characterised by social implosion and fragmentation. This 'neo-liberalism', in which the underclass is segregated from society, stands in stark contrast to global cosmopolitanism.

Dahrendorf (1994: 15) views the term 'underclass' as a misnomer that is simply a convenient way to describe the victims of social exclusion:

> The underclass does not pose a class problem. Technically, the name underclass is wrong. Classes are conflict groups based on common interest conditions within a framework of relations.... The underclass on the contrary is a mere victim. It is unlikely to organise and defend the many similar yet not really common interests of its members.

Jordan (1996: 199) has commented on this issue that 'whether or not there exists a "class" of individuals with identifiably distinctive interests, strategies, and cultural practices, the very fact that influential commentators and populist politicians have been able to form public opinion and mobilise political action around such a concept suggests latent groups'.

The use of the term 'underclass' by the New Right to attack the welfare state, on the basis that it promotes a dependency culture, has made many commentators critical. They view the term 'underclass' as abusive and potentially racist (Levitas, 1998: 14–21). Charles Murray, the neo-conservative social policy analyst from the US on a visit to Britain in 1990 described himself as 'a visitor from a plague area come to see if the disease is spreading' (Murray, 1990: 3). He described the disease as one 'whose values are contaminating the life of entire neighbourhoods' through undermining both the work ethic and the family ethic (Murray, 1990: 4). On a second visit to Britain in 2000, Murray further explored his concept of an 'underclass': 'By underclass I do not mean people who are merely poor, but people at the margins of society, unsocialised and often violent' (*Sunday Times*, 13 February 2000).

The British Prime Minister, Tony Blair, uses the term 'underclass', repeatedly portraying its members as victims of both economic and moral failure: 'often their life is marked by unemployment, poor education, crime, drug abuse and family instability' (cited in Levitas, 1998: 155). Mr Blair has concluded that the 'underclass' is living 'without any sense of shared purpose' with the rest of society, whereas 'to be a citizen of Britain is ... to share its aspirations to be part of the British family' (cited ibid.: 156).

It is, therefore, not surprising that the 1990s witnessed a reopening of the debate on the nature of citizenship and a reassertion of its duties and obligations at the expense of rights and entitlements. The implications of the idea of citizenship have led Dahrendorf (1994: 13) to comment that 'there may be a case for emphasising obligations as well as rights, but once they lose their unconditional quality, the door is open not just for the invisible hand of the market (which can be benevolent) but above all for the visible hand of rulers who tell people what to do when'. In the case of minority groups, who experience social exclusion at its most extreme (gypsies, HIV/AIDS victims, asylum seekers, refugees, etc.), Dahrendorf's point has particular resonance.

Global trends are towards increasing inequality, sometimes referred to as the 'Silent Depression', with the poorest fifth of the world's population sharing on average little more than 5 per cent of wealth, while the richest fifth possess 40–60 per cent. In the USA, incomes for high school dropouts have declined by 23.3 per cent since 1973, high school graduates have experienced a 17 per cent drop in income and even some college students (who have not studied to degree level) have had a fall in income of 7.3 per cent. At the other end of the social spectrum, 1 per cent of the nation's richest households have 40 per cent of the country's wealth (Cohen, 1995).

In Britain, the Rowntree Foundation *Inquiry into Income and Wealth* (1995: (1) 6) concluded that 'income inequality in the UK grew rapidly between 1977 and 1990 reaching a higher level than recorded since the war'. This increase was exceptional in international terms and was due to multiple causes: rising unemployment, widening tax differentials, decreasing benefits and a more regressive tax regime. It impacted particularly on marginalised communities and ethnic minorities. The Joseph Rowntree Inquiry suggested that this sharp increase in inequality was a threat both to the social fabric and to economic efficiency.

In terms of the threat to the social fabric the central theme of the Rowntree Inquiry (1995: (1) 33) is that 'the living standards and life opportunities of the poorest.... are simply unacceptably low in a society as rich as ours'. It adds: 'our central concern is with the failure of the poorest 20–30 per cent of the population to benefit from recent economic growth – not just out of concern for those directly affected, but also because of the damage done to the overall social fabric, and to the economy when a substantial group has no stake in its performance' (Rowntree, 1995: (1) 38). The Inquiry (1995: (1) 34) warned:

> Regardless of any moral arguments or feelings of altruism, everyone shares an interest in the cohesiveness of society. As the gaps between rich and poor grow, the problems of the marginalised groups which are being left behind rebound on the more comfortable majority.

This warning raised seminal issues about the need for social cohesion that go to the heart of the postmodern concern about fragmentation and social disintegration. Social cohesion is under stress in an insecure and fractured society with fewer and fewer shared values and common interests (Dahrendorf, 1995: 16). Levitas (1998: 22) views these discourses of social exclusion and social cohesion as indicative of the growing influence of European social policy over national and ideological vocabularies. In reality, the debate in continental Europe about social cohesion is directly paralleled by an Anglo-Saxon debate about social capital. Both devolve on the issue of trust and the need to promote a more virtuous society. This is an age-old humanist debate. The World Summit for Social Development convened by the United Nations in 1995 at Copenhagen is a significant example of a growing global concern about the relationship between wealth creation and social cohesion.

Civil society, trust and civic humanism

Both civil society and civic virtue are concerned with defining the relationship between the individual and the social and are firmly rooted in the intellectual traditions of Western civilisation. They are visible in the doctrines of natural law and the political philosophies of classical Greece and republican Rome. The Dahrendorf Report (1995: 16–17) advised that 'social cohesion is brought about by a thriving civil society which gives all citizens a basic common status, creates a sense of belonging, engenders civic pride, and encourages participation in common concerns of a public nature'.

The Greek word *arete* is translated as 'virtue' and means the quality which entitles any institution or individual to be called good. Plato divided human virtue into four elements: wisdom, courage, temperance and justice. For Plato, justice is simultaneously a part of human virtue and the bond that joins people together in society. It is virtue that makes an individual both good and social. This construct is the first and fundamental principle of Plato's political philosophy. The Italian Renaissance philosopher, Machiavelli, reflecting on the practical lessons to be learned from the fall of the Roman Republic, cites civic virtue in a people as the essential ingredient for a free society. He equates virtue with vigour in both the human body and the body politic, and concludes that where civic virtue is lacking the people are corrupt and tyranny is inevitable. For Machiavelli, the two great forces that govern society are fortune and virtue. Fortune is a capricious power, incalculable and often irresistible, influencing human destiny from without. But people are not simply the victims of fortune; they can seek to control their own destinies. The power that enables then to do so is civic virtue, and the more virtuous a people, the freer the society.

Civic humanists of the Renaissance period maintained that civic virtue was essential to the maintenance of 'the civil life'. As Thomas Starkey (1533: 27), put it in his *Dialogue*, 'the civil life consists of living together in good and political order, being ever ready to do good to another, and as it were conspiring together in all virtue and honesty'. That is the moral in the tale of civic virtue, which is as true today as it was in earlier historical epochs.

Not surprisingly, during the 1990s a new debate began about the values of civic trust. In this debate the good society has been recast as civil society. This development essentially represents a swing back towards collectivism, since it promotes a new form of communitarianism (Etzioni, 1994; Fukuyama, 1995). However, to describe this trend as a reassertion of the collectivist values of the welfare state would be simplistic. What the 'new communitarianism' of the exponents of civil society seeks to do is to reconcile the globalised market with a form of active citizenship in which the individual seeks to achieve a moral commitment through involvement in the community. In a sense this is a crosscutting definition that defies the distinction between individualism and collectivism. That is both its strength and its weakness.

The exponents of civil society in the contemporary debate about the moral economy of welfare view reciprocal responsibility and social well-being as the basis of 'social capital'. Fukuyama (1995: 26) asserts that:

> Social capital is a capability that arises from the prevalence of trust in a society or certain parts of it. It can be embodied in the smallest and most basic social group, the family as well as the largest of all groups the nation, and in all other groups in between. Social capital differs from all other forms of human capital insofar as it is usually transmitted through cultural mechanisms like religion, tradition or historical habit.

Social capital, therefore, comprises the institutional relationships of a vibrant civil society, based on solidary individualism and active citizenship, from extended families to neighbourhood networks, community groups to religious organisations, youth clubs to parent-teacher associations, local business to local public services, playgroups to the police on the beat (Borrie Report, 1994: 307–308). At the heart of civil society are empathy, compassion, trust and participation. This is the basis of the 'good society' that we all yearn to belong to in the midst of uncertainty, scepticism, disillusion and institutional fragmentation. Consequently, the pluralisation of lifestyles and the search for meaning has stimulated a revitalisation of the concept of civil society as a means for resolving the problems of contemporary society. Perhaps the greatest of these problems is social exclusion, because it embodies a fracture in society that contains the seeds of its disintegration. Social exclusion leads to distrust, diminishing the quality of life for everybody. It also leads to oppressive social policies, such as zero tolerance policing, which undermine democratic values. Trust, democracy and humanism are interdependent in the body politic.

Trust, inclusion and social work

Trust is the basis of an inclusive society. The Irish *Green Paper on the Community and Voluntary Sector and its relationship with the state* (Department of Social Welfare, 1997: 25) observes that:

> It is important to create a culture and society which respects the autonomy of the individual. In such a society, individuals are given the opportunity to realise their potential and to take potential for themselves and others. This means creating a climate which supports individuals and groups to make things happen rather than have things happen to them. Such a culture respects diversity and community solidarity. Interdependence is built on trust and dialogue.... All people, but especially those who are at present excluded, must be facilitated to participate in dialogue about problems, policy solutions and programmes' implementation. For dialogue to take place with Government agencies, officials must ensure that there is openness and trust and that there is flexibility towards new interactive ways of responding to issues and concerns of those who are excluded.

The Green Paper is part of Ireland's National Anti-Poverty Strategy, which seeks to address the challenge of social exclusion. Whereas American and British discourse during the twentieth century has been grounded in the Anglo-Saxon belief that voluntary associations, churches and communities should be free and autonomous, the Irish perspective is more European. It views the relationship between the voluntary and community sector and the state as an essentially symbiotic one (Silver, 1996: 112).

During the 1990s there were signs of a growing movement towards a partnership between the voluntary sector and the state in Britain (Lewis, 1999). It is notable that the New Labour government in Britain published a *Compact on Relations between Government and the Voluntary and Community Sector in England* (Home Office, 1998). Social work in continental Europe is deeply embedded in the voluntary and community sector, with close links to the churches, as well as having humanist and socialist associations. In the United States, Canada and Australia, and most developing countries, the voluntary and community sector also play a vital role in the delivery of personal social services, along with state agencies, e.g. criminal justice, education, social assistance, special employment, health and housing. This organisational form is the global paradigm for social work (Jordan, 1997: 18).

British social work, on the other hand, as demonstrated in Chapter 3, has evolved as an integral part of the welfare state – the fifth social service. The particularism of British social work can also be attributed to Lockean notions of contract based upon political and market relations. British social work in postmodern society therefore faces two profound dilemmas. First, its impulses are contradictory. Jordan (1997: 10) writing in the British context, comments that 'there is a contradiction at the heart of social work, because it is spawned by market-orientated economic individualism, yet its values are those of a caring, inclusive, reciprocal community that takes collective responsibility for its members'. Second, the emergence of the enforcement state, epitomised by workfare, has undermined the value base of social work. Jordan (1997: 10) concludes: 'Social work is the spirit of community in the clothes of Hobbesian third party enforcement – a caring face in the service of Leviathan'. This is somewhat of a caricature. Government in Britain has thought it essential to decouple the Probation Service from social work, because it perceived the latter as subversive of retributive justice. The Home Secretary, Jack Straw was reported to be planning to rename the Probation Service 'the Community Rehabilitation and Punishment Service' with probation officers being transformed into 'Community Punishment Officers' (*Guardian*, 8 December 1999). Jordan's analogy between social workers and 'blue helmeted UN troops serving as peacekeepers in a civil war' is more persuasive. The challenge is trust. The role is ambiguous:

> They [social workers] are often denounced, and sometimes attacked by both sides. They are open to manipulation and exploitation by the combatants, and their work is always morally compromised. (Jordan, 1997: 10)

Commercialisation poses further challenges to social work, notably in Britain and the United States. The abandonment of the profession's historic mission to the poor in favour of therapeutic individualism is indicative of this influence. Moreover, the emergence of the 'contract culture' that turns welfare into a commodity, to be bought and sold in the market-place, threatens the very basis of trust. Commercialisation involves the privatisation of 'the social'. Solidarity is therefore removed from provision of care. In an era of state enforcement and privatisation, it is difficult for social work to promote trust. To return to Jordan's blue-helmeted UN peacekeeper analogy, social work cannot afford to appear to stand by and adopt a position of neutrality in the face of exclusion and social injustice. Social work is challenged to negotiate between the state and civil society. This means renegotiating its own role and task in order to promote social cohesion, trust and social harmony. What does such a negotiation involve?

French social workers have demonstrated some of the possibilities. The French have developed their own version of 'the third way', reconciling socialist commitment to the value of solidarity with humanist concern for individual rights.

Instead of the Lockean individualised centractualism that dominates British welfare discourse, the French emphasise the Durkheimian concept of the social bond between the state and the poor. The French have harnessed republican notions of fraternity to working-class commitment to mutualism, in order to forge the ideal of 'integration', 'cohesion' or 'solidarity' (Silver, 1996: 21). A policy of 'insertion', epitomised by the very popular guaranteed minimum income, Revenue minimum d'insertion (RMI), provides the necessary dynamic. Delahaye (1994: 245) defines insertion as 'the dynamic process by which an individual in a situation of exclusion acquires and finds a recognised place in the heart of the society while internalising the social functions whose mastery ensures automony'. Essentially, the policy of 'insertion' is about participation in society. While recipients of RMI are required to sign a *contrat d'insertion* which frequently focuses upon employment, in some cases the form of participation is negotiated with a social worker and involves issues of 'daily living, behaviour and family relationships' (Levitas, 1998: 22). The French approach underlines the importance of communitarianism in the practice of social work. The challenge of trust raises axial questions for social work practice regarding individualism versus communitarianism.

A heated debate took place in British social work on this issue of community responsibility following the publication of the Barclay Report in 1982. It concluded: 'the Working Party believes that if social needs of citizens are to be met in the last years of the twentieth century, the personal social services must develop a close partnership with citizens focussing more closely on the community and its strengths' (Barclay, 1982: 198). Instead a client-centred individualised approach emerged, geared towards a reactive service and preoccupied with risk management. No doubt the ascendancy of neo-liberal thought in Britain during the 1980s played a key role in the rejection of the communitarianism espoused by the Barclay Report. A more atomised society had become preoccupied with risk.

Social work, risk management and dangerousness

Giddens (1999) in his BBC Reith Lecture series 'Runaway World' made risk the theme of one of his lectures. For him, 'risk refers to hazards that are actively assessed in relation to future possibilities' (Giddens, 1999). The word 'risk' appears to be the product of modernity being associated with the voyages of Western explorers in the sixteenth and seventeenth centuries. Risk, as Giddens points out, is 'inseparable from the ideas of probability and uncertainty'. In relation to social policy, Giddens (1999) comments: 'The Welfare State, whose development can be traced back to the Elizabethan Poor Laws in England, is essentially a risk management system', and, he adds, 'those who provide insurance, whether in the shape of private insurance or state welfare systems, are essentially redistributing risk'. Beck in his influential book *Risk Society* (1992) writes that what is new is not risk *per se* but our consciousness of risk and our capacity to control it.

Risk management is central to idea of welfare and the practice of social work. Roche and Tucker (1997: 4) have observed that taking responsibility for someone else's welfare has traditionally involved a number of core activities with citizens:

♦ looking after them;
♦ making sure they are safe;
♦ meeting their physical needs for food, shelter and so on;
♦ supporting them in resolving their personal difficulties;
♦ teaching them appropriate forms of behaviour and discipline where necessary.

The emergence of risk has also been associated with the prediction of danger-ousness in individuals and families. Yet research into the prediction of violence does not inspire confidence, according to Parton (1995: 139): 'the empirical sup-port for the prediction of violence is very poor'; he adds that 'such difficulties lead to the statistical problems of "false negatives" and "false positives"', which 'clearly ... has enormous implications for civil liberties' and he concludes that 'those who oppose such developments generally stress the importance of indi-vidual rights of people likely to be subjected to intervention'. Dangerousness and desert have become reflexively connected in postmodern welfare discourse, justi-fying risk management strategies intended to control.

Social work in postmodern society is engaged in risk management with a series of high profile client groups including children 'at risk', young offenders, the mentally ill in the community and the homeless and rough sleepers. These social groups challenge the limits of welfare and highlight the changing environment of risk and trust in which the perception of dangerousness has reframed both public policy and social work practice.

Children 'at risk'

Child protection has emerged as one of the most sensitive areas of risk manage-ment in postmodern society. Ferguson (1997: 221) writes: 'a radically new pro-fessional risk consciousness in child protection is traced to late modern existential crises associated with death and sexuality and the emergence of manufactured risk, which is known and experienced by social workers as risk in the context of radically uncertain futures for children'.

After two decades of child abuse inquiries the social work task has been reframed by risk management, with 'welfare' being replaced in the discourse by 'protection'. In practice social work has become a policing exercise, intrusively investigating the child care standards of the socially excluded (Parton, 1991, 1994; Thorpe, 1994, 1997). Parton (1995: 176) in *The Politics of Child Abuse*, concluded: 'the problem has thus been constructed with strong moralistic over-tones which support paternalism whereby it is assumed that child abuse is one of the worst, if not the worst, manifestations of the decline in the family and the social order more generally'. In this sense child abuse has become the archetypal example of a new discourse of problematisation that allows the socially excluded to become a site of disciplinary power.

The UK Department of Health (1995) in a document called *Child Protection: Messages from Research*, suggested that there needed to be a shift back towards prevention, family support and 'children in need'. However, in the context of fiscal rectitude and morally based discourses of problematisation, it is difficult to see how emphasis in child care policy can be easily recast. Waterhouse and

McGhee (1998: 282) note the paradox that 'a child's chances of gaining access to resources may, therefore, be likely to be significantly increased through the imposition of legal order'.

The *Guardian Weekend* of 12 February 2000 in a report on child sexual abuse entitled 'The End of Innocence', asserted that 'nearly half the sexual abuse suffered by children is inflicted on them by other children'. It was suggested that children as young as five years old may be guilty of child abuse. The report cited the NSPCC as its source of information, stating that it calculates 'that 40% of abuse on children is committed by other children'. It noted that in 1997, the last year for which statistics were available, more than 1,000 young people were found guilty or cautioned for sexual offences in Britain. While the number of children on the Sex Offenders Register is unknown the report estimated that 'there are probably around 200'. The *Guardian* enquired: 'In this new, unsettling universe, is our children's normal sexual development being criminalised?' The answer must be that society's preoccupation with risk is undermining the legal and social status of childhood and criminalising children in growing numbers. The 'end of innocence' might more accurately be described as the 'end of childhood'.

Young offenders

This emphasis on legalism has also become the hallmark of the treatment of school truants and young offenders, who are increasingly viewed from the perspective of dangerousness and social risk. Fuentes (1998: 20) comments from a US perspective:

> In the past two decades, our collective attitude toward children and youth has undergone a profound change that's reflected in the educational and criminal justice systems as well as in our daily discourse. 'Zero tolerance' is the mantra in public (state) schools and juvenile courts, and what it really means is that to be young is to be suspect. Latino and black youth have borne the brunt of this growing criminalisation of youth. But the trend has spilled over racial and ethnic boundaries, to a degree. Youth, with all its innocence and vulnerability, is losing ground in a society that exploits both.

Killings by youths of their classmates in Springfield, Oregon and Jonesboro, Arkansas, during 1998 caused a wave of public revulsion. It paralleled the earlier killing of the toddler Jamie Bulger, in February 1993, by two ten-year-olds in Britain. However, instead of seeking to understand the causes and meaning of these terrible incidents, a mood of revenge and retribution has been the hallmark of public reaction. The then Conservative British Prime Minister, John Major, urged the country in the light of the tragic event of Jamie Bulger's death, 'to condemn a little more and to understand a little less' (cited in Jones and Novak, 1999: 1). The European Court of Human Rights ruled in 1999 that Jamie Bulger's two killers had had an unfair trial. A *Guardian* editorial on 17 December 1999 declared: 'child killers may be exceptional but they still deserve the protection extended to all other child offenders. Vengeance is not justice.' When one Texas legislator called for the enforcement of the death penalty for children as young as eleven, Fuentes (1998: 20) noted: 'he's got plenty of support, because this is the

era of crime and punishment and accountability for all constituencies without
wealth or power to shield them'. Compassion and care are demonstrably in short
supply in Britain and the United States where child offenders are concerned.

In a growing climate of moral panic in postmodern society the image of the
young offender as portrayed by the media is that of a folk devil. Not surprisingly
this widely shared public perception of the young offender has been accompanied
by a growing disenchantment with what is believed to be the soft (i.e. welfare)
policy options represented by social workers. Critics of welfare, purporting to
represent popular opinion, have harnessed this *angst* to their campaign to restruc-
ture the current juvenile justice system. Paradoxically, they have found support in
the arguments of the libertarian advocates of natural rights, who have increasingly come to question the moral basis of the welfare concept. Arguing that in
practice some supposedly welfare dispositions have become suspect in libertarian
terms, they accept that it may be justifiable to lock children up as retribution for
their deeds, but question our warrant to confine them until they become better
people. Thus the concept of welfare is simultaneously presented by its critics as
a permissive policy and a denial of natural rights. Social workers have reeled
under the double burden of alleged permissiveness coupled with perceived
ineffectiveness on the one hand and moral doubt on the other. It is in this climate
that the case for a juvenile justice system informed by justice principles has
gained widespread support. Justice means a return to classical criminology based
upon the idea that punishment should fit the crime. The fractious 'justice versus
welfare' debate has been a key component of populist politics for the past two
decades, paralleling the rise of the New Right and the retreat of the Old Left.

The 'justice versus welfare' debate is, ultimately, a debate about means rather
than ends. Stripped of its abstract philosophical rhetoric, it is a dialogue about how
best to achieve conformity with the law amongst young offenders. One side advocates care and protection, the other duty, retribution and punishment. However,
questions of age and social circumstances have been a consideration in court proceedings for juveniles for nearly a century: welfare principles are deeply embedded in the system. In Scotland a welfare model has been retained because it works;
but in England and Wales a fundamental shift took place during the Thatcher and
Major years of Conservative government. The White Paper *Young Offenders* (1980)
signalled a hardening in official attitudes towards young offenders. However, it
was not until the Criminal Justice Act, 1991, and the Crime (Sentences) Act, 1997
that the full magnitude of the shift towards a justice model became fully evident.
The Crime and Disorder Act, 1998 introduced Anti-Social Behaviour Orders that
can be applied to any behaviour 'likely to cause harassment to the community'.
This policy, which includes the adoption of the American practice of curfews, as
well as exclusion and the restriction on the movement of young people, curtails the
civil liberties of younger citizens. Young people are not the only citizens considered dangerous by an increasingly Leviathan state.

The mentally ill in the community

The *Independent* on 15 November 1999, announced 'tough new controls on
potentially dangerous patients discharged from psychiatric hospitals'. In keeping

with the philosophy of welfare reform in the UK, a radical reform of the Mental Health Act, 1993, is envisaged. Under these proposals patients discharged from hospital are to be given an order specifying where they should live and a care plan. Patients who fail to adhere to the terms of the order will be returned to hospital for compulsory treatment. Ministers presented this policy shift as 'a third way' between institutionalisation and community care.

The *New York Times* on 23 May 1999 published a major investigative article entitled '*Bedlam on the Streets*' by Michael Winerip. It summarised the failed potential of community care for the mentally ill:

> with the introduction of antipsychotic medication, state hospitals nation-wide began releasing patients into the community. There was a good deal that was hopeful about this; by then many state hospitals had become snake pits. Yet the states never created the outpatient services that were supported to replace those hospitals, landing many of the seriously ill on the streets. (Winerip, 1999: 45)

Winerip concluded, sardonically, that the reason the mental health system behaves so irrationally is usually money. There is a push to close state hospitals because that saves money, but there is no incentive to build the badly needed community housing to replace them, because that costs money (Winerip, 1999: 49).

This article was dealing with New York, one of the richest cities in the world, but it might have been anywhere. The disturbing reality of community care of the mentally ill is that it fails to provide tangible support in the community, leaving many vulnerable people homeless. The public's reaction is to panic at the perceived dangerousness of the mentally ill unsupervised on the streets. In the United States, many of them end up in prison; Winerip (1999: 46) notes: 'there are now far more mentally ill in the nation's jails and prisons (200,000) than in state hospitals (61,700)!'

In Britain under the Mental Health Act, 1983, social workers are required to assess need for appropriate services and engage 'in activities geared towards reducing the risk of harm, maximising independence and improving quality of life' (Thompson, 1998: 301). Yet the system is failing because of a lack of resources. *The Report by the Social Exclusion Unit on Rough Sleeping in England* (Social Exclusion Unit, 1999: 4) recorded that 'some 30–50 per cent of rough sleepers suffer from mental health problems' and added: 'the great majority (88 per cent) of those with mental health problems became ill before they became homeless'.

Homelessness and rough sleeping

On 15 November 1999, the *Independent*, in an editorial comment on homelessness and rough sleeping, critically assessed New Labour strategy:

> 'Don't give money to beggars; it only encourages them.' That is advice that really divides people. It is perhaps the fundamental emotional and philosophical divide between right and left in politics. For the right, you have to be cruel to be kind: if you gave them good-quality sleeping bags, the homeless would rather sleep rough than in a crummy hostel. For the left, you have to respond morally to the need in front of you: as long as there are people out on the streets, for whatever reasons, they should be helped.

This was written after Louise Casey, the Labour government's 'homelessness tsar' had denounced charities and the *Big Issue* magazine for perpetuating the problem of homeless and rough sleeping by short-term tokenistic support. Ms. Casey's deeply iconoclastic attack on charity exposed the need for a long-term solution. She declared: 'We are going to be as tough on ourselves in Whitehall about delivering on prevention as we will expect our partners to be in delivering real and lasting solutions on the street' (*Guardian*, 18 November 1999).

The *Report by the Social Exclusion Unit on Rough Sleeping in England* (1999: 1) concluded that there are about 2,000 people sleeping rough in the street every night, and up to 10,000 people sleep rough during the course of the year. Rough sleepers were largely composed of people with backgrounds in institutional care. Between a quarter and a third had been in local authority care as children. About 50 per cent were ex-prisoners. A quarter to one-fifth had served in the armed forces (Social Exclusion Unit, 1999: 3–4).

The Prime Minister, Tony Blair, voiced public fears when he stated in the foreword to the Social Exclusion Unit report: 'many people feel intimidated by rough sleepers, beggars and street drinkers, and rough sleeping can blight areas and damage business and tourism'. The SEU Report advocated a 'joined up solution' based upon better co-ordination of services, with the objective of reducing the number of homeless and rough sleepers by two-thirds as early as 2002.

One of the problems with this focus on rough sleeping is that it conceals a much larger problem of homelessness. This is exacerbated by a lack of shared definition of what homelessness means. Official UK estimates put homelessness at 125,000 in 1995. Independent estimates put the figure much higher, suggesting that much of the problem is concealed (Walker and Walker, 1998: 53). The preoccupation with risk and the damage associated with rough sleeping has distracted public attention from the scale and insidiousness of homelessness.

In the United States, New York's homeless are being required to work in order to maintain their places in shelters, under new rules introduced by Mayor Giuliani. The link between work and shelter was the defining principle of the deterrent Poor Law system that was abolished in New York in 1896. In the classic Poor Law tradition those who refuse to work for their shelter will be refused welfare and their children taken into foster care. Steven Banks, of the Coalition for the Homeless, said, 'it's extraordinary, with the weather coming now, that the city wants to put vulnerable New Yorkers on the streets' (*Guardian*, 27 October 1999). It is very difficult to see this policy shift as anything other than a move towards the coerced marginalisation of the poor introduced by Latin American dictatorships in the 1970s (Oxhorn, 1995).

Social work, exclusion and power

Lishman has poignantly encapsulated the challenge to social work posed by social exclusion:

> Social workers engage in complex decision-making, often about relative risks, safety, harm and protection. They do so in the context of a breakdown of consensus about

social and collective responsibility and a rise in the value accorded to individual choice and responsibility. Paradoxically, 'society' is simultaneously experiencing widespread economic insecurity and increasing marginalisation and vulnerability; in particular in relation to people who are unemployed, in poverty or homeless, or have mental health problems. Social work is closely interlinked with these changes, and social workers' dilemmas and actions reflect and symbolise wider preoccupations with insecurity, safety, marginalisation, risk and control. (Lishman, 1998: 90–91)

The problem for social work is that its reformist vision, based upon a policy of controlled inclusion as opposed to coerced marginalisation, was complementary to the practices of the welfare state. In the postmodern era, when the New Right constantly attacks the welfare state for creating a dependency culture, social work is in the front line of criticism. This constitutes its essential vulnerability.

But it has a further problem that also characterised its period of relative professional success. It is not trusted by the socially excluded clients it seeks to help. Jones and Novak (1999: 84–85) observe:

> The view of social work from below has been largely negative. There is a widespread sensibility in many working-class neighbourhoods that social workers are to be avoided because of their powers to remove children or commit people to mental hospitals. There is very little trust.

Black people are, in addition, alienated by social work's failure to respect the integrity of matriarchal family care (Jones and Novak, 1999: 85). Social workers have a tendency to espouse a static notion of the 'normal family' based on a two-parent marriage (Allan, 1997: 58). This culture blindness further alienates social workers from service users.

Institutionalised child abuse has been revealed as an endemic problem in children's homes in both Britain and Ireland and has created a major public scandal. While the Catholic Church was deemed to be responsible in Ireland for the mismanagement of children's homes, social work has been held culpable in Britain. The sense of public revulsion at this betrayal of trust by those charged with the care and welfare of the most vulnerable in society has profound implications for the future of social work. The Pindown scandal in a Staffordshire children's home, involving an abusive disciplinary regime that lasted for six years between 1983 and 1989 with the apparent acquiescence of social workers, has become symbolic of social work's failure to care for the most vulnerable in society. The Waterhouse tribunal on the systematic abuse of children in care in North Wales revealed that child abuse is an endemic feature of institutionalised provision. The *Observer* of 20 February 2000, in an editorial comment enquired:

> Was the Waterhouse tribunal about the past or the present? Its report into the abuse of children in public care in North Wales came out last week. Its details – the awful human treacheries and tragedies – are still emerging day by day. But is this report just about 'then' or also about 'now'? Or could Waterhouse even be revealing the future for 'looked-after' children, a future which will not be much safer than what went before?

The *Observer* answered its own rhetorical question, concluding:

> Some problems will not go away. The most fundamental is the connection between male sexuality and the sense of power over weaker beings. Waterhouse shows how tightly physical cruelty and sexual abuse are woven into the thrill of authority. Equally durable is the human tendency not to ask questions in case the answers are disturbing. The neighbours didn't ask what Belsen was for; the North Wales bureaucrats did not inquire about what went on behind the shrubs.
>
> But there are also solid grounds for hope. By far the most important change is about knowledge. Britain and Ireland have been through a decade in which shattering revelations about the abuse of children 'in care' streamed from every TV set. Back in the Seventies and Eighties, there was no name for what was happening to them. Now it is 'child abuse', a famous crime, a red handle they can grab for.
>
> A lot is being learned. Nine out of ten 'looked-after' children in England and Wales are in foster homes. It's recognised that where bigger institutions exist, there must be gender balance in the staff as well as the inmates, that they must be independently 'visited', as prisons are, that children in care must have access to the outside world. Merciless vigilance against abusers is still needed. So is a campaign to persuade children that they have rights. But the worst may be past.

The greatest challenge that confronts contemporary social work is the need to build trust with its client constituency and the public at large. The current perception that social work is purely a regulatory activity, intruding into family life, disempowering vulnerable people, is deeply damaging. Abuse of vulnerable people challenges its right to exist. The belief amongst minorities that social work represents cultural domination combined with cultural disrespect raises crucial questions. If social work is to meet these challenges it needs to build trust. Its current approaches to practice demand radical reappraisal. The personalisation of social problems is inadequate in the light of the catalogue of abuse that has been visited upon the weakest and most vulnerable people in society. Radical disparities in power, as the *Observer* notes above, are often the explanation for abuse.

Empowerment, community and inclusive practice

Mullaly (1997: 164–181) has suggested a series of practice principles intended to build trust between social workers and service users: acknowledging that the personal is political; empowerment, consciousness-raising, normalisation; collectivisation, redefining and dialogical relationships. He argues that these principles provide the basis for an inclusive or 'structural' approach to practice. Mullaly is inviting social work to break out of its traditional theoretical frameworks, which are very personalist in orientation, and consider the politics of social work. He notes that: 'the traditional split between micro and macro social work practice has served to weaken the link between the personal and the political, which is at the heart of social work' and adds: 'although they may reflect the current political reality of separating the personal, they do not reflect the social reality of people's lives or the reality of good social work practice' (Mullaly, 1997: 165). Mullaly contends that the curriculum in social work training and restricted agency mandates are responsible for the split and that they result in the political immobilisation of social work.

In the ensuing analysis of empowerment, community and inclusive models of practice the author will draw upon the international literature and his own local experience of involvement in the Cork Northside Education Initiative. This initiative was intended to open up opportunities for Northsiders to become skilled in community development and social action strategies. Like many cities, Cork is divided, with the Northside community experiencing high levels of social exclusion. The overall objective of the Cork Northside Education Initiative was to counter the disempowering effects of marginalisation and social exclusion through commodity development and social education.

For poor communities and groups who are excluded from commodity consumption, political participation and cultural capital, social services are of particular importance. Yet, paradoxically, social services are most constrained in disadvantaged communities. Empowerment is *per se* the antidote to social exclusion. Empowerment has four basic characteristics, according to O'Sullivan (1993: 195–196):

1 **Instrumental:** knowledge, communication and literacy skills;
2 **Expressive:** confidence, assertiveness, freedom from dependency;
3 **Critique:** the capacity to question the society in which one lives and engage in a critical reading of reality;
4 **Activist:** the motivation to take action to change society in the light of critical awareness.

The Brazilian adult educator, Paulo Friere, sees 'conscientisation' as residing at the heart of the empowerment process. Conscientisation and empowerment are, therefore, essentially one and the same thing (Friere, 1972). However, it is a complex process. Onyx and Benton (1995: 50) note that 'the concept of empowerment is located within the discourse of community development, connected to the concepts of self-help, participation, networking and equity', and that 'empowerment means the taking on of power, at both individual and social levels'.

The people of the excluded Northside community in Cork share this vision of empowerment. Feedback from a seminar at Knocknaheeny/Holyhill Youth Centre on 28 January 1995 states:

A second point was that it was important for the community themselves to define their needs. It could involve a way of thinking about society and their perceptions about how society works. They may need assistance with this process but it was important that they did the thinking themselves and this is where the idea of empowerment came in: actually defining what your needs [are] and how you would address them. There must be a common vision, and [people must] try to get as close as possible to a common vision. Again, it must represent the wishes of all the people. (Cork Northside Education Initiative, 1995)

Empowerment-based community development initiatives are not new: they have been practised throughout the century. Key examples are the Antigonish Community in Canada and the Highlander Project in the USA, which played an influential role in the civil rights movement in the 1960s. Several of the earliest European community development workers were trained at the Antigonish community.

The process of community development 'involves stimulating communication between people with a view to social action for the ultimate purpose of transforming individuals and society for the better' (O'Sullivan, 1993: 59). The feedback from the seminars on the Northside of Cork was quite succinct in relation to community perceptions of the role of community development:

> Community development involves a way of thinking as well as a way of acting. It can involve analysis of how society works, how this affects communities, and what communities can do to bring about change in society. It is important to keep this aspect of community development in mind, as it can often be neglected when people talk about the skills communities need to undertake activities at local level.
>
> Communities have a wealth of skills which can be put to use in the community development process. Communities may, however, need help with certain tasks. For example, if a community is successful in accessing funding for a project or task, it may require assistance in managing and spending this money. Training and information from outside sources may also be needed. It is vital, however, that skills are transferred from outside agencies to communities, so that communities may become more independent and self-sufficient. There is also a need for advice on strategies or actions which have proved successful in other places, so that communities may be aware of what is being done outside of their own area and may learn from those experiences. (Cork Northside Education Initiative, 1995)

What is clear from the above analysis is that empowerment is both a goal and a process for overcoming exclusion and cultural disrespect.

This consideration differentiates community development from other social work methods. Empowering practice within the community involves a dialogical relationship geared towards consciousness-raising. Mullaly (1997: 71) observes: 'much of consciousness-raising occurs in the form of political education whereby structural social workers, in the course of their daily service efforts, attempt to educate service users about their oppression and how to combat it'. This dialogical relationship is a democratic one rather than the traditional hierarchical professional relationship. It eschews 'the big professional–small service-user model'. Rather it is based upon a shared humanity. It leads to the 'normalisation' of the helping relationship in which the service user is no longer seen as the problem – and becomes a citizen rather than a client. The core problematic of social work is consequently redefined.

Hardcastle et al. (1997: 5) have asserted that: 'without community knowledge and skill, the social worker is limited in the capacity to understand and assist clients in shaping and managing the major forces that affect their lives, and in the ability to help clients empower themselves to develop and manage personal and social resources'. They view community development skills as providing 'the "social" in social work' that distinguishes it from cognate professions, such as counselling. Empowerment radically reframes social workers' relationships with service users.

Community provides the context because it replaces individualisation with collectivisation. The emphasis on the collective group, as opposed to the individualised self, underlines the 'social' as a value in the helping process. Mullaly (1997: 175) explains: 'This value is a recognition that people are social beings who depend on one another for the satisfaction of most of their primary and social needs'. The communitarian approach to social work has close links to the radical social work movement of the 1960s and 1970s and to earlier initiatives (notably the settlement movement). It aims to define social work in 'social' terms. The links with political radicalism are clearly evident. However, within Europe there are 'social economy' initiatives grounded in the ecological concept of sustainability, that share this approach to community-based social work. It is compatible with both the European Union's emphasis on social cohesion and Anglo-Saxon concerns with promoting social capital. Empowerment promotes trust and social integration. This is the essence of its communitarian ethos.

Social economy, sustainability and inclusive practice

European advocates of the social economy approach to community-based social work acknowledge their inspiration in the settlement movement in the United States. They also note the inspirational role of earlier European settlers in the American Midwest, who managed to adapt and redesign community bonds and systems of social solidarity in the face of the raw forces of 'robber-baron' capitalism. Hull House in Chicago and Jane Addams were emblematic in this regard (Elsen and Wallimann, 1998: 151). Communitarianism has deep roots in social work practice.

   In the wake of globalisation, a renewed free market capitalism is evident in Europe, tearing communities asunder and leaving people's lives shattered and their worlds fragmented. European countries grounded in the more inclusive tradition of the social market economy have been seeking to adapt, by emphasising the importance of the social economy in sustaining communities in their attempts to deal with these economic changes. Elsen and Wallimann (1998: 157) assert: 'social economy provides people with an alternative which is work intensive, equitable, and integrative', adding, 'it is based on the principles of grass roots democracy and can be facilitated through community-based social work'. They argue that community-based social work needs to adjust to changing the economic reality of globalisation by widening its focus to incorporate sustainable economic life in communities beset by unemployment, marginalisation and poverty. The social economy approach to community development, based upon the idea of sustainability, stands in marked contrast to contemporary social policy trends defined by the calculus of risk. It stresses the need to act locally while thinking globally (Shanahan and Ward, 1995: 80).

   Elsen and Wallimann (1998) identify several examples of community-based business enterprises and federations of social co-operatives in Switzerland, Germany and Italy. All of these social economy initiatives share a number of core principles or 'steps'; as Elsen and Wallimann (1998: 155–156) put it:

> The first step involves thought and action in core areas of development as a means of focusing individual efforts on the internal and external possibilities for development and on the possibilities of working in combination with others and as a network in a local

community.... The second step involves systematic anchoring in the community as conscious integration and reintegration of economic efforts in the social and cultural structures of the community.... The third step involves the development of an 'autonomous' grass roots sector in a regional network.

Social economy initiatives do not share the same goals and principles as market economy. They are guided by humanism, co-operative endeavour and a commitment to sustainable development in a community context. As the Basle Social Economy Project, in Switzerland, put it: 'The way to save the physical and socio-cultural basis for human existence is to be found in the construction of a social economy' (cited in Elsen and Wallimann, 1998: 157).

The European Union has played a key role in promoting the concept of social economy as a basic community development strategy in a series of poverty programmes. One example of EU anti-poverty strategy is Forum: the North West Connemara Rural Development Project, based in Ireland's disadvantaged west coast at the extreme periphery of Europe. This project was established under the European Union Third Poverty Programme 1989–94. Its aims were to:

- develop locally based activities which will improve the lives of people in north-west Connemara, particularly the disadvantaged;
- work out new partnership arrangements between statutory, voluntary, community and private bodies;
- empower local people and the development of sustainable action programmes;
- integrate the experience gained into mainstream public policy and practice. (Combat Poverty, 1995)

Many of the successful features of this programme, which includes the development of local co-operatives and allied social economy activities, have been adopted in the Irish government's National Anti-Poverty Strategy, which was initiated in 1997 with a commitment 'to building an inclusive society'. In 1998 there were ninety community development projects in Ireland.

In Britain the Commission on Social Justice (Borrie Report) in 1994 endorsed the concept of social economy. It emphasised 'the need to build linkages between the economic, human and social capital investments required to achieve sustainable regeneration' (Borrie Report, 1994: 325). The Borrie Report pointed to several successful community development projects in the United Kingdom based upon the principles of social economy, notably Bootstraps in the London Borough of Hackney, the Miles Platting and Ancoats Development Trust in Manchester and the activities of the Belfast Action Teams. The Commission on Social Justice asserted:

It is difficult to exaggerate the change in thinking and working required of central government and civil servants, away from the top-down approach towards one rooted in the needs and skills of local communities. The Fabian notion that governments know better than citizens cannot stand. The future lies in a new partnership, where national and local governments share power with their citizens, enabling local people to use the skills, which are now being wasted. (Borrie Report, 1994: 326)

It advocated that 'the focus of a new, bottom-up regeneration strategy should be Community Development Trusts, established in the most disadvantaged areas to bring together residents, voluntary organisations, religious and other groups, and local authority councillors and officers' (Borrie Report, 1994: 328).

The successful Northern Ireland community development activist, Paddy Doherty, of the Inner City Trust, explained to the Commission on Social Justice:

> Standing in the vacuum between private enterprise, unwilling to become involved because of the lack of profit on the one hand, and government on the other, and harnessing help from both sides, we can fill that vacuum.... The best vehicle to fill the gap is the development trust movement. (Borrie Report, 1994: 328)

President Clinton's community empowerment agenda in the United States reflected similar principles, including new programmes to provide access to capital; credit and banking services for poor communities; the extension of small business support to inner city and ethnic minority businesses; public/private partnerships for economic development; a concentration on the educational capital in an area; and a new infrastructure programme to reconnect disadvantaged communities. His community development programme has been described as 'the most significant neighbourhood revitalisation initiative since the Model Cities programme of the 1960s' (Wievel and Gills, 1995: 127).

Paradoxically, Wievel and Gills (1995: 134) note during that neo-conservative presidencies of Reagan and Bush, which withdrew funding from urban areas, community development not only survived but flourished. This was because of the 'new federalism' characterised by decentralised government, greater emphasis on local decision-making and volunteerism. Wievel and Gills (1995: 136) conclude:

> Thus the community-based development movement is in a reasonably good position to have a positive effect on domestic policy. With the relative decline of labour as a political force and in the absence of a progressive national movement among the underrepresented minority groups, the community based development movement has filled a vacuum as a significant player in public policy formation over the past decade.

In South Africa today community development has become an important aspect of social reconstruction. However, the community development movement has had to struggle against the legacy of apartheid, which sought to destroy civil society. In a transitional society, where endemic injustice and poverty have for so long militated against trust and capacity-building, the challenge to community development is a considerable one in the new democratic political order. As Taylor (1995: 171) puts it: 'when people have been denied access to education, health care, housing and work over many years, it is not difficult to understand why the slightest provocation from groups who are competing for power and material resources can lead to intense battles'. Nonetheless, there is considerable evidence that the ANC-led government is tackling the task with energy. The South African Development Education Programme (SADEP) is addressing the challenge of providing community development workers with the skills necessary to promote bottom-up decision-making processes in social reconstruction.

Inevitably, there are sceptics such as the Dutch sociologist, Benno Galjart (1995), who characterises the social economy approach as an exercise in counter-development, largely dependent on non-governmental organisations. He is open to criticism for underestimating the role of the state and particularly the European Union. Nonetheless, Galjart (1995: 21) makes the limitations of the social economy approach to community development clear in an incisive critique:

> Not only is it illusory to think that Schumpeterian entrepreneurs will suddenly arise among the poor. To expect a group of poor people to refrain to a large extent from relying on markets, and hierarchy, as organising principles, relying only on trust, is to burden them with additional difficulties.

Galjart's point is that the social economy approach to community development is essentially a utopian enterprise. However, there is a considerable body of evidence to the contrary. The long established success of the co-operative movement, credit unions and mutual organisations attests to this fact. O'Gorman (1995: 209–210) commenting in a Brazilian context, where community development and the social economy approach have been closely interlinked, notes:

> Community group processes began to sustain and guide the varied range of self-help and popular movement activists, as a constructive form of social contestation, a 'utopia of society', a solidarity in group cohesion and social ferment not dependent on a specific social formation. 'Base' community experiences, although limited to local outreach work, stood as providing an alternative to society's dominant values of individualism, personal ambition and inordinate market competition.

A British community worker, Paul Henderson from the Leeds Community Development Foundation, makes a similar point to the Commission on Social Justice:

> Community development does not offer a panacea to the deep-rooted social and economic problems of British society. But it can help to bring forward the language and political agenda of communities which are exhausted and suspicious of external agencies. It can be a means of keeping hope alive and kicking. (Borrie Report, 1994: 325)

However, Galjart is right to point out the vulnerability of excluded groups and individuals in the age of global capitalism. There is a need for the state to assist the socially excluded by making its policies and practices socially inclusive. Poverty proofing is an important strategic consideration in this regard.

Poverty proofing, social work and welfare rights

What is poverty proofing? It can be defined as a process by which statutory bodies (e.g. social work agencies) assess policies, programmes and practices at design, implementation and review stages in relation to their anticipated impact on poverty and the social and cultural inequalities that cause poverty, with a view to poverty reduction. Some policy initiatives may result in positive outcomes for some 'at risk' social groups and negative outcomes for others. There is a need to tease out such policy anomalies at design and review stages. The participation of social workers and involvement of user groups in this process is essential rather than top-down management directives, if an inclusive approach to practice is envisaged.

Poverty proofing, arguably, needs to be an integral part of agency policy formulation. It should be included in the preparation of statements of strategy and organisational plans; in the preparation of agency annual budget proposals and project estimates; in manuals, handbooks and procedural guidelines; in quality control and annual audits.

Social workers have a key role to play in poverty proofing their agencies' policies and practices in the promotion of inclusive practice. This strategy creates an important bridge between the professional, the agency and the service user. Particular user groups need to be identified in the poverty proofing exercise: the homeless and rough sleepers; children in families at risk; lone parents and marginalised women; unemployed (especially long-term unemployed people); ethnic minorities, asylum seekers, refugees, HIV/AIDS victims; the elderly, especially in households headed by retired persons; people with disabilities.

The Irish National Anti-Poverty Strategy has made poverty proofing a core element of its approach to promoting inclusive practice (National Anti-Poverty Strategy, 1999). It clearly has potential as an approach to developing inclusive practice in social work. But there are constraints. The term 'poverty proofing' tends to define the responsibility in the context of agencies' social liability, rather than promoting the potential of service users as actors in their own emancipation. Radicals will no doubt have concerns for the potential for 'assistentialism', i.e. the pacification of the poor. However, a poverty proofing strategy based upon user involvement should allay these concerns. User involvement in poverty proofing that is genuinely empowering needs to be based upon democratic community development principles. It envisages the user as being involved in the key steps in the process:

- identification of need;
- identification of options and strategies;
- decision or choice of action;
- mobilisation of resources;
- the action itself. (Onyx and Benton, 1995: 51)

Ultimately, national and local policies need to be 'joined up' in the pursuit of poverty proofing.

The former Director of the Child Poverty Action Group, Professor Ruth Lister (1998: 16) comments that 'despite the involvement of a growing number of British local authorities in anti-poverty strategies over the past decade and the significant increase in the number of "poor clients", poverty appears to have slipped off the social work and social service users' agenda'. She notes that, despite encouragement from the Central Council for Education and Training in Social Work (CCETSW), there is resistance in British schools of social work to welfare rights training, resulting in the voice of social workers and social services departments on behalf of the poor being at best 'muted'.

Reisser (1996: 243) also detects a growing apathy towards the poor amongst American social workers: 'Political efforts seem to be too unbalanced in favour of professional protection as opposed to advocating for change on behalf of and with the poor and oppressed'. She is concerned about the impact of social work education on the perception of professionalism amongst the student body. Reisser advocates a more pluralistic approach to training that encompasses both private and public issues. She concludes: 'There must be a better fit between the purpose of social work, which deals with the intersection of private and public issues, and what most social workers do, which is deal with individual problems (private issues). Both poverty proofing and welfare rights are important ingredients in any anti-poverty strategy'.

Conclusion

Social work in postmodern society has had to confront the challenge of social exclusion. This challenge is manifest in the paradigms of trust and risk that define the social and moral context of social work. Risk has created an environment in which there is a perception of dangerousness. Marginalised groups receive increasingly harsh treatment in a society characterised by coerced marginalisation that is revisiting Poor Law forms of regulation and control. Social work has found itself at the sharp end of this new environment. Its challenge is to redefine its mission in a manner that promotes trust and humanistic responses to risk. Inclusive practice has been suggested as an appropriate social work response to social exclusion. The concept of inclusive practice is closely connected to the idea of empowerment and user involvement. Community development is an essential ingredient in inclusive practice because of its associations with consciousness-raising, democratic dialogue and empowerment. The concept of social economy is also important in inclusive practice, empowering communities to think global while acting local. But service users need to operate in the context of agency policies that are supportive of inclusive approaches to practice. Poverty proofing based upon the principles of bottom-up planning and service delivery is an approach that sets out to address social exclusion. Ultimately, there is a need for joined-up solutions involving national, local and regional government, social agencies, professionals and service users in the pursuit of inclusive practices.

6

Civil Society, Citizenship and User Participation

The decline of the welfare state is matched by the degeneration of the nation-state paradigm. Increasingly, we are witnessing the placelessness of power and the powerlessness of place. Paradoxically, there is a growing interest in global forms of governance and local capacity-building. The intellectual foundations of a new paradigm of governance are already evident in the work of sociologists such as Jürgen Habermas and Manuel Castells. Political developments, notably the European Union, suggest a federalist paradigm of international governance in the making. As the nation state is hollowed out politically and ideologically, cosmic optimists look to these new forms of governance as the paradigm of the future. Essential to this unfolding transformation in governance is a growing interest in civil society, active citizenship and participation. This chapter sets out to explore the implications of changing paradigms of governance for social work with reference to civil society, citizenship and user participation. The implications of a politically more variegated society are important for social work in its broadest sense, which includes service users, volunteers, community activists and professionals.

Civil society, globalisation and the state

Barber (1998: 14) writes that 'without civil society, citizens are suspended between big bureaucratic governments they no longer trust and private markets they cannot depend on for moral and civic values'. This statement invests a lot of credibility in the social and moral potential of civil society. It envisages the civic domain as essentially democratic, providing 'free spaces' where citizens can take control of democracy, learning the competencies of social responsibility and participation. Keane (1998: 6) has defined civil society as 'an ideal-typical category that both describes and envisages a complex and dynamic ensemble of legally protected non-governmental institutions that tend to be non violent, self-organising, self-reflexive, and permanently in tension with each other and with state institutions that "frame", constrict and enable their activities'. This definition places a very positive construction on the concept of civil society and its potential for good. Essentially, Keane (1998: 69) notes, civil society has become 'a positive

synonym for voluntary association, diversity and liberty, amongst its supporters
on the political left'. He further asserts: 'so we see the waxing moon of civil society
and the beginnings of a world-wide search for new equilibriums between state
and non-state institutions' (1998: 34). For Keane, civil society is forging a new
language: 'so striking is the popularisation of the term that it could even be said
that the language of civil society is currently undergoing vertical and horizontal
globalisation' (1998: 32). He concludes: 'this development was wholly unexpected
and it has consequently filled some with the millenarian hope that the Age of
Civil Society is nigh' (1998: 65).

Events at the World Trade Organisation (WTO) meeting at Seattle, in December
1999, lend unexpected support to Keane's thesis that civil society is 'a waxing
moon'. Hundreds of non-governmental organisations came to Seattle to protest
and observe, endorsing the perception of 'a new global ideology of resistance to
corporate expansion' (*Observer*, 5 December 1999). In an editorial comment the
Observer, reflected on the options for the WTO's future:

> One way ahead is to give the WTO a much narrower, trade-orientated remit which
> might command more support. Another is to listen to this new, populist protest genera-
> tion. 'Civil Society says the corporate agenda is invalid'. These curious words introduce
> the first serious opposition to global capitalism since the Cold War. Seattle, it seems,
> was only a prelude. (ibid.)

Professor John Gray, an influential political scientist, observed that the demons-
trators 'showed that in many crucial areas power has passed to the forces of an
emerging global civil society' (*Guardian*, 22 December 1999). Clearly, the 1999
Seattle protest represented a kind of victory for humanity over global capital, a
fin de siècle triumph of decency over cupidity. It suggests the emergence of an
embryonic global politics to challenge the global market. For example the pro-
testers at Seattle accused the WTO of encouraging 'the exploitation of our planet
and its people by the global capitalist system' and demanded 'alternative social
and economic structures based on co-operation, ecological sustainability and grass
roots democracy' (*Observer*, 5 December 1999). This critique sounds highly evocative of the forging of a humanist agenda to match the conditions of postmodernity. It would appear that there are grounds for believing that the 'Age of Civil
Society is nigh', as Keane suggests. On the other hand mainstream analysts will
undoubtedly regard Seattle as simply a pothole on the road to global market
capitalism.

Furthermore, Keane's optimism is challenged by more sceptical commentators. Rieff (1999: 11) declares:

> When we put our faith in civil society, we are grasping at straws. Apart from a few prin-
> cipled nationalists, libertarians and Marxists, most well intentioned people now view the
> rise of civil society as the most promising political development of the post-cold war
> era. By itself, that fact only points to how desperate we are, on the cusp of the millen-
> nium, to identify any political paradigm offering some realistic prospect for a more
> humane future.

Rieff (1999: 12) goes on to provide a searing critique of civil society, arguing that
any idea that simultaneously enjoys the support of the US government and the

European Union poses no threat to powerful vested interests: 'Far from being oppositional, it is perfectly in tune with the Zeitgeist of an age that has seen the growth of what proponents like Bill Clinton and Tony Blair are pleased to call the "third way" and what might be called Thatcherism with a human face.' He accuses the advocates of civil society of being 'the useful idiots of globalisation' assisting the privatisation of democracy-building: 'further undermining the state, they undermine the only remaining power that has at least the potential to stand in opposition to the privatisation of the world, commonly known as globalisation' (Rieff, 1999: 12). Rieff asserts that in a world consisting of etiolated nation states, putting society's faith in local concerns and single issue campaigns represents a return to pre-democratic forms. He concludes that civil society 'is, indeed, the new medievalism, with the leaders of the NGOs as feudal lords.... Yet as things stand it is this unaccountable, undemocratic congeries of single-interest groups that is being proposed as the only viable alternative to the nation-state.'

Clough (1999: 16), who shares Rieff's scepticism about the limitations of civil society, warns: 'attempting to create twenty-first century versions of twentieth-century institutions founded on seventeenth-century assumptions is a recipe for failure'. He argues that we exist in a world where the nation-state paradigm is being eroded and replaced exponentially by the market and civil society, but insists that much progress needs to be made before a clear alternative form of governance will be achieved. Clough (1999: 18) makes several important suggestions:

1 That government at local, national and international levels needs to become more inclusive, collaborative and adaptive in its dealings with civil society.
2 Civil society, for its part, must recognise that partnership with government brings new obligations to be democratically accountable in forging an ethic of global governance.
3 Civil society can do much to promote with government the elimination of poverty, oppression and war.

The relationship between civil society, globalisation and the state raises profound normative questions that ought to inform any discussion of the meaning of citizenship and participation in postmodern society.

Welfare, civil society and voluntary action

At the core of the contemporary debate about civil society is the relationship between welfare and citizenship. Much of this debate has devolved on a crude distinction between individualism and collectivism. The moral and emotional meanings attached to both terms have obscured as much as they have enlightened. Inherent in the debate about these social forms lies a deeper distinction about alternative conceptions of the self, the good life and human potential and purpose. As Marquand puts it:

> On the one side of the divide are those who view the self as a static bundle of prefer-
> ences and the good life as one in which individuals pursue their own preferences with-
> out interference from others. On the other are those for whom the self is a governing and
> developing moral entity and the good life one in which individuals learn to adopt higher

preferences in place of lower ones. On one side of the divide stress is laid on satisfaction; on the other on effort, engagement and activity. (*Guardian*, 28 October 1996)

In this prescient comment, Marquand essentially differentiates between the independent citizen and the active citizen. The active citizen forms the cornerstone of civil society, since s/he has embraced a form of solidary individualism that addresses the imperative of the common good.

The renewal of civil society has been associated with demands for a larger role for voluntary welfare provision in both Western society and the former Soviet Bloc. The voluntary sector is perceived as (1) an alternative to state bureaucracy and professional elitism and (2) a public space between government and market. Civil society in its reinvigorated form is presented by its advocates as a democratic movement based on the concept of active citizenship in the welfare state. The emphasis of active citizenship is on participation in the decision-making process, leading to empowerment of the citizen (Etzioni, 1994).

According to the concept of civil society, communities, neighbourhoods, voluntary associations and churches are the basic building blocks of society because they teach civic virtues such as trust and co-operation (Putnam, 1993; Etzioni, 1994; Fukuyama, 1995; Keane, 1998). These 'new communitarians' promote the fostering of intermediate institutions, i.e. families, neighbourhoods and schools, in civic society. They view these as the source of moral and social cohesion in the globalised market society. At the same time they regard a revitalised civil society as a bulwark against an overweening welfare state that, in their view, has lost its legitimacy because of its remote bureaucratic structure and domination by professional elites. As Landry and Mulgan (1995: 6) put it:

> Associational life in the form of family networks, networks of interest groups and others have often provided an important glue through which the individual and the group have been bound together in some larger whole. Traditionally, this 'civic' realm has provided the means for people to transcend pure individual self interest in the name of the public good. More recently, as the state has lost its legitimacy as the upholder and arbiter of that public interest, other types of civic association have come to seem more important.

Salamon suggests that 'a virtual associational revolution' is taking place throughout the world, creating a global voluntary sector. It is defined by several core characteristics:

- ◆ structured organisations [that are]
- ◆ located outside the format apparatus of the state
- ◆ not intended to distribute profits from activities to a set of shareholders or directors
- ◆ self-governing
- ◆ involving significant private, voluntary effort. (Salamon, 1994: 5)

The impetus for the global associational revolution has come both from the bottom up and from the top down. Eastern Europe provides the most dramatic example, with organisations such as Solidarity in Poland and the Civic Forum Movement in Czechoslovakia capturing the imagination of the world. Less well reported were the environmentalist movements in Eastern Europe during the Communist era, for example the Danube Circle, which opposed the siting of a hydroelectric plant on the Danube, on the grounds that it would cause acid rain in East Germany, by tying thousands of bed sheets to apartment roofs and then recording the pollution accumulated. These activists in Eastern Europe (including the Soviet Union) described 'their efforts as the creating of a "civil society", a society in which individuals have the right not only to speak out as individuals, but also to join together in organisations' (Salamon, 1994: 5).

This pressure for bottom-up change through voluntary organisation was perhaps most dramatic in Eastern Europe because it brought down the Communist form of government and its hegemonic system of control. However, the 'virtual associational revolution' was by definition a global movement touching most continents. The so-called urban popular movement in Mexico and elsewhere in Latin America is characteristic of grassroots political activities against government oppression in the Americas. In Africa a 'new wind' of change has also given rise to grassroots political and environmental organisations, notably in Nigeria; these are usually of a non-profit voluntary nature. Chopko, the Indian environmentalist movement, arose from a spontaneous effort by rural residents to protect an endangered forest by literally linking their arms around it.

Support in the West for the expansion of voluntary organisations was distinctive because of its top-down character and its association with the scaling down of the welfare state. Neo-conservatives were at the forefront of this process, notably Margaret Thatcher in Britain and Ronald Reagan in the United States. Reagan opposed 'Big Government' *per se*. Thatcher took a more radical line by calling for the dismantling not only of the welfare state, 'but also [of] the organised voluntary sector and leave social care wholly to volunteers' (quoted in Salamon, 1994: 8). She described volunteers as 'the heart of all our social welfare provision' (ibid.). Support for voluntarism has not been unique to neo-conservative governments. The Socialist President of France, François Mitterrand, sought to liberalise taxes on 'social economy organisations' during the 1980s. However, such organisations in France (as in Germany) are 70 per cent supported by public funding, creating a symbiotic relationship between the state and the voluntary/ community sector.

Critics of civil society point out that the real emphasis is on the dutiful citizen engaged in self-help. In the context of the atomised individualism and fragmented social order we live in, there is an element of unreality about the larger claims made for the concept of civil society as an alternative to state welfare. As Kramer (1981: 283) puts it:

> Voluntarism is no substitute for services that can best be delivered by Government, particularly if coverage, equity and entitlements are valued.... there is a danger that those who have jumped on the bandwagon of the era of limits, signalling the end of the welfare state by advocating more voluntarism, are being co-opted by others who share less concern with social justice than with tax reduction.

Clearly, it is quite unsustainable to suggest that the needs of the most disadvantaged can be met by the voluntary sector. Civil society based purely on the principle of private altruism would not be a civilised society. Indeed, there is no essential link between civil society and civilised society – contrary to Paine's view. Civil society has had a chequered political history. The Nazi Party undermined the Weimar Republic in Germany by infiltrating local organisations, and it should not be forgotten that the Mafia is an intermediate institution.

Arguably, civil society that is genuinely civilised is meaningless outside a welfare state ethos in contemporary Western civilisation. To suggest that Rotary Clubs, Red Cross chapters and local community groups can provide social protection in the era of globalised capital would not be a tenable position. However, civil society connected to generative political strategies, based on more complex ideas of equality and a more empowering concept of citizenship, is a vibrant and powerful means of civic renewal in an era of social fragmentation. The EU Comité des Sages (European Union, 1996: 14), which addressed the future of civic and social rights in Europe, shares this vision, stating that while in a global economy competitiveness is a 'fixed imperative', it 'cannot be improved by dismantling the welfare state'. Instead it called for developing social rights and 'rejuvenating social dialogue'.

Pluralism is at the core of this vision. *The Report of the Commission on the Future of the Voluntary Sector* (1996: 22) in the UK observed in this regard that 'the pluralism that is a characteristic of a healthy civil society implies a diversity of ideas, institutions and interests that sometimes appears chaotic'. This 'creative chaos', as the distinguished German sociologist Professor Ralf Dahrendorf has put it, goes to the heart of the democratic contribution that the voluntary sector makes to the dynamic of civil society. The respected British social policy scholar, Professor David Donnisson told the Commission on the Future of the Voluntary Sector (*Report*, 1996: 22) that:

> What could become damaging tyrannies and abuses should be kept in check, partly by strong democratic civic leadership, which establishes and polices the limits of tolerable behaviour and ensures that groups that might be neglected gain a hearing and partly by competition between agencies expressing different interests and views. If this system includes a sufficiently rich and well informed mixture of agencies capable of working in these ways and power holders in the public and private sectors are capable of responding to them, it will help to make the society which it operates more democratic.

The Commission (*Report*, 1996: 15) itself concluded that 'the relationship between voluntary bodies and democratic institutions can be seen in different ways – either as a contribution in their own right to the vitality of civil society or as a check on abuses of power'.

The EU Comité des Sages (European Union, 1996: 53) went a great deal further, asserting that:

> democratic consultation must give due weight to the traditional social partners but cannot be restricted to them alone. It must also encompass new players, and in particular non-Governmental organisations.

What is clear is that the voluntary sector is characterised by a dynamic diversity that enhances the well-being of civil society, outside the confines of the market and the state. Citizens contribute to the voluntary sector both as individuals and collectively, informally and formally through organisations, and without payment or as salaried staff. Voluntary organisations exist at national level and at local community level, in myriad forms both large and small. Some are traditional and paternalistic; others are transparently democratic, controlled and operated by users. These groups define the 'community sector'. Many voluntary organisations have close partnership relationships with the state, often depending on statutory funding for survival. Yet others challenge the state through new social movements (environmental, peace, gay and lesbian, feminist, anti-racist, etc.) that some see as 'a people's opposition'. In this diversity lie the strength and weakness of the voluntary sector and, indeed, the limitations of civil society. The future is in this diversity but not as an alternative to the welfare state. The mainstream of the voluntary sector in the social market economy is clearly shaped by its symbiotic or partnership relationship with the state. Only in liberal market economies such as the USA, where the state contributes 10 per cent of funding, are things different. However, as Lewis (1999: 256) observes: 'In the late 19th century the voluntary sector took the lead in establishing the nature of the partnership; in the late 20th century, government has been in the driver's seat'.

Civil society and reflexivity

Where do civil society and active citizenship fit into the structures of postmodernity? We have already noted the changing nature of the postmodern project in the West. It is, however, impossible to ignore the momentous events of 1989, when the Communist world collapsed. This raises challenging questions about the future. Will the historical symbiosis between capitalism and democracy that characterised the West be generalised on a global scale? Should we not see the return to nationalism, Fascism and racism in Europe precisely as a reaction to this process of global unification? What future has civil society as a vehicle for social action and change in this new social order?

One can take the pessimistic view and envisage the future role of voluntary and community activists in terms of defensive politics as governments increasingly temporise with racists in relation to asylum seekers and refugees, cut wages and unleash the full forces of the unbridled market. As social divisions widen between class groups, gender groups and ethnic groups, voluntary and community activists can seek to advocate the cause of social justice by helping the socially excluded to challenge fundamental inequalities. The politics of participation can become the touchstone of voluntary action and active citizenship in the twenty-first century as the emancipatory political dreams of the twentieth century disappear into the realms of historical curiosity. That is the pessimistic scenario. It suggests a vital but Sisyphean role for civil society in the future.

On the other hand, one can embrace a more cosmically optimistic view of the future of the world and the role of civil society. The political changes we are witnessing at the start of the new millennium are due to the reflexive nature of modernity. Reflexivity is variously defined by sociologists. Giddens (1991: 20) states that:

Modernity's reflexivity refers to the susceptibility of most aspects of social activity, and material relations with nature, to chronic revision in the light of new information or knowledge. Such information or knowledge is not incidental to modern institutions, but constitutive of them – a complicated phenomenon, because many possibilities of reflections about reflexivity exist in modern social conditions.

Beck et al. (1994: 6), commenting from a German perspective, have declared that 'reflexive modernisation means self-confrontation with the effects of risk society that cannot be dealt with and assimilated in the system of industrial society – as measured by the latter's institutionalised standards'.

If the analyses of these theorists of reflexivity are correct, we are entering a new era with greater potential for change than ever envisaged before. The nature of this change ironically defies control, suggesting boundless potentialities for reframing the core social issues. The argument of Beck et al. (1994) that social confrontation is seminal to the process of reflexivity is illustrative.

Beck et al. contend that postmodern society (or risk society, as they term it) 'is by tendency also a self-critical society'. We are all aware that we live in an era of radical doubt. There are no longer taboos or sacred cows. In this society, self-criticism abounds. As Beck et al. (1994: 11) put it:

Insurance experts (involuntarily) contradict safety engineers. While the latter diagnose zero risk, the former decide uninsurable. Experts are undercut or deposed by opposing experts. Politicians encounter the resistance of citizens' groups, and industrial management encounters morally and politically motivated organised consumer boycotts. Administrations are criticised by self-help groups. Ultimately, even polluter sectors (for instance, the chemical industry in the case of sea pollution) must count upon resistance from affected sectors (in this case the fishing industry and sectors living from seashore tourism). The latter can be called into question by the former, monitored and perhaps even corrected. Indeed, the risk issue splits families, occupational groups from skilled chemical workers all the way up to management, often enough even individuals themselves. What the head wants and the tongue says might not be what the hand (eventually) does.

Beck et al. conclude that the multiple antagonisms, despite their diffuse and ambivalent natures, are 'hollowing out the political co-ordinates of the old industrial society'. Latterly, Beck (1997: 98) has argued that we are reinventing politics: 'in short a double world is coming into existence one part of which cannot be depicted by the other: a world of symbolically rich political institutions and a world of often concealed political practices (conflicts, power games, instruments and arenas)'.

Arguably, this cosmic optimism is warranted. The Cold War era was characterised by a petrification of criticism. The ideological glue that held society together, East and West, throughout the twentieth century has now dissolved. As noted above, in postmodern society, traditional class structures, family patterns and belief systems are all breaking down. However, this does not, as cultural pessimists suggest, leave a vacuum with nothing tangible to take the place of traditional forms. New forms are emerging. Emancipatory politics are being complemented by life politics. The women's movement, gay and lesbian movement, the ecological movement and the anti-corporate movement are indicative of the intersection of the traditional politics of change with the new politics of community, which adds lifestyles and existential security issues to the political agenda. Social movements and protest groups have become the vehicles of social and political action that is increasingly taking on a globalised form. While the traditional notions of civil society, based upon paternalism, have become redundant through the disembedding of traditional society, new possibilities exist for re-embedding in the new structures of post-industrial society and the new technologies which have transformed communication. The role of civil society in colonising the future must be pivotal. In a world of constant confrontation and self-criticism, civil society cannot but prosper as a vehicle for alternative political action if it adapts to the new forms of discourse. The twenty-first century promises to be more challenging for civil society and for active citizens who have an unprecedented opportunity to colonise the future.

But there are substantial grounds for caution. Putnam, in his celebrated essay, 'Bowling Alone' (1995), has demonstrated that active citizenship and civic engagement, in the US, are becoming highly problematic in an increasingly atomised and individualised world. Stokes and Knight (1996: 8) have suggested that the traditional modes of voluntary participation in the UK are in decline, e.g. trade unions, mutual aid associations, the churches and political parties. Green (1993) in his study, *Reinventing Civil Society*, has argued that the welfare state has undermined civil society and that it is imperative to create a space for the re-emergence of the civic virtues of solidarity, service to others, duty and self-sacrifice. He concludes:

> We must refresh our understanding of the moral case against the welfare state. Much of what we call the welfare state should be returned to civil society, especially education and health care, not to save money, nor to improve efficiency, but above all to prevent the suppression of opportunities for bringing out the best in people through service to others. (Green, 1993: 152)

The problem with Green's analysis is that so far as welfare is concerned the relationship between civil society and the welfare state, in the form of the voluntary sector, is a symbolic one. The humanism of the voluntary sector is only possible with the beneficence of the state. However, the strength of the voluntary sector lies in its reflexivity and its variegated forms, that allow it to adapt to changing socio-political needs. This has led to a renaissance of voluntarism in the UK, in an age when welfare pluralism is certainly nigh.

The rebirth of voluntarism

In November 1998 a national compact between the voluntary and community sector and the state was announced for England (Home Office, 1998). The redefinition of the voluntary sector as 'the voluntary and community sector' is indicative of its increasing democratisation. The national compact was the culmination of these reviews of the voluntary sector during the 1990s. The first was produced by the Home Office and sought to concentrate on the issue of 'efficiency', which had become a core theme of the New Public Management approach that transformed the business of government during the 1980s and 1990s (Home Office, 1990). The second review was the Centris Report, an independent document published under the auspices of the Home Office (Knight, 1993). The third was the *Report of the Commission on the Future of the Voluntary Sector* (the Deakin Report), an independent review published in 1996.

All of these reviews took place within the context of the application of market principles to the public sector, which in turn sought to impose this philosophy on the voluntary and community sector through the 'contract culture'. Lewis (1999: 261) has observed that historically this represents yet another shift in statutory and voluntary relations diverging from the late nineteenth- and mid-twentieth-century trends:

> This third shift in the statutory–voluntary relationship did not amount to a return of the kind of balance of 'separate spheres', experienced at the turn of the century, but rather involved the creation of a completely new relationship. Central government sets the fiscal conditions that limit the room for manoeuvre on the part of voluntary organisations. New Public Management approaches were making a major impact on the voluntary sector and many argued that market-style contracts involved instrumentalism on the part of the government, which undermined the independence of voluntary organisations.

Lewis (1999: 257) considered that some voluntary organisations have never in reality been independent and are 'linked to the state in ways that smack more of fusion than partnership'. Yet the 'third shift', as she depicts it, represents an attempt by the state to regulate the voluntary sector through controlling its resources and reshaping its purpose. The implications for the maintenance and development of an ethical civil society are profound. Much of the débâcle in Eastern Europe during the 1980s devolved on the state's control of civil society, which was perceived as an affront to liberty. In the current circumstances the threat to civil society's ethical base has been relocated to the theatre of the West, with market values setting the agenda for the state's relationship with the voluntary and community sector. Lorenz (1994: 122) comments in regard to the British Conservative administration's (1979–97) approach to civil society:

> The British approach amounts to a colonisation of civil society by political interests, as is evident from the enforced adaptation to the principles of the market economy, i.e. cost-effectiveness in the social services. This is an ideological imposition equivalent to that of communist ideology 'suspending' the autonomy of civil society.

The suggestion is that the Leviathan state, whether socialist or capitalist, is the enemy of civil society and the antithesis of liberty.

The Report of the Commission on the Future of the Voluntary Sector (1996: para. 1.3.16) took up the issue of the importance of civil society for the maintenance of liberty:

> In a democracy, voluntary action is a badge of citizenship. The opportunity to come together and take action jointly for purposes you have chosen yourselves is one of the characteristics that defines a free society. The act of participation may sometimes be as important as the end result.

As a whole the Report represented a significant attempt, according to Lewis (1999: 264), 'to get across to government that voluntary organisations are not just contractors, but are embedded in civil society with goals of their own'.

New Labour and communitarianism

The New Labour government, elected in May 1997, viewed partnership with the voluntary and community sector as a key component in its 'third way' strategy to forge a new social model for a new century. In its compact with the voluntary and community sector, the New Labour government describes its core philosophy in terms of 'voluntary and community activity' being 'fundamental to the development of a democratic, socially inclusive society' (Home Office, 1998: para. 5). The New Labour government promised 'to recognise and support the independence of the [voluntary and community] sector, including its right within the law, to campaign, to comment on government policy, and to challenge that policy, irrespective of any funding relationship that might exist, and to determine and manage its own affairs' (para. 9.1). New Labour has promised to move away from the centralised command and control system of the 1970s and the focus on markets of the 1990s, towards a more democratic and equal partnership. The Department of Health in its document *Modernising Social Services*, published in 1998, acknowledges the importance of partnership in promoting a mixed economy of welfare.

At the heart of New Labour's 'third way' philosophy is an espousal of communitarianism. In his preface to the *Compact on Relations between Government and the Voluntary and Community Sector*, Tony Blair commented on the value of the contribution citizens make to the development of their own communities. By doing so, they promote citizenship, help to re-establish a sense of community and make a crucial contribution to our shared aim of a just and inclusive society (Home Office, 1998: 1). Lewis (1999: 265) has suggested that Blair's vision of the role of the voluntary sector in a communitarian society 'has much in common with the much earlier ideas of C.S. Loch and Bernard Bosanquet'. The parallels with the COS are in my view real, but not quite so direct as Lewis suggests. A more accurate historical comparison would be with the ideas of Alexis De Tocqueville, the formative influence on American thinking on civil society. The Tocquevillean philosophy has been given contemporary expression by the American sociologist, Amitai Etzioni. Etzioni's influential book, *The Spirit of Community*, published in 1994, declared that as communitarians:

> We suggest that free individuals require a community, which backs them up against encroachment by the state and sustains morality by drawing on the gentle prodding of kin, friends, neighbours and other community members, rather than building on government controls or fear of authorities. (Etzioni, 1994: 15)

He argues that encroachment wears many disguises but argues that 'we must be able to tell the difference between a British (or other) occupying force and social workers' well intended attempts to help the most vulnerable members of the community' (Etzioni, 1994: 165). Etzioni describes himself as a 'responsive communitarian', arguing that it 'leapfrogs the old debate between left-wing and right-wing thinking and suggests a third social philosophy' (Etzioni, 1997: 7). This third way philosophy rejects the market liberalism of the New Right, the liberal/libertarian stress on individual rights, and the top-down managerialism of the welfare state (Hughes and Mooney, 1998: 74).

Etzioni contends that social obligations in the civic realm are being undermined by the entitlements of the welfare state. He argues that the pursuit of welfare is better served at the moral level through giving the community and the family back its moral voice. In essence, Etzioni is arguing for the remoralisation of society. Here, there are real parallels with the COS in the nineteenth century in the moral authoritarianism of Etzioni's vision. The concern is that the community is being turned into a moral policeman (Levitas, 1998: 127). Alternatively, communitarianism may be viewed as the blueprint for a more just and decent society, based upon social obligation.

Justice, decency and social obligation

The clash of ideologies between the rampant free market values of the Right and the Left, fragmented into the traditional social politics of the welfare state, neo-Marxism and the identity politics of multiculturalism, occludes a deeper problem. There is a crisis of belief in the welfare state. It is partly due to the declining influence of the radical humanist values, traceable to the Enlightenment, that have shaped it.

A welfare state reflects not merely the values of a democracy but the image it has of itself as a just and decent society. The welfare state is based on the ideal of social obligation, in which the entitled citizen has a right to have his or her needs met. Increasingly, this concept has been broadened into a set of rights or expectations that some commentators argue are no longer realisable, creating a pervasive sense of disillusionment with government. The problem, as Melanie Phillips (1997: 13) has put it, is that in a consumer culture 'rights' have been translated into 'wants'. She holds politicians responsible for this development:

> Politicians have refused to speak the language of priorities essential to all responsible Government. They have refused to exercise political leadership and to stand for a concept of common good. They have treated people not as citizens with reciprocal duties to each other and to their society but as consumers with an inalienable right to obtain whatever they desire. They have created a culture of escalating and never realisable rights which has destroyed social cohesion by setting up competition between interests and eroded the duty to take responsibility for ourselves and our families.

Phillips's critique of the welfare state is somewhat overstated: it ignores the systematic reduction in expectations and downsizing that have taken place over the past two decades. Nonetheless, there is an important underlying truth in Phillips's argument: a just society, based on social rights, is not necessarily a decent society. The issue of welfare rights has dominated the debate about the welfare state in recent decades, to the exclusion of other values, notably the ideal of social obligation. Rawls's influential theory of social justice has given intellectual coherence to this perspective in liberal democratic society. The problem is, however, that the Rawlsian view places rights within a highly individualist context, ignoring the larger communitarian context. Ignatieff (1999: 10) has commented that there is a considerable gap between justice and decency in the welfare state, which in his view institutionally humiliates its claimant population:

> Indeed the welfare state makes a practice of recognising the right to relief, but in a humiliating manner. Such humiliations are not casual or accidental. They may be consequent and deliberate, an attempt to discourage the unemployed from claiming what is their due. Justice between tax payers and claimants is often held to require the imposition of some deterrent effect in the way we deliver benefit. The deterrent effect may not be unjust, but it is certainly indecent.

A society that practises institutional humiliation in order to control access to entitlements by linking welfare to the principle of deterrence is the very antithesis of a decent society.

So what can be deduced from the various critiques of the welfare state? Has it failed? Should it be abolished? Is social obligation achieved only through voluntarism? If one accepts the neo-conservative critique, then civic virtue belongs exclusively to the realm of personal initiative, and the welfare state has failed and should be abolished. However, neo-conservatives do not argue that there is any obligation to help a stranger (Murray, 1984). Rather, welfare is a matter of personal prudence, moral sentiment and religious virtue, as opposed to social rights or obligations. On the other hand, if one accepts the view that an unqualified welfare rights paradigm is the only basis for social justice, questions arise about the finite nature of resources and the need for a contractual basis for welfare, in which individual citizens also have obligations towards the community.

How does one resolve this ideological conflict? The New-Zealand-based sociologist, Ian Culpitt, has suggested a reassertion of the ideal of social obligation as a way forward. He argues that 'the current welfare rights paradigm has no theory of obligation and has only facilitated the proliferation of need claims' (Culpitt, 1992: 34). According to Culpitt, 'what any defence of the welfare state must argue is not for a renewal of the moral imperative for individuals to care but that it is the practical recognition of mutual vulnerability that leads to a sense of obligation'. He concludes that 'personal and social obligations that respect individual vulnerabilities are not ultimately moral demands upon the arbitrary beneficence of individuals but social demands that recognise the legitimacy of such vulnerabilities' (Culpitt, 1992: 46–47). New Zealand, which first introduced the welfare state in the 1930s, has recently abolished it, leaving the poor to the vagaries of providence.

Culpitt's concept of social obligation is important because it eschews the individualisation favoured by the welfare rights paradigm and neo-conservatives in favour of a more communitarian view of welfare based on reciprocity. It links justice to decency in defining social obligation. Furthermore, Culpitt's concept of social obligation acknowledges a close interdependence of individual and society. However, it does not insist that this relationship must be mediated entirely by the state. There is room for welfare pluralism in a society that is both just and decent.

In this context, a civilised society that is democratic rather than paternalistic emerges. Moreover, recipients of welfare are the dependants neither of philanthropists nor of state bureaucrats, but entitled citizens within a democracy that acknowledges its social obligations.

This removes much of the philosophical basis underpinning the conflict between political partisans. As Culpitt (1992: 36) puts it:

> Much of the clash between left and right depends on the classic dualism of public/ private. Both political philosophies attempt to prove that their ontological view is not only superior but is the only possible one. However, there are systemic connections between the idea of private and public worlds and the 'meaning' of this ontological division resides outside the rigidity of the internal logic of the separate arguments.

We can therefore conclude that the basis for taking the welfare state project forward into the new millennium depends on moving the argument beyond the welfare rights issue that has dominated late twentieth-century debate. The EU Comité des Sages (European Union, 1996: 45) has made a useful contribution in this regard, advising against 'handing down rights from on high: Rights should be evolved in a democratic process based on the principles of active citizenship.' This wise advice links entitled citizenship with rights to obligations, and ultimately places trust in the people. The EU Comité des Sages (1996: 45–46) also comments that 'the process by which rights evolve is almost as important as their content: rights which are jointly worked out by a democratic process over an adequate period of time will be more readily respected than those formulated by experts'. The Comité des Sages concludes that 'citizenship is not merely a collection of rights: it is also a way of living, of recognising one's obligations to others, of participating in society, through a multiplicity of relationships with its members'.

Communitarianism, civic participation and social inequality

The communitarian philosophy that informs the 'third way' is predicated upon the notion of increased civic participation and engagement in social life. Communitarians are concerned about the 'cancerous effects' of market individualism in community life (Tam, 1998: 3). Currently, about four million adults in Britain are engaged in formal volunteering (*Report of the Commission on the Future of the Voluntary Sector*, 1996: para. 1.4.16). Informal volunteering involves many more people. In addition, there are approximately 620,000 paid employees in the voluntary and community sector. This represents a significant level of civic participation. However, formal volunteering tends to be skewed towards the middle classes, although people from lower socio-economic groups are equally likely to be involved in informal volunteering. Similarly, ethnic minorities (especially black people) are less involved in formal volunteering but are active in more informal voluntary activities in the community (ibid.: para. 1.4.17). The divide between classes would seem to reflect the division between the more paternalistic tradition of the voluntary sector and the more egalitarian tradition of the community sector. It is in the community sector that the democratic potential of civil society exists. The *Report of the Commission on the Future of the Voluntary Sector* (1996: para. 1.3.25) comments upon the evolving nature of the third sector from paternalism to community action. It suggests that it is becoming increasingly part of the social economy it purports to represent:

> Some community action involves not an intrusion upon, but a rediscovery of democracy. It is concerned with direct participation, not representation at one remove, through the ballot box. It can provide a 'voice for the voiceless'. There are important lessons to be learned from feminism, both in the content of the action taken – battered women's hostels and rape crisis centres – and its form ('the personal is political'). The lessons have been applied by the disability lobby, with its emphasis on organisations of, not for disabled people.

Manifestly, substantial progress is being made in the development of civic equality. The paradox is that this progress takes place against the social inequality built into the project of globalised market capitalism. The challenge that progressive politics, epitomised by New Labour, has set itself is 'to do something about poverty without radical fiscal adjustment or redoing the class structure' (*Guardian*, 6 December 1999). The evidence (as demonstrated in Chapter 4) is that the gap between rich and poor is widening. This is the fundamental flaw in the communitarian approach of the New Labour government. The new deal for communities in Britain, Sure Start, directed at pre-school children, health action zones, and 16- to 18-year-olds who have dropped out of school, is not uniformly based across the country. Moreover, the emphasis is upon extending opportunity rather than promoting social equality.

The positive contribution offered by communitarianism is that it reframes the relationship between the users of social services and the providers in a democratic and empowering market. In this regard it has profound implications for the way social work will define its role and task in the new millennium. Ife (1997) has called on social work to rethink its professional project. Civil society provides an important focus for any such debate.

Power and social work's dual mandate

The dual mandate defines the role and task of social work as promoting the interests both of the state and of the service user whom they are intended to help. This dual mandate makes social work by definition a politicised activity. For some practitioners this has involved a high degree of sensitisation to the implications of the use of professional power. Others (the majority) prefer to avoid the implications of the dual mandate by adopting an individualised therapeutic approach that locates social work in the apolitical world of psychology and the personalisation of social problems. However, they are making an implicit choice that is itself political, since it assumes that the professional task of social work is neutral. Moreover, the individualised therapeutic approach seeks to ignore the social background which gives rise to the client's request or referral for help in the first instance. Zavirsek (1999: 69) observes: 'For these social workers, power means something negative, always connected with manipulation and control, and social work remains defined as work that primarily requires "neutrality" towards people'.

Power is at the centre of the professional relationship with service users. What does power mean? Giddens (1989: 52) has defined it in the following terms:

> By power is meant the ability of individuals or groups to make their own concerns or interests count, even where others resist. Power sometimes involves the direct use of force, but is always also accompanied by the development of ideas ... which justify the actions of the powerful.

In other words, power does not necessarily depend on physical force but more often is manifested through ideas, which legitimise the actions of the rulers. Power is, therefore, a subtle force that pervades all aspects of our lives.

Our understanding of the nature and the meaning of power has been transformed by the French philosopher, Michel Foucault. He was less concerned with the formal or 'juridical' manifestations of power and instead focussed on the everyday expressions of power in human relations, which are at the root of social control because they enforce discipline.

In his influential study, *Discipline and Punish*, published in 1977, Foucault examined the changing nature of punishment between the eighteenth and nineteenth centuries. He argued that the focus of punishment moved from the body to the mind. The public spectacle of the gallows was replaced by the regimented carceral regime of the penitentiary, where discipline held sway. Donzelot in *The Policing of Families* (1979), developed Foucault's arguments, demonstrating that therapists and social workers had become key mediators of a disciplinary social order that operated through control of the mind. Sheridan (1980: 218–219) observed in relation to Foucault's concept of power:

> There are certain categories of person – children, prisoners, the 'insane' – whose ability to exercise power is severely limited, but few members of these groups do not find some means of exercising power, if only on each other. Power is not, therefore, to be identified with the state, a central apparatus that can be seized.... factories, housing estates, hospitals, schools, families, are among the more evident, more formalised of such 'micro-powers' [local centres of power].

Foucault in *Power/Knowledge* (1980) suggests that power and knowledge are inextricably connected. State power depends on knowledge gleaned from surveillance of the population, which is carried out not only by the security apparatus, but through the health and social services carefully documenting the private lives of citizens. Conversely, citizens can be empowered by knowledge of the basis of governance and participation in the decision-making process.

Croft and Beresford (1997: 273) have argued that 'social work is increasingly marginalised publicly and politically, amid growing professional fears that it is tied to authoritarian welfare policies'. They argue the case for a user-led social work committed to the principles of autonomy, participation and inclusion. The emphasis on empowerment and participation advocated by the proponents of civil society offers a very positive agenda for addressing the problems of state bureaucracy and professional elitism that threaten the legitimacy of the welfare state in the eyes of its service users. Furthermore, the over-extended welfare state can greatly benefit from the services of volunteers. The professional challenges of civil society, particularly the social movements it has generated, have been delineated for social work by Lorenz (1994: 127).

> They call for limits to professionalism by putting the experienced volunteer, the use of 'the person who has been through it' against the power and elitism of certified experts. They value process and participation rather than technical efficiency and success as the key to self-directed learning and change. They search for identity, personally and collectively, by way of questioning the oppressive use of labels and attributes.

Given that social work is quintessentially a personal social service, located in the arena of community care, voluntarism in the context of a civil society that defines a social domain makes sense. However, the volunteer cannot be a substitute for a well trained professional in a risk society, any more than charity can be a substitute for state welfare benefits. What civil society can offer is greater participation and the recognition of the rights of the service user. Lorenz's emphasis on participation goes to the core of the imperative to democratise the personal social services and make them inclusive of user and community organisations.

The *Report of the Commission on the Future of the Voluntary Sector* (1996: para. 4.6.1) asserts that 'user involvement is the key to the future' if that concept of user involvement has been 'extended to the public sector to involve users and communities in the development of services and to take some responsibility for the development of user and community based organisations and capacity' (1996: para. 4.6.3). The Report concludes that user and community organisations 'express user involvement in terms of participation of overcoming exclusion and/or articulating social service requirements beyond services for immediate needs' (1996: para. 4.6.4).

The emergence of the service users' movement has had important implications for social work practice. Organisations such as Parents Against Injustice (PAIN), Voice of the Child in Care and the National Association of Young People in Care, Mindlink, Survivors Speak Out (SSO) and UKAN have represented the rights of service users and highlighted the shortcomings of social work in meeting their needs (Croft and Beresford, 1997; Barnes, 1997).

In the era of growing disability awareness, the 'people first' emphasis on self-advocacy has transformed perceptions of service users. Professional sympathisers have been part of this development that is replacing the medical model with a social model based upon users' rights as citizens to autonomy and respect. In the emergence of the users' movement there is the promise of a new paradigm for social work. Croft and Beresford (1997: 276) assert:

> Social care service users, on the other hand, are changing the terms of the social work debate. They are asking fundamental and important questions like why social work, what is it for, how is it to be accountable, what would it look like, and they are beginning to offer their own answers to all of these. They have developed new demands, models and theories which are having a growing impact on public policy and which point to the reconception and reconstruction of social work and social services. They place the emphasis on people's human and civil rights and the relation between the individual and society, and the service system and society.

Social work, participation and user rights

The emerging debate in postmodern society about citizens' rights and public service accountability – frequently called participation – has major implications for the role and task of the social worker in terms of engendering trust. In the past, while consumer relations in the private sector were mediated by contract, such rights were either abrogated in the public sector (e.g. in transport) or replaced by a service delivery system in which rights depended on administrative discretion (e.g. in the public health sector). Social workers, who have always regarded respect for the individual as a basic canon of practice, have found themselves frequently at odds with the impersonal, managerial ethos of the public service sector. They have gained a reputation for being 'questioning' employees, with divided loyalties which often put them on the side of the client at the expense of their duty to the agency. Social workers have not enjoyed this conflict between their professional and administrative cultures – they are often deeply demoralised by it. This underlying conflict has been exacerbated by the 'tyranny of the immediate', where overworked social workers in crisis situations have had to reconcile agency procedures and accountability structures with their professional values, under intense pressure.

The unidimensional nature of human relations, which characterises the public sector (and many traditional voluntary) social service agencies, is under strong attack in postmodern society in most European democracies, where transparency and accountability are the order of the day. Social workers are well placed to play a major role in adapting public services to consumer needs.

What does participation mean in practice? It is not easy to explain since it envisages a new language of communication with social service users. Social workers, long pilloried for their jargonised 'socio-babble', may be well placed to contribute to the development of this new language from their rich lexicon of person-orientated terminology. Within these linguistic limitations, it is possible to identify the key features of participation.

First, as a starting point, participation puts the limelight on front-line producers of social services, on the users, and on the relationship between them. On these producers will depend the quality of the service delivered and its potential for empowerment. Social workers, nurses, teachers and other public service professionals are recognised as the embodiment of official contact between the state and the consumer in the delivery of social services. Participation envisages not merely augmented professional status and authority for such front line workers, but delegation of administrative responsibility, training in information gathering and applied research techniques, as well as a policy evaluation role.

Second, essential to participation is the need to redefine professionalism to include working with the 'user' – which is a better word than 'client' or 'consumer' since it recognises that the user is an active participant rather than a passive dependant. Paradoxically, service delivery systems and traditional concepts of professionalism have tended to reduce users to a passive role, often to the point of treating them in a degrading manner as supplicants. Developments in preventive health have underlined the possibilities of user participation. Prevention lies at the core of participation, though it is being reinterpreted in the reactive language of risk. Social workers can take the opportunity to empower clients in defining and solving their own problems. The mushrooming of community groups in recent years is indicative of the growing movement towards giving power to the public and the politics of recognition. In some instances, a community group may run a quasi-public facility directly, e.g. a community centre. In other cases, such groups serve (1) as channels of information; (2) as fora for discussion and consciousness-raising; and (3) as a method of bringing pressure on the state to improve the quality of its public services. What is manifest from the emergence of these community service users' movements is that, in reality, people have moved far from the traditional professional model of individual passive consumers, who do not know what they want, being served by all-knowing professionals who make rational decisions about what they need. This development puts the role of the public service professional, notably the social worker, in a new light, as supporter and adviser as much as provider.

Third, participation envisages a new social economy of public service delivery. This involves (1) decentralisation of decision-making and (2) open networks of communication. Professional units (e.g. social work teams) then require a degree of administrative autonomy, clearly delineated, within which they can take decisions, and to which user groups can relate. It is increasingly being appreciated by policy analysts and service providers that:

1   the imperative of economies of scale, which produced large organisations like social service departments, often exhibits diseconomies of organisation;
2   over-centralised decision-making leads to administrative sterility;
3   power must be devolved to smaller units if effective service delivery is to take place.

The notion of small, autonomous decision-making units is not new in social work. The patchwork approach described by Hadley and McGrath (1980) two decades ago foreshadowed this concept – though they were arguably more preoccupied with community self-help than empowerment. The Barclay Report (1982) in the United Kingdom pointed in the same direction, offering the blueprint for a community-based model of social work.

However, the notion of decentralisation of a measure of decision-making to autonomous units is not sufficient in itself. A second fundamental issue arises. Can these autonomous units co-operate to produce an effective system of service delivery or do they ultimately have to be controlled by a strong, centralised management structure? Open networking within and between agencies has proven highly effective in some societies. This envisages a transparent structure, with both central and local government ensuring that community links are maintained and open and accountable service delivery structures established.

Fourth, participation envisages more democratic forms of reorganisation where the user has a direct input in policy formation. This can occur through involvement in management committees, advisory groups, and, at a more micro-level, in case conference decisions that directly affect users' personal welfare. User involvement can also take place through user assessments and studies of social services. Participatory research models provide an opportunity for professionals and users to work together in defining problems, identifying solutions, and measuring the effectiveness (outcomes) of policy strategies. Partnerships between provider and user lie at the heart of the empowerment process.

Finally, participation amounts to defining a new public service ethos, characterised by democratic and inclusive values and devolution of power to service providers and users. As an organisational model, it is in harmony with social work values and provides a much more flexible method for responding to human needs. The current political preoccupation with open government and public service accountability, with a view to promoting trust, suggests that participation is firmly on the agenda. Increasingly, it will be necessary to acknowledge that the public has a dual relationship with the social services: as users and as citizens. A new paradigm of professionalism is essential if social work is to flourish under this new public service ethos, at the interface between civil society and the welfare state.

Participation, community and social work

Closely connected to participation is the concept of community, which has been in decline in social work practice in recent decades (Hardcastle et al., 1997: 8). The idea of community which is central to civil society represents a powerful symbol for integration in the fragmented and polarised conditions of postmodern society. It is not a new idea, since it is deeply rooted in classical civilisation, but its meaning has been adapted to suit the purpose of the times. In the modern world, community stands in opposition to atomised individualism, symbolising the possibilities of co-operative and mutualistic social action in a tradition that goes back to Robert Owen, Peter Kropotkin and P.J. Proudhon. Community offers the possibility of 'we' as opposed to the 'me-myself alone versus ourselves together'. This makes it a very seductive philosophy that attracts support from across the political spectrum.

Hughes and Mooney (1998: 72) have commented:

> Community is symbolic, it appears almost as magical. Communities are always imagined. Perhaps they exist as a necessary fiction, through which attempts are made to make sense of the world, whereby links are forged and though which mobilisation and resistance to marginalisation and exclusion can be conducted. But alongside the awareness of diversity and differentiation, ideas of community continue to have a deep moral resonance. Community is a fundamentally political concept. As such it is saturated with power.

Community is viewed by its advocates as a wholesome concept concerned with promoting 'the good' in society. Critics perceive a potential for limiting human freedom in the idea of community and view it as an essentially illiberal world view (Holmes, 1993). In reality the elasticity of the concept of community allows diverse intellectual and political traditions to lay claim to it as a unifying symbol.

Hardcastle et al. (1997: 9) write of the decline of community engagement that 'the decay of social work's skills and commitment has accompanied the erosion of America's community spirit and social commitment'. They conclude that 'it is reflective of the "me-ism", the libertarian, self-centred philosophy presently rampant, and the social isolation and fragmentation of contemporary America'. Their remarks might as easily have been addressed to the United Kingdom, Canada, Australia, New Zealand or Ireland. The growth of the consumer society, and the new managerialist ethos of the personal social services, has undermined our faith in community. This decline in public commitment is reflected in social work's professional drift towards an individualised therapeutic approach and the growth of private practice. Moreover, the replacement of the social politics of the welfare state by identity politics tends to change the emphasis from community as a basis of integration to communities of interest that differentiate themselves from others by their gender, ethnicity, sexual orientation, disability, age, etc. This creates a problem of essentialism where communities of interest can reject outside support as an unwelcome intrusion, including that of professional sympathisers.

Community politics can often be highly charged, frightening professionals and administrators, who fear that they may be compromised. But this is part of the professional social work challenge in postmodern society. As the old paternalistic certainties that defined the relationship between professionals and users evaporate in the more democratic and sceptical conditions of postmodernity, new skills are needed for new times.

Lane (1999: 143) has linked community development to a postmodernism of resistance, declaring:

> Being respondents to context rather than imposers of already established formulae for action need not mean working in an ethical vacuum of an 'anything goes' postmodernism where all views must be accepted as having equal value. We are not forced to work with people whose causes we oppose, and who do not respect our values or those of others – we too, have the right of speech and the right of refusal. Whilst we cannot assume a unitary set of ethics about which there is universal agreement, we can hold on to our personal ethics.

She argues that in the era of economic rationalism and the contract culture 'community development is under siege as a process-orientated contextually sensitive means of promoting participation in civil society and politics' (Lane, 1999: 146). Funders are setting the professional agenda, compromising social work's mission to operate at the axis between the state and civil society.

If the profession of social work wishes to engage with civil society in the era of the 'shrinking' state, then it must develop the capacity to communicate with the 'subjugated voices' in the community that continue to be its constituency and *raison d'être*. Lane (1997: 147) concludes:

> The challenges inspired by postmodernism can lead us to ever-more creative practice. For the last half of the twentieth century, we have built some solid practice castles from modernity. I believe it is time to move on from those ageing, modernist structures, and their generalised 'models', 'competencies' and narrow 'scientific' ways of knowing. It is time to immerse ourselves in ever-changing networks and domains. We are uncertain about many things but we have memory, personal ethics and the magic of speech.... We are confident that community, though fragile, is possible.

The re-emergence of civil society poses new challenges to social work. There is a clear argument that it should reinvent itself in more democratic forms to retain its relevance in postmodern conditions. This assumes a genuine partnership between the state and civil society (i.e. the voluntary and community sector) that is predicated on the postmodern concept of the enabling state. As the state retreats from its traditional role as provider of social services under the 'third way' strategy, the third sector takes on a heightened importance as the instrument of community renewal in partnership with the state. Giddens, in *The Third Way* (1998), argues that 'government can operate in partnership with agencies in civil society to foster community renewal and development'. It is in these interstices that social work can find a distinctive professional mission that promotes the values it espouses and empowers those it has traditionally sought to serve. This is a particularly complex task in a consumer society where the meaning of citizenship is being redefined.

Consumerism, user participation and citizen's charters

In the language of the market that dominates the global market economy, the citizen is a consumer. This makes the citizen highly vulnerable to the overweening power of both public and private corporate bodies. The neo-conservative answer has been the Citizen's Charter closely identified with the former British Prime Minister, John Major. It was intended to empower the consumer citizen.

The idea is not a new one. Its history goes back to Magna Carta (The Great Charter) agreed between King John and his barons at Runnymede in 1215. It represented the beginnings of an accountable state and is the basis of the British Constitution. The charter idea re-emerged in the nineteenth century, when the rising working class sought to make the state more attentive to its needs, in a People's Charter. While the Chartist movement failed, it laid the foundations for subsequent progressive political reforms, including universal suffrage and secret ballots. During the twentieth century, Charter 77 pointed to the discrepancy between law and reality in communist Eastern Europe.

The UK Citizen's Charter was launched by the Conservative government in 1991 as a ten-year plan, with six key principles which 'sought explicitly to improve the quality of services delivered to the public by encouraging organisations to put customer service first while also acknowledging public responsibility' (Humphreys, 1998: 40). They were:

1   Setting Standards
2   Openness and Information
3   Choice and Consultation
4   Courtesy and Helpfulness
5   Putting things Right
6   Value for Money (Humphreys, 1998: 40–41)

Many other governments quickly followed suit, introducing charters geared towards making public service organisations more accountable:

United Kingdom – *Citizen's Charter* (1991)
Portugal – *Public Service Quality Charter* (1992)

France – *Public Service Charter* (1992)
Canada – *Declarations of Quality Service Principles* (1994)
USA – *Customer Service Standards* (1995)
European Union – *Citizens First* (1996)
Australia – *Putting Service First* (begun in 1997; not completed)

The introduction of the Citizen's Charter in Britain was greeted with considerable scepticism as a top-down statutory exercise in improving consumer relations at the expense of genuinely participative citizenship. As Barnes (1997: 38) put it: 'The Citizen's Charter had the effect of confusing two entirely different concepts: that of a consumer of specific services, and membership of a specific political community which defines the status of citizenship'. The New Labour government, elected in May 1997, acknowledged public scepticism regarding the charter concept:

> In the past too many charters were drawn up from the top down, and there was little or no consultation with those who used the services. Too many were vague and unspecific.... In short, they did not put the user first. (Cabinet Office, 1998)

However, the Citizen's Charter, despite the change in government in the UK, still exists, but there is an important change in emphasis from customer to service user. Instead of the charter being done away with by the Labour government it has been revamped, renamed, and, in fairness, reimagined. New Labour's *Service First* charter has an increased number of public service delivery principles;

1   Set standards of service
2   Be open and provide full information
3   Consult and involve
4   Encourage access and promote choice
5   Treat all fairly
6   Put things right when they go wrong
7   Use resources effectively
8   Innovate and improve
9   Work with other providers
    (Cabinet Office, 1998)

Taylor (1991) enquires whether Citizen's Charters were in fact 'the big idea of the nineties'. For him the debate is essentially around the issue of customer satisfaction versus citizen participation and empowerment. The subtext is that Citizen's Charters represent either a market imperative or a democratic imperative. In the age of the consumer citizen, it is not easy to disentangle these two components, given that public life is being increasingly privatised. Nonetheless, there are core issues in the process, notably whether a charter is a top-down market exercise or a bottom-up democratic exercise, that determine its democratic authenticity. The UK Cabinet Office advises:

> Don't underestimate the time, effort and cost of consultation. But this is always well spent if it ensures that your service better meets people's needs. Most organisations find that consultation has many positive benefits, including a better understanding of views, and greater job satisfaction for staff. (Cabinet Office, 1998: 19)

The importance of consultation and participation is emphasised by the UK Cabinet Office as the essence of good charter-making. Nine key questions are suggested to guide user participation in the consultative process:

1 How will you consult users and potential users?
2 Are the methods you have chosen the most suitable for your purposes and convenient for your users?
3 Have you allowed plenty of time for the consultation?
4 Who will do the consulting?
5 Will your consultation include people from different areas, and different ethnic and social backgrounds?
6 Have you identified and clearly communicated the issues that you can have an effect on and improved those that you cannot?
7 How will you consult and involve people at all levels in your organisation?
8 How will you consult other local service providers with whom you work?
9 How will you give feedback to users and staff?
  (see Cabinet Office, 1998: 19)

The UK Cabinet Office also advises:

> If you are producing a charter for the first time, you may also find that users will respond more positively it they have an early draft to consider. It is often much harder to generate ideas from a blank piece of paper. But take care not to be too prescriptive or inflexible. (1998: 18–19)

Charters can be very important in local authority social provision. They put the local authority in touch with user views on service delivery issues and create the possibility of the reflexive development of services in the light of expressed needs. For example, in New Zealand, Wellington City Council have commented on the advantages of service user inputs:

> Feedback from those consulted is analysed with the expectation that new ideas and new perspectives (previously not considered) are thrown up for further investigation or ideas that had originally been suspected are confirmed. The outcomes of this analysis can then be incorporated directly into the decision making process. They become key factors in that process. (Wellington City Council, 1999)

Goodlad (1993: 34) has suggested that an inclusive approach to charter-making resting upon the principle of citizen participation can change the way local government acts and how it is perceived:

> This model emphasises the community development and empowering opportunities of local government, in which they operate as a training agency, resource centre and support service for local community groups.

The creation of local citizen's charters designed to augment users' rights is only the beginning of the process. Charters need to be updated regularly. As the UK Cabinet Office puts it:

> You should use the opportunity to evaluate with users the success (or otherwise) of your charter. Remember, charters are for the benefit of users. To be effective they need to be up to date and meet users' needs. (Cabinet Office, 1998: 12)

The importance of citizen's charter in some countries, notably the United Kingdom and New Zealand, arises from the extreme policies of marketisation pursued by ideologically led governments. They have transformed the nature of governance, which has impacted particularly heavily upon the way local authority social services carry out their role and task.

In the United Kingdom the Conservative government passed the National Health Service and Community Care Act, 1990. This measure shifted the boundaries of community care further towards the community; made local authority social service departments the 'lead agency' and introduced a consumerist philosophy based upon market principles. The post of care manager was created, with the task of designing and monitoring care packages tailored to the needs of individual service users. Services were to be provided within a 'mixed economy' of welfare, either purchased from independent providers or from the resources of the social services department. However, the emphasis was strongly placed upon the development of the independent sector composed of voluntary organisations (which had always existed) and private 'for profit' companies (Barnes, 1997).

Social service departments were given a strategic role, being required to produce community care plans in collaboration with the National Health Service and other relevant agencies. As part of this process, social service departments were required to consult with service users and carers. In this way services were expected to become more sensitive to the needs of consumer citizens. The introduction of new complaints procedures and 'arm's length inspection units' for residential services, composed of service users and providers, furthermore emphasised the engagement of the citizen consumer (Barnes, 1997: 28).

Local authority social services departments in Britain have consequently been reconstituted as 'enablers'. This represents a shift in the balance of the social services delivery system away from the state and towards the market. The implications for social work are significant, involving a new emphasis on competence at the expense of professionalism. Social workers are no longer the arbiters of social care. The care manager can be selected from any of the professions involved in the provision of social care.

Local authorities have interpreted their role as 'enablers' in different ways. Three models have emerged: (1) enabling market development; (2) enabling personal development and (3) enabling community development. While the intention of the Conservative government had been to drive community care towards the market, some local authority social service departments have interpreted their role as enabling authority differently. The emphasis on personal development stresses the importance of individual welfare and is compatible with traditional casework. A community development emphasis on the other hand recasts the enabling role of the local authority in terms of forging a healthy civil society. Wistow et al. (1994: 135) note the need of 'the mobilisation and support of community-based resources, especially those of the informal and local voluntary sectors, in order to foster participation and democratise decision-making.'

This model of the social services department as enabling authority has the potential to return social work practice to the community-based approach favoured by the Barclay Report (1982). It may also open up new paradigms of practice. Much depends on the routes that local authorities pursue in recasting themselves as 'enablers' of community care. Social work can influence these developments by putting 'the community' back into community care. If the deprofessionalisation of community care is to be resisted, then social workers will need to come up with a distinctive role for themselves and vision of community care. It is not at all clear whether a deeply demoralised social work profession in the United Kingdom has the will and capability to meet this challenge. The nature of social work education and training will be critical, since social workers need to have a sound grasp of the political context and potential for change in their role and task. A mission that increasingly depoliticises social work does not offer grounds for optimism.

The growing recognition of user rights, participative practices and the emergence of the charter movement has important implications for professionals. It redefines the relationship from the significant status of 'client', 'patient', 'resident' to the more empowering status of consumer and citizen. Consumer suggests choice. Citizens require the professionals to acknowledge the need for equality in their treatment of service users. In an era when the social work profession has moved away from its historic mission to the poor and oppressed towards promoting professional agendas, citizen's charters and user rights help to redress the balance in favour of the service user. Clearly, this has the potential to reshape the profession of social work in a more democratic form.

Citizenship and social work: rethinking the agenda

Professor Ruth Lister, former Director of the UK Child Poverty Action Group, observes: 'user involvement represents a more active form of social citizenship in which welfare state users are constructed as active participants rather than simply the passive bearers of rights or the recipients of services' (Lister, 1998: 15). There is a reluctance in social work to open to these more democratic approaches to practice. For example, Clare Evans, Director of Wiltshire and Swindon Users' Network, asserts: 'despite the rhetoric, social services departments are still finding it difficult to change their style, culture and systems to put people who receive services at their centre of thinking' (cited ibid.). Evans's comments underline the problems in promoting the idea of partnership in the social services in general and with service users in particular. Yet a more democratic and participative paradigm of social work demands an openness to partnership and participation.

There are important precedents in the United Kingdom through which poor people have been given a voice. For example, Church Action on Poverty's 'Local People: National Voice', the Independent Citizens' Commission on the Future of the welfare state (composed of service users) and the UK Coalition Against Poverty, all put the empowerment of the subjugated voices of the poor at the top of their agenda. Lister (1998: 16) advises that 'social workers need to think about their role in that partnership and in facilitating poor service users to make their voices heard as citizens'. This arguably requires a paradigm shift in social work practice, which is currently immobilised in the hierarchical management structures of social services departments in the United Kingdom and elsewhere. It will not be achieved without a re-embedding of civil society at the centre of the social work task, involving new partnerships between the statutory and the voluntary/community sector.

Taylor (1996: 68) comments that 'a focus on citizenship also has the potential to resolve the tensions between diversity and solidarity'. When service users are made stakeholders their status is moved beyond the language of labelling as client, recipient, survivor, or even customer or consumer, to citizen. Citizenship implies a language of inclusion, a movement beyond the disempowering relationship with the service provider of being a parent with a child on the 'at risk' register, an offender on probation, a person sectioned under mental health legislation, a sufferer from HIV/AIDS, a council tenant or a claimant. Taylor (1996: 57) asserts 'there is a fundamental difference between people who feel themselves defined and confined by their use of particular services ... and those for whom the use of a particular service, however important, does not define their whole identity and lifestyle'. The language of service provision encodes its social meaning, constructing its users as either supplicants or citizens.

The language of 'user participation', 'partnership' and 'stakeholding' has been incorporated into the mainstream of social policy and service provision. It is about giving users a voice and a stake in services that purport to promote community care. If caring is about alleviating suffering and relieving anxiety, development is about capacity-building that empowers service users to take independent control of their own lives and communities. It is empowerment in the knowledge that the state will support them in an ethical and healthy civil society that promotes democracy and social inclusion. This does not necessarily mean displacing professionalism. Most citizens value professional support and advice, but they wish it to be accountable to the public it serves. There are few professions (if any) so connected to and dependent upon its users for legitimation as social work. It has defined itself as both a profession and a movement with the social and moral purpose of helping the poor and oppressed. The future of social work depends on rethinking its agenda in the context of participative practice (Reisser, 1996: 250–251).

Conclusion

This chapter has set out to deconstruct the concept of civil society. It set the analysis in the context of the hollowing out of the nation state as a declining 'shell institution' and the emergence of embryonic alternative institutions of governance and movements for augmenting democratic rights. Voluntarism has been closely analysed in terms of its changing nature over time. The communitarianism of the New Labour government and its advocacy of partnership with the voluntary and community sector was scrutinised. The implications for social work practitioners of the emergence of more democratic forms in the user's and community movements has been considered. A new paradigm based upon participation and community engagement has been discussed as the future strategy for social work in a more democratic society. The suggestion is that service users need to be acknowledged as citizens first and clients second – multiculturalism underlines the need for a critical concept of citizenship at the centre of social work relationships with service users. We will now turn to the consideration of that question.

7

Multiculturalism, Feminism and Anti-Oppressive Practice

Multiculturalism is an issue that transcends politics, social theory and professional practice. It represents a wide range of ideas that are not easy to define. Quite simply, in terms of social theory, multiculturalism means a double focus on equality and distinctiveness (Blum, 1998: 73–79). Nancy Fraser has played a central role in theorising multiculturalism. Her ideas have been widely debated because they have profound implications for established concepts of equality. Fraser (1997: 11) records the political and ideological tensions between 'the eclipse of a socialist imaginary centered on terms such as "interest", "exploitation", and "redistribution"' and 'the rise of a new political imaginary, centered on notions of "identity", "difference", "cultural domination" and "recognition"'. She sets herself the task 'of developing a critical theory of recognition, one which identifies and defends only those versions of the cultural politics of difference that can be coherently combined with the social politics of equality' (Fraser, 1997: 12). Fraser (1997: 26) concludes that a transformative politics of recognition (that deconstructs group identities) combined with a transformative politics of redistribution (based on the principles of socialist solidarity) can 'blur' and 'destabilize' group differences, 'helping to redress some forms of misrecognition'. This means going beyond the 'surface' reallocations of resources of the welfare state and the 'surface' reallocations of respect of mainstream multiculturalism. Fraser's analysis is clearly a very challenging one and underlines the radical implications of the multicultural debate for social work practice.

In this chapter the meaning of multiculturalism will be explored in terms of political ideology. The influence of new social movements on changing the focus of the social work debate *vis-à-vis* the potential of radical political action will be addressed and the impact of feminism considered. Disability awareness will be discussed as a user movement that is promoting progressive political action. Finally, the chapter will examine the emergence of anti-discriminatory and anti-racist practice in social work.

Deconstructing multiculturalism

Monoculturalism is essentially an ethnoracialised Europeanism, based upon the dominant idiom in modern civilisation. European imperialist expansion carried its cultural hegemony to the four corners of the world. The Cold War divided the world into East and West, reflecting another deeper cultural and economic division between North and South. At the end of the Cold War, a global culture largely dictated by American values and taste emerged. While the core values of mono-culturalism continue to be in the ascendant, countercultural pressures in the form of new social movements have challenged this orthodoxy with a pluralistic vision called 'multiculturalism'. But 'multiculturalism' has many variants, signifying its colonisation by diverse political ideologies.

Multiculturalism is based upon transformative discourses that envisage the deconstruction of difference in an emancipatory social environment. In a social environment that is genuinely multicultural, differences of geographical background, economic class, race, religion, culture and gender are redefined. Moreover, multiculturalism challenges those universalising norms that regulate meaning (Goldberg, 1995: 30). On the face of it this seems to be a utopian task but it is underpinned by a serious political purpose.

Multiculturalism is ultimately about the politics of recognition. Taylor (1994: 75) comments:

> The thesis is that our identity is partly shaped by recognition or its absence, often by the misrecognition of others and so a person or group of people can suffer real damage, real distortion, if the people or society around them mirror back to them a confining or demeaning or contemptible picture of themselves. Non recognition or misrecognition can inflict harm, can be a form of oppression, imprisoning someone in a false, distorted and reduced mode of being.

Recognition is mediated through forms of signification, i.e. through modes of intelligibility and ideological frames of sense-making that organise individuals and groups into socio-economic hierarchies of power and privilege (McLaren, 1994: 55–56). This takes us to the core of multiculturalism.

Monoculturalism and multiculturalism are essentially polar ends of a continuum. At one end is the idea and practice of cultural domination; at the other end the idea of emancipation. Xenophobia is the antithesis of multiculturalism. Its influence amongst politicians is evident in countries such as Austria, where Jorg Haider's Freedom Party pursues an openly racist agenda. Xenophobic politics in Austria, Bavaria, northern Italy and Switzerland takes an overt form. In other countries xenophobia manifests itself in a more hidden way. For example, in France, Pierre Bourdieu notes an encoded xenophobia in the utterances of politicians:

> You don't need a degree in political science to discover in their silences and in their discourse that they do not have much to set against the xenophobic discourse which, for some years now, has been working to generate hatred out of the misfortunes of society – unemployment, delinquency, drug abuse etc. Perhaps for lack of convictions, perhaps for fear of losing votes by expressing them, they have ended up no longer talking about this false problem, which is always present and always absent, except in conventional stereotypes and more or less shamefaced innuendoes, with their references for example to 'law and order', the need to 'reduce (immigrant) entries to the lowest possible level' or to clamp down on 'clandestine immigration' (with occasional references, to give a progressive tinge to 'the role of traffickers and employers who exploit it'). (Bourdieu, 1998: 16)

In Britain, Stuart Hall has been at the forefront of the debate about multiculturalism. He argues that during the 1980s there was a drift towards populist authoritarianism and the emergence of 'the law and order society'. In this reconstituted reality the 'Black Mugger' has become a cultural symbol for all that is wrong in society. Middle England has come to symbolise the ideal society. Hall (1998: 13) observes: 'Middle England is a place of mind, an imagined community' defined by its exclusive membership. Politics and culture have become closely enmeshed in postmodern society.

Multiculturalism and political ideology

There are a variety of political forms of multiculturalism: conservative or corporate; liberal; Left-liberal and critical and resistance (McLaren, 1994). While these variants have overlapping elements, the categorisation of multiculturalism into different ideological components is important because of its political contextualisation.

Conservative or corporate multiculturalism is essentially monoculturalism. It is intimately connected to imperialism and colonialism. It presupposes the superiority of Euro-American civilisation and in particular Anglo-Saxon cultural and linguistic forms. Globalisation is a modern manifestation of cultural imperialism, promoting a common popular culture as the dominant world idiom. In this assimilationist view of the world, whiteness becomes 'the invisible norm by which other ethnicities are judged' (McLaren, 1994: 49). Its own ethnicity is denied: only non-white cultures are 'ethnic', according to this social construction of culture. Furthermore, the prescription of English as the 'official' global language reinforces this cultural dominance.

Finally, conservative multiculturalists presuppose the superiority of Western intellectual traditions, cosmologies and education systems. Manifestly, conservative multiculturalists take a view of the world that is rooted in Social Darwinism and rests upon the notion of racial superiority. Apartheid and racial segregation are essentially the extreme end of a continuum of cultural and ethnic domination rooted in the idea of white superiority.

Liberal multiculturalists promote the idea of natural equality between racial groupings: Anglo-Saxon, African-Caribbean, Asian, etc. The assumption is that all races share the same intellectual potential to be equal within the capitalist system. What liberal multiculturalism does not allow for are the inbuilt inequalities that result from the social and educational structures that allow whites to be advantaged within the current political order. McLaren (1994: 51) asserts: 'This view often collapses into an ethnocentric and oppressively universalistic humanism in which the legitimating norms which govern the substance of citizenship are identified most strongly with Anglo-American cultural political communities'. Dominelli (1988: 53) takes a similar view, arguing that liberal multiculturalism in social work is a 'euphemism for racism.... Conceptualizing society in these terms assumes different racial and cultural groups are already equal, thereby defining racism away rather than dealing with it, and obscuring the necessity of having both black and white social workers confront racism as a structural and endemic feature of British society.'

In its defence, liberal multiculturalism is also the language adopted by the UN's Universal Declaration of Human Rights. It values tolerance and equal dignity above all else: this is the essence of its universalism. Liberal multiculturalism is deeply rooted in the humanist tradition. It, therefore, embraces a common cultural heritage with social work, sharing the same value base. Its influence in social work is consequently substantial, putting tolerance at the forefront of the professional agenda.

Left-liberal multiculturalism seeks to address the problems arising from the liberal stress on 'sameness' between racial groups. It suggests that this view neglects the importance of difference and cultural diversity, which it celebrates. The problem with the Left-liberal perspective is that it tends to promote 'essentialism', which ignores the reality that difference is the product of history, culture and power. Moreover, it tends to exoticise difference, leading to romantic cultural misrepresentation. From the perspective of professionals, such as social workers, this emphasis on the essentialisation of cultural difference can become problematic in practice, because it leads to exclusionary identity politics. Social workers' resistance to trans-racial adoptions is a topical example of essentialisation. Professional sympathisers often misread the cultural complexity of their position, which results in media parody.

Critical and resistance multiculturalists take a more radical view. In contrast to Left-liberal multiculturalists, critical multiculturalists argue that differences are produced as the result of ideological influences and the reception of cultural signs. The politics of signification is fundamental to this perspective. Socio-economic structures, based upon group domination, require systems of signification by which citizens are ordered into hierarchies of power and privilege. In this process binary constructions of meaning (such as white/black, male/female, good/bad, normal/deviant create a regime of representation, where negative cultural meanings with the status of norms are attached to subordinate groups. For example, the portrayal of black people as welfare mothers, drug pushers, gang members, etc., not only creates a symbolic social division. It legitimises police brutality and welfare discrimination.

Resistance multiculturalists go beyond the Left-liberal multiculturalist preoccupation with celebrating difference and seek to 'transform the social historical conditions in which meaning-making occurs' (McLaren, 1994: 58). Fraser (1997) in her critical theory of recognition argues that the goal of resistance multiculturalism is the deconstruction of difference. She takes the binary division between heterosexual and homosexual as an example. Fraser argues that queer theory represents an archetypal model for a transformative politics of recognition. Queer theory does not seek to support the integrity of gay identity within a pluralistic framework of tolerance of sexual difference. Fraser (1997: 24) comments:

> Queer politics, in contrast, treats homosexuality as the constructed and devalued correlate of heterosexuality; both are a reification of sexual ambiguity and are codified only in virtue of each other. The transformative aim is not to solidify a gay identity but to deconstruct the homo–hetero dichotomy so as to destabilise all fixed sexual activities. The point is not to dissolve all sexual difference in a single, universal human identity; it is, rather, to sustain a sexual field of multiple, debinarised fluid ever-shifting differences.

Organisations like Outrage practise queer politics, aiming to expose the normative basis of sexual division in political debate and to destabilise established dichotomies between 'gay' and 'straight' identities. Critical and resistance multiculturalism points in the direction of a revolutionary praxis based upon the deconstruction of difference favoured by groups such as Outrage. It suggests that assimilationist and cultural diversity approaches may be fragmenting in postmodern society where both conservative and liberal perspectives are being challenged by critical multiculturalism.

Social work education, multiculturalism and cognitive praxis

Multiculturalism has become a critical debate within social work. Fong et al. (1996: 25–26) comment:

> The final question raised by the current state of racial category deconstruction is a theoretical one with implications for social work that are not fully clear. Social workers are in the habit of locating their clients along analytical axes, of which race and class are two. Traditionally, race has been seen as a biological attribute (with obvious social ramifications), whereas class has always been understood to be socially constructed. Most of the recent work on race concludes, however, that it is not a biological fact at all, but rather a social and political construct that uses physical markers. Race, therefore, must be considered a social consequence and not a cause of human behavior.

They conclude that multiculturalism will pose social work with one of its greatest challenges in the twenty-first century. This suggests that the politics of recognition is going to be one of the dominant concerns of social work during the new millennium. Two key considerations arise for social work: professional consciousness and education. The dominant discourses of social work education are governed by a civic unconscious that determines the normative structures of practice. In essence, the traditional strategic concerns of social work practice have been based upon the remoralisation of the poor for the disciplined practice of citizenship. Critical multiculturalism suggests that social workers need to intellectually engage with the issues of difference and citizenship, in a manner that detaches practice from monoculturalist norms.

Traditional social work practice within the welfare state rests upon a compromise between social classes. Furthermore, traditional social work accepts the compromise, favoured by mainstream liberal multiculturalism, of respecting existing ethnic identities as equal and combating discriminatory and racist practices within the welfare state. Critical multiculturalism challenges social workers to interrogate the value assumptions of their approach to practice and assess the principles in the name of which they act. If social workers are to avoid narrative repression (i.e. undermining service users' identities) they need to be capable of challenging discursive hierarchies of meaning in their practice.

This implies that at the point of professional identity formation in training, the issues of difference and citizenship need to be fully deconstructed in the curriculum. First, the received texts of social work literature must be challenged by counter-texts that interrogate the dominant tradition of Western humanism in social work. Cultural respect is only possible when alternative cultural traditions, cosmologies and their position in the hierarchy of cultural status production have been analysed. Second, bivalent division (e.g. white/black, male/female, heterosexual/homosexual, able-bodied/disabled) need to be challenged, along with the associated institutionalised forms of discrimination (e.g. white superiority, patriarchy, homophobia, ableism). There is clearly an imperative for social workers to be grounded in an understanding of culture based upon critical citizenship. Gould (1996: 37–38) asserts in reference to the imperatives for social work education in America:

> Fundamentally, multiculturalism presents a paradigm that goes beyond intercultural learning and multicultural competency. Its vision of an ethnically complex society provides a prescriptive rather than a descriptive model.... In this respect, there is a difference in degree, if not in kind, between multiculturalism and any one ethnic or cultural perspective. Multiculturalism is built on an organising principle that puts the onus on both the dominant community and community members of colour to consider the fact of their 'ethnic psychological captivity'.

However, Gould (1996: 33–34) notes that multiculturalism is a 'devalued norm' in social work, which implicitly endorses the value of 'Anglo-conformity'. She concludes:

> Despite the fact that the profession, in principle, has endorsed the value of implementing a multicultural curriculum, there was always an unease involving the mission of social work – whether social work education was trying to achieve a kind of rainbow collectivist society by teaching required courses. (1996: 39)

The experience of implementing an 'anti-racist' practice curriculum in the United Kingdom by CCETSW underlines the complexity of addressing multiculturalism in social work education and training. Dominelli (1997: 162–170) has charted the failure of this initiative, despite well intentioned support from CCETSW. Interest in multiculturalism arose from the anti-racist and anti-sexist programmes promoted by the Greater London Council (GLC) during the 1980s. Ethnic minorities and women's groups felt empowered to campaign for fundamental attitudinal change, based upon the politics of recognition.

Problems quickly emerged in terms of the inability of universities to successfully negotiate this multiculturalist educational task. In part there was a lack of resources. There was also often a lack of comprehension about what was required in terms of curriculum design and content. At a deeper level there were profound epistemological problems, common to cultural studies in general in universities. Anti-racist practice challenges some of the most hallowed principles of liberal humanism, upon which the idea of the university in Western society rests. Social work courses in the United Kingdom are often short (e.g. two-year diploma courses); 50 per cent of the course is spent in practice and the curriculum is already overcrowded. Preparation for anti-racist practice requires considerable theoretical input that seeks to explore the cultural complexities of its underlying principles. Simplistic understanding is open to the charge of propaganda.

Dominelli (1997: 167–168) claims: 'Leading white male social work academics have opposed the requirement to introduce anti-racist social work into the curriculum'. Searching questions were asked in the media that brought social work education into considerable disrepute (Phillips, 1993). The thrust of the critique was that multiculturalism was promoting intolerance in the curriculum, putting social work education seriously at odds with the liberal humanist tradition of the university. Part of the problem was a failure to understand that both 'oppressor' and 'oppressed' have power (even if only the power to resist) and this involves ethical obligations.

The critical tradition in Western knowledge since the days of Socrates has had its detractors (e.g. Aristophanes). It is incumbent upon educators to practise the tolerance they preach. Fearless questioning in pursuit of the truth necessitates a profound compassion and belief in humanity. It also requires a true appreciation of the educational task as the ultimate act of liberation: 'knowledge sets you free'. Bowdlerised attempts to introduce multiculturalism into the social work curriculum are profoundly self-defeating: they are at odds with the value base of social work, which is rooted in liberal humanism. Multicultural education in social work needs to look at the variegated political approaches involved; oppressive systems of signification in everyday culture; the politics of recognition and its informing values and the application of these principles to social work practice. Unless multiculturalism is explored in the context of the deep structure of learning in the humanities, egalitarian discourses will not emerge in practice. Practice competencies that are rooted in surface structures of meaning have little or no validity, are not likely to stand the test of time and the pressures of institutionalised racism within the social system.

Social work education needs to develop a cognitive praxis designed to explore 'border identities'. McLaren (1994: 67) observes: 'Borders can be linguistic, spatial, ideological and geographical', adding: 'they not only demarcate otherness but stipulate the manner in which otherness is maintained and reproduced'. Border identities are at the core of multicultural understanding. Cognitive praxis assists multicultural understanding through the acquisition of knowledge and experience from a series of intercultural encounters. It implies intercultural movement but perhaps more importantly the confrontation with difference. This is, according to McLaren (1994: 68), a challenging educational task:

> As multicultural educators informed by critical and feminist pedagogies, we need to keep students connected to the power of the unacceptable and comfortable with the unthinkable by producing critical forms of policy analysis and pedagogy.... It is important, as critical educators, that we do not manipulate students simply to accept our intellectual positions nor presume at the same time to speak for them.

Ultimately, multicultural education is about the exploration of the cultural spaces where border identities are constructed, whether linguistically, epistemologically or inter-subjectively. In essence, it is an exercise in decolonisation (McLaren, 1994: 69).

New social movements: new social work?

The transformative impact of new social movements on social work practice is opening up new vistas. Over the past thirty years new social movements have emerged championing causes as diverse as feminism, anti-racism, gay rights, disability awareness, grey power, peace and the environment. They pose a challenge to conventional politics organised around political parties (Byrne, 1997). New social movements have created political and cultural spaces where identity politics can flourish. As such, the social politics that dominated most of the twentieth century, embodied in the welfare state, is rivalled by a new political agenda. Progressive politics, so long concerned with class inequalities and redistributive justice, has become more complex, embracing a diverse set of agendas, including the politics of recognition. In this changed political, social and cultural landscape, social work is challenged to reinvent itself in new forms suited to the climate of the times.

The struggle within social work to discover a new identity, role and function is a major professional preoccupation. Social work has always been defined by diversity and eclecticism. It is unlikely that it will ever achieve a standardised form, given the variety of methods (casework, groupwork and community work) and settings (health, child care, probation, voluntary and community sector, etc.), that constitute its field of activity.

The new social movements are making a vital contribution to this renewal and redefinition. Feminist social work has reshaped women's relationship with the welfare state and generated new practice paradigms. Disability awareness has brought the impact of a social movement, that is simultaneously a service user movement, into the centre of the definition of progressive practice. Similarly, grey power is transforming cultural attitudes towards the elderly and raising awareness of the need for generative welfare strategies that support dignity and independence in an ageing population. Anti-racism challenges institutionalised discrimination in our society and demands new practices. Gay rights have heightened our awareness of the relationship between sexuality, culture and power.

New social movements have raised crucial issues for social work that could transform its approach and deconstruct the traditional division between the individualist and community orientations. These are a recognition (1) that citizenship is gendered, (2) that the personal is political and (3) of the need for anti-discriminatory practice. We may also be witnessing the emergence of a global civil society that is reordering the relationship between equality and difference. Social work must adapt to these powerful social and cultural changes that represent a deepening of democracy. Feminists have been at the forefront of these developments.

Feminism, citizenship and social work

Dominelli and McLeod (1989) assert: 'at the heart of feminism is a very simple idea: that there are not two sorts of people in the world, the superior and the inferior, or in terms of power relations, the dominant and the subordinate. We are all equal irrespective of our gender'. This powerful statement exposes a fault line in our political culture: citizenship is gendered. Lister (1997: 66) observes that 'the ostensible gender neutrality of the term "citizenship" disguised the gender division constructed in its name, both historically and to-day'.

The 1970s represented the renaissance of the women's movement, which in an earlier era struggled for universal suffrage. Quickly, the study of gender issues became a major preoccupation across the campuses of the Western world. But in villages, towns and cities across the globe there was also a spontaneous emergence of women's groups, concerned with issues as diverse as equal opportunities, domestic violence, rape, abortion and health. Out of these localised groups emerged campaigns (e.g. the right to choose) and initiatives (rape crisis centres and women's refugees) as well as the sense of solidarity in the face of oppression.

The publication of a series of books – notably Betty Friedan's *Feminine Mystique* (1965), Kate Millett's *Sexual Politics* (1971) and Germaine Greer's *The Female Eunuch* (1971) – transformed women's vision of their role in society. Civil society became the space in which the women's liberation movement (as it was originally called) took shape and set about renegotiating the basis of the political and social order. Citizenship was at the core of the feminist critique that sought equality on the basis of democratic participation. Patriarchy (i.e. the systematic subordination of women by men) became the focus of feminists' attempts to unpack the established meanings of citizenship. However, more recently feminists have become divided about the use of the term 'patriarchy' and there is more general acceptance of the alternative term 'sexual division of labour' (Bradley, 1996: 92–95). The term 'phallocentric' is also employed as a symbol of the cultural dominance of the male gender.

Social citizenship, embodied in the institution of the welfare state, has been a particular target of feminist criticism. Feminists noted the lack of attention to women's rights in welfare discourse. Elizabeth Wilson (1997: 9) in a pioneering study *Women and the Welfare State* concluded: 'Social welfare policies amount to no less than the state organization of domestic life'. Fiona Williams (1989: xii) in *Social Policy: A Critical Introduction*, defined the scale of the feminist contribution to rethinking the social policy agenda:

> Much of this work offered new dimensions to key questions in social policy analysis: issues of caring, dependency, needs, of the relationship between work and income, of the relationship between the providers and users of welfare provision, as well as theoretical questions about the relationship between patriarchy, capitalism and the state.

A feminist social policy has delayered women's inequality within the welfare system and the workplace and a growing appreciation of the complexity of the equality issue has emerged. Jane Lewis (1998: 90) notes: 'aiming to treat women the same as men will not do'. More sophisticated welfare responses are required that recognise the intersecting inequalities of gender and class.

While the relationship between feminism and social policy is beset by complexity, feminism has unlocked generative aspects of social work. Feminism has exposed women's exploitation as carers. This has profound implications for the personal social services in a society where 'informal' systems of caring are often promoted. Moreover, social work, like health visiting and housing inspection, is historically located in women's attempts to push out the boundaries of the public sphere, revealing 'the feminisation of poverty' to a denying male public. Clients of social workers are overwhelmingly female. The profession continues to be populated by women, though arguably still dominated by men (Mullender, 1997: 42). Social work and feminism, consequently, share much in common, although the practice of social work is open to the charge that it reinforces women's domesticity and, consequently, oppression. For example, the influence of Bowlby's theory of material deprivation on social work practice during the post-war years was widespread. It served to justify the dismantling of the extensive level of child care provision developed during the Second World War, when women's labour was essential. Yet when the silence surrounding women's oppression was broken female social workers responded with new approaches and new practices. Many recognised the problems of domestic violence, rape, misrecognition and devalued cultural status as common to all women in varying degrees regardless of class position. While feminists are often criticised for promoting the interests of middle-class women, the agenda they have pursued suggests otherwise. Essentially, feminism has challenged a gendered social and political order, demanding fundamental change. This affects the interests of all women in society, regardless of social status. The ultimate aim of feminism is to deconstruct the bivalent power structures that have enabled a gendered hierarchy to exist in society through the institution of patriarchy.

The cultural and economic forces which are reshaping women's role in society are complex. Suzanne Moore (1998: 19) in an article published in *Marxism Today*, entitled 'The Cultural Revolution', observes:

> Of the cultural revolutions that have had the most effect on all our lives, feminism has proved remarkably resilient even to sustained attacks on it. Changes in women's lives have been driven by a curious mix of the quest for personal freedom and the demands of an economy that seeks cheap and flexible female labour. Culturally speaking, it seems that even for women who do not define themselves as feminists, feminism has brought about an increase in the demands and expectations of women, yet it has not produced either the men to satisfy these demands or a society in which these expectations can easily be met.

A powerful backlash from cultural conservatives, most notably the well organised religious Right in the United States, places major obstacles in the way of feminism's agenda. This social movement defeated the Equal Rights Amendment (ERA) designed to enshrine gender equality in the American Constitution. In Britain, 'the back to basics' campaign of the Conservative government during the 1990s underlined a growing cultural dimension in politics. The personal has become political, giving rise to culture wars.

The personalisation of the political by the feminist critique is very important in terms of social work's epistemological basis. Individualised approaches to social work have traditionally been seen as apolitical in contrast to community-orientated approaches. The politicisation of the personal blurs this distinction. White (1999: 109) comments: 'In advocating such an approach, feminist social work texts have rooted their analysis in the belief that feminist social workers and women service users have common experiences of oppression'. Dominelli and McLeod (1989: 147) have noted the importance of 'fostering awareness of the common material interests between women social workers and their clients'. However, White (1999: 110) argues that this emphasis on shared experiences, common material interests and equality is inherently problematic. It ignores status hierarchies, organisational contexts and can serve to marginalise black women, older women and lesbians.

Moreover, there is a problem in accommodating feminist social work within statutory settings, since there is a basic contradiction between the emancipatory agenda of feminism and the role of a welfare state that reinforces patriarchy. Theorists of feminist social work take different positions on this question. Dominelli and McLeod (1989: 114) suggest a transformative agenda for feminist social work:

> Against such an agenda for change, feminist initiatives in practice by now amount to an identifiable, extensive and widespread programme for action. This includes the impact of feminist work from bases external to statutory social work on statutory practice itself; direct practice from a feminist perspective with clients in statutory social work on a one-to-one and small group basis; feminist social worker support groups; trade union action, and attempts to tackle the male-dominated management pyramid.

This transformative strategy challenges the traditional basis of social work.

The politics of disability

Oliver (1990: 3) has demonstrated that the definition of disability is highly problematic:

> Disabled people too have realized that dominant definitions of disability pose problems for individual and group identity and have begun to challenge the use of disablist language. Whether it be offensive (cripple, spastic, mongol, etc.) or merely depersonalizing (the handicapped, the blind, the deaf, and so on), such terminology has been attacked, and organizations of disabled people have fostered a growing group consciousness and identity.

Cultural images reflect either the 'tragic' or 'heroic' dimensions of disability. Both are profoundly disempowering to disabled people, highlighting that definition is ultimately not a semantic issue but a political one. Oliver (1990: 11) argues the case for a social theory of disability, but one that 'must be located within the experience of disabled people themselves and their attempts, not only to define disability but also to construct a political movement amongst themselves and to develop services commensurate with their own self-defined needs'. This is a very important assertion of the political nature of disability: i.e. its social meaning subordinates citizens with physical or sensory impairments to a second-class status in the political culture.

Independence is a core issue in defining the status of disabled people. Oliver (1990: 91) comments:

> Professionals tend to define independence in terms of self-care activities such as washing, dressing, toileting, cooking and eating without assistance. Disabled people, however,

define independence differently, seeing it as the ability to be in control of and make decisions about one's life, rather than doing things alone or without help.

The politicisation of disability is associated with the emergence of the disability movement. The United Nations Year of Disabled People in 1981 triggered the development of a social movement. Internationally, Disabled People International (DPI) acts as a global organising body for the disability movement. Nationally, disabled people's organisations have also flourished, such as the British Council of Organisations of Disabled People (BCODP), composed of local coalitions of disabled people, which had over one hundred affiliate organizations by the mid-1990s:

> By any standard this numerical growth is remarkable but there are four reasons why it was even more remarkable than appears at first sight. Firstly, all organizations con- trolled by disabled people suffered from chronic under-funding throughout the decade, even from national and international agencies which are supposed to support such developments. Secondly, many politicians, policy-makers and professionals had no faith in the viability of a new movement which was being built by people who had so far seemed passive and dependent. Thirdly, the new movement was built in the teeth of opposition from the traditional voluntary organizations who, up to then, had been in control of disability and this opposition was often active rather than passive. Finally, because of the disabling environments that disabled people encounter, the difficulties involved in simply funding ways to meet, communicate and organise, should not be under-estimated. (Oliver, 1996: 43)

At the centre of the disability movement's ideology is the social model. This has driven disabled people on to the streets to protest against discrimination and to demand equal citizenship. Barnes (1997: 59) asserts: 'The social model defines both the philosophy and the strategy of the disability movement'.

The decision of disabled people to organise on an autonomous self-advocacy basis was a vital step towards democratic participation and away from indepen- dence on paternalistic voluntary organizations to represent their interests. It signalled an important claim to full citizenship rights, traditionally denied in the culture of dependency that informed the state's attitude towards disabled people. Empowerment through self-advocacy has been the guiding strategy of the disabi- lity movement in the developed world, involving campaigning for equal rights and against eugenic policies and the use of inhumane weapons (e.g. landmines) (Burden, 1998: 236–237). Social rights are also at the top of the disability move- ment's agenda, notably the right to a real home, to worthwhile jobs, autonomous relationships and basic income support (Booth, 1997: 154–159).

Barbara Lisicki, a leading member of Direct Action Network (DAN), has defined what the disability movement means from an activist perspective:

> I don't think anyone knows for sure what a movement is but essentially what we are talking about is a set of ideas and an analysis which people can support in different ways. I always think of the movement as a set of people that have somehow made a connection with a set of ideas. The disability movement is obviously a set of ideas that presents a challenge to dominant ideology that says disabled people are burdens on society and that they should be taken care of but the disability movement is also about people

who have a right to a life. (Evidence to the Commission on the Future of the Voluntary Sector, 1996: 44)

The disability movement has sought to change the political landscape by focussing its attention on issues as diverse as civil rights, the social model, independent living, the benefits system and positive disability imagery.

Critics challenge the disability movement's legitimacy to speak for its constituency – Vic Finkelstein, a founder and first Chair of BCODP, is forthright in his response to this criticism:

> We shouldn't deny that it is a minority of disabled people who belong to the BCODP. If you say there are 7 million disabled people in Britain, obviously only a tiny minority are politically active in [the] disability movement. We shouldn't deny that. The BCODP reflects a tiny minority, but the Thatcher government was elected on a minority of the electorate. (Evidence to the Commission on the Future of the Voluntary Sector, 1996: 45)

The disability movement is having a significant impact on politics and society. For example, in Britain in 1995 the Disability Discrimination Act was passed, making it an offence to discriminate against disabled people. In service terms, the emergence of centres for independent living (or for integrated living) known as CILs, have created alternatives to traditional residential provision. The 1990 NHS and Community Care Act has enabled disabled people to argue the case for becoming their own care managers and determining needs and resource requirements (Barnes, 1997: 62). The disability movement has demonstrably unleashed a move towards empowerment, autonomy and equal citizenship amongst its constituents.

Ageism and the grey movement

The fastest growing demographic group in the developed world is that of the elderly. In an era when social rights, in the form of pensions and social security benefits, are under attack from a resurgent New Right, the capacity of the elderly to fight back is vital. In the United States the American Association of Retired Persons (AARP) has proven to be a potent political force. The 'Gray Movement', as the social movement comprising elderly people is called in the United States, has been instrumental in staving off cuts in the social security budget and maintaining medical benefits during the era of welfare reform. The American Association for Retired Persons (AARP) is the main pressure group.

In Britain, the National Federation of Old Age Pensions Associations, founded in 1939, and the British Pensions and Trade Union Action Group, formed in the 1970s, have been less successful. During the 1990s, when local pensioners' action groups affiliated to the National Pensioners' Convention (composed of 1.5 million members) a new political consciousness emerged amongst the elderly. This resulted in a successful attempt to oppose the introduction of Value Added Tax (VAT) on fuel and signalled a determination to organise on issues of vital interest. Campaigns to resist ageism in the policies of the National Health Service have provided ongoing focus for action (Barnes, 1997: 63–67).

The former leader of the Transport and General Workers Union (TGWU), Jack Jones, as President of the National Pensioners' Convention Council, expressed open dissent when he declared:

> The treatment of frail elderly people in Britain today is a scandal crying to high heaven.... As a community, we should care for them as passionately as a good family cherishes its own parents. It should be a major objective of society to secure the relief of poverty, to provide dignity of security, and to enhance the quality of life of all our elderly citizens. (cited in Barnes, 1997: 67)

Anti-discriminatory practice

Anti-discriminatory practice is rooted in multiculturalism. Thomas and Pierson (1995: 16) define it as follows:

> A term used widely in social work and probation work, and in social work training, to describe how workers take account of structural disadvantage and seek to reduce individual and institutional discrimination particularly on grounds of race, gender, disability, social class and social orientation.

Thompson (1997: 238) observes: 'A basic feature of anti-discriminatory practice is the ability/willingness to see [that] discrimination and oppression are so often central to the situations social workers encounter'. He views the need to be sensitive to the existence of discrimination and oppression as a basic social work concern. The power of human agency vested in the social worker offers a choice between transforming or reinforcing discriminatory practices within the social system through promoting social justice, equality and user participation. Jordan (1990) views anti-discriminatory practice as a moral imperative in an unjust society. This view suggests that social workers cannot simply be technicians of state power but should become moral arbiters of justice in the social order.

Social workers employ anti-discriminatory practice methodologies through enabling individuals to overcome individualised and institutionalised prejudice. They also seek to empower service users to tackle the social context that embeds and defends institutionalised discrimination. By decontextualising practice, traditional individualised social work ignored discrimination. It was viewed as beyond the remit of the care worker. This served to reinforce monoculturalist 'Anglo-conformity'.

Anti-discriminatory practice democratises the professional relationship with the service user and redefines it as a partnership. Thompson (1997 : 241) has identified the core elements of this partnership:

- Defining needs to be met, problems to be solved;
- Deciding how best to meet the needs/solve the problems;
- Implementing and reviewing such decisions;
- Agreement on termination; and
- Evaluating intervention.

He adds: 'A clear assessment, developed in partnership with the client(s), which takes account of the patterns of discrimination and the experience of oppression, is an essential first step in ensuring that subsequent intervention is not distorted by discriminatory assumptions or oppressive practices' (Thompson, 1997: 243–244). Thompson's perspective is rooted in liberal multiculturalism.

Burke and Harrison (1998: 238) formulate what they call an 'anti-oppressive practice' approach in more critical multiculturalist terms, arguing that effective work involves a perspective that:

- is flexible without losing focus;
- includes views of oppressed individuals and groups;
- is theoretically informed;
- challenges and changes existing ideas and practice;
- can analyse the oppressive nature of organisational culture and its impact on practice;
- includes continuous reflection and evaluation of practice;
- has multidimensional change strategies which incorporate the concepts of networking, user involvement, partnership and participation;
- has a critical analysis of the issues of power, both personal and structural.

Essentially, it is impossible to disentangle anti-discriminatory and anti-oppressive practice from political ideology. The multiculturalist perspective that informs anti-discriminatory practice shapes its form and content. Inevitably, statutory social work settings are more likely to adopt liberal multiculturalist perspectives. In civil society voluntary and community groups are likely to be more directly influenced by social movements and adopt a critical multiculturalist perspective.

Conclusion

Multiculturalism and feminism have had a profound impact on the way social workers view their role and task. At the core of this politics of recognition are the intersecting forces of equality and difference, propelling social workers in the direction of more democratic forms of practice. But there are inherent contradictions. The welfare state has long been based upon patriarchal assumptions. Statutory practice settings resist politicisation. But when the personal becomes political, it is impossible to draw the line between the two. This serves to destabilise established social work practice paradigms and suggests new possibilities for the future.

8

Futurescapes

This book started by posing the question: 'Postmodernity: the End of Social Work?' It has argued that the historic paradigms of social work are being replaced by contemporary paradigms that open up new spaces and sites for practice in civic social work. The core argument has been that postmodernity does not mean the end of social work but its reconstruction. This has necessitated an examination of the various cultural shifts that have shaped social work throughout its history. In this final chapter it will be argued that social work is confronted by three options in postmodern society:

1 **Marketisation:** Social work accepts and adjusts to market-led change in a future characterised by a combination of consumerist welfare, deprofessionalisation and the redefinition of social work as social care.
2 **Radical resistance:** Social work opposes these changes by identifying itself with global struggles against capitalism, the defence of human rights and the advocacy of solutions to world poverty.
3 **Social inclusion:** Social work defines its role in terms of civic engagement with the most vulnerable citizens as a basic democratic imperative grounded in socially inclusive practice.

Marketisation – consumerist social work

Social work is increasingly influenced by the consumerist visions of welfare in a burgeoning social care market which is redefining social work as social care. Some commentators welcome this transformation and advocate the abolition of social work and its replacement by social care. An article in the *Guardian*, on 22 May 2000, suggested that this would be a popular proposal in the New Labour manifesto for the next election:

> Labour should propose to abolish social workers. The idea would win easy headlines and pander to popular prejudice, but also make much sense.
> Rightly or wrongly, the term 'social worker' is irredeemably tainted. Associated with political correctness, the failings of municipal socialism and 20 years of care scandals, it is a real deterrent to recruitment into the social care sector. By redefining and renaming the role, the profession could make a fresh start.

The move should be coupled with the extension of care management – as designed for work with elderly people – into children's services. Vulnerable children would in effect have a personal champion, holding a budget and able to commission the services best suited for the individual. For 'interfering social worker' read 'enabling care manager'.

The impact of marketisation on professional social work has been profound. Hugman (1998) attributes this to the pervasive influence of New Right philosophy, which has reconfigured welfare in the language and image of the market, defining welfare as a 'product'. He concludes:

> It is in this context that the reformulation of welfare as a form of production legitimates the withdrawal of the state from direct provision, to the more indirect roles of subsidy and regulation, while at the same time encouraging private providers to enter the scene in larger numbers than previously. This is so whether the providers are not-for-profit non-governmental agencies or profit-making companies. The beneficiaries of this move can be seen as these agencies and companies who are able to enter the (quasi-) market, as well as the government which is able to divest itself of direct institutional control. The claims for such changes also include the direct users of services who, it is argued, benefit from choice (created by competition), which leads to greater responsiveness and improved quality, and so to more efficient services. (Hugman, 1988: 101–102)

Welfare has succumbed to globalised capitalism with enterprise values and corporate organisational forms informing the logic of social service delivery. Marketisation has promoted the rise of corporate managerialism and the decline of traditional concepts of professionalism. On the face of it, social work is being marginalised in a social care industry that is being remodelled on business lines.

We are witnessing the emergence of consumerist social work. Much of this book has concentrated on the ideas of citizen and community in terms of emerging social work paradigms that promote social justice. The concept of the service user as a consumer has dominated the 1980s and 1990s. It has reconfigured the relationship between the citizen and the welfare state. Clarke (1998: 14–15) observes in reference to the changes wrought by consumerist welfare: 'In the process, ideas of altruism, collectivism and mutuality were momentarily derided as concealing or distracting from the real human motivations of competitive and possessive individualism'. He concludes: 'At root, this view of "economic man" saw the defining feature of human behaviour as the wish to do better and the wish to own property.' Apart from this ideological justification, the proponents of the market argue that it is capable of much greater efficiency than the state. Moreover, they contend that the market is dynamic and innovative in contrast to the dependency culture promoted by the welfare state. The market, according to its exponents, promotes choice, enabling the consumer to 'shop around' for the best service.

Ultimately, the consumerist vision of welfare depends on purchaser power. Money determines access. Without money the consumer cannot purchase the service. This makes the notion of choice for some citizens highly problematic. What is the consumerist welfare solution to this dilemma? Clarke (1998: 24) notes: 'the classical answer to this problem is that of the Poor Law: the benefits or services provided by public authorities or the state should be of a level and quality sufficiently low to dissuade all those but the absolutely desperate from relying upon them'. In other words, the principle of 'less eligibility': i.e. the conditions of welfare recipients should be lower than those of the most disadvantaged worker. This logically means the end of welfare for the poor and the restoration of the punitive Poor Law regime. The question is: 'is this acceptable in a democratic society?' In the United States the Republicans' 'Contract with America' clearly either thought so or believed that the poor had forfeited their right to citizenship, because of their dependent status. In Britain, the treatment of refugees and asylum seekers suggests the emergence of a similar vein of thought. William Hague, the Conservative leader, has led this populist backlash. In a speech to the Police Federation Conference at Brighton in May 2000, Mr Hague took a similar hard line on offenders: 'We shall only turn the tide of rising disorder and lawlessness if we stop treating crime as an abstract problem and criminals as victims of society' (*Independent*, 19 May 2000).

Consumerist social work in a socially differentiated welfare system would appear to be a highly problematic concept. Social workers clearly can transform themselves into therapists and counsellors and sell their services to those capable of paying for them in the private market. They can also become social entrepreneurs in a privatised welfare system, where social care is offered on a commercial basis. There are also opportunities in the not-for-profit voluntary sector to provide social services within a market context. Social workers can harness the innovative potential arising from such private–public partnerships in a manner that seeks to blend market realities with humanistic values. But there are inherent tensions in the concept of consumerist social work. As Clarke (1998: 47) puts it: 'At the core of these arguments is the tension between entitlements to being treated as a full and active citizen as opposed to being treated as a diminished person with "special needs".' More fundamentally, consumerist social work is divorced from social citizenship rights. At best service users can avail of procedural rights by recourse to law, if they can afford it. Market values and social work are inherently conflictual. This has pushed some social workers towards suggesting radical resistance.

Radical resistance: social work as political action

A radical resistance approach to marketisation, informed by what Mullaly (1997: 127) calls a conflict perspective, involves two imperatives: (1) to provide practical humanitarian care to the casualties of a global capitalist social order; and (2) at the same time, to further the democratisation and restructuring of society along socialist lines. However, it is difficult to see how social work can carry on radical resistance within a nation state that is either privatising social services or operating quasi-markets. It seems axiomatic that radical resistance has to be carried on outside the state in civil society. Mullaly's (1997) advocacy of socialism as a transformative strategy in postmodern conditions is questioned by some commentators. Naomi Klein, a key figure in the anti-globalisation movement, argues that it deserves 'the chance to see if, out of the movement's chaotic decentralised multi-headed webs, something new, something entirely its own can emerge' (*Guardian Weekend*, 23 September 2000).

Hugman (1998: 120) cautions: 'Yet the success of New Right governments in reconstructing the welfare state through the reduction of the direct role of the state in funding and provision raises questions about the extent to which prole-tarianisation as a strategy can enable caring professions to be effective in their opposition'. It seems likely that the main theatre of radical resistance in post-modern conditions lies outside the state, in community action, welfare rights work, co-operatives, self-help groups and organisations dedicated to building an ethical civil society. Moreover, as events at Seattle in 1999 and Prague in 2000 suggest, radical resistance is increasingly taking a globalised form. This has positive features in terms of harnessing international professional co-operation for change.

Beck (1997: 157) observes: 'professions are de facto agents in a global society of specialists and this real existing supranationality predestines them to be agents of global solutions'. Beck's point is an important one. Professions clearly have a global role: they have the power to influence the global agenda. As Beck (1997: 156) puts it:

> Vocations and professions – understood as 'brand name products' on the labour market, as commodity like, licensed competence – are the guardians of a certain form of nor-malised subpolitics. Personal-social identity is tied in these 'labour force patterns' to the right and duty to arrange the substance of work. Occupational groups possess the productive intelligence and the power to arrange things in society.

Social work has an important global role to play in defending human rights and promoting solutions to world poverty.

Global social work must therefore address both human rights and the economic issues that lie at the root of injustice. Mullaly (1997: 129–130) distinguishes between radical humanists who aim to change consciousness along Frierean lines and radical structuralists who seek to transform the social structure through politi-cal mobilisation. However, he concludes that they are two sides of a coin: 'In short, structural social work incorporates both these radical traditions into its theory base, recognising that they constitute a dialectical whole rather than distinct and contradictory approaches' (1997: 131).

There is a further issue that devolves on the question of the basis of radical resistance. Should it be focused on economic issues based upon class and regional inequalities? Or should it also take a cultural form shaped by the ideas of critical multiculturalism and anti-oppressive practice? Feminism, anti-racism, and the movements for gay rights, disability equality challenge fixed identities. Radical resistance activities on the part of social workers would need to destabilise culturally based inequalities that assign stereotypical identities to and practise discrimination against minority groups. But they also need to expose global economic inequalities and the exploitation of labour in the Third World. Finally, radical resistance in a global context involves defining global civil society through the use of professionalism as political action in the interest of the poor and oppressed. Ultimately, this is a question of social inclusion and the nation state is likely to remain the main theatre of action. This gives social work a vital civic role.

Social inclusion: civic social work

Social inclusion as a strategy for social work is based upon an approach to practice that seeks to empower service users as citizens. Social work's capacity to survive depends upon its legitimacy as an authentic 'humanistic voice', rather than simply a conservative profession conveniently wrapping itself in the rhetoric of the market. A global strategy based upon radical resistance to market forces would not protect social work from the challenge of *clientisation* within the nation state. Brown (1997: 102) points out that: 'It has long been recognised that the process of clientisation is a distinctly modern form of state power that has threatened the citizen's position'.

In spite of strong resistance from radical social work practitioners to clientisation and dependency, the structures and practices within social services organisations nonetheless reproduce relations of inequality that disempower the most vulnerable citizens in society. Whilst the values of social work are humanistic, an unequal relationship of service provider and client-recipient are inherent in its discursive structure, predominantly based upon the individualisation of social problems. The challenge of postmodernity is to break out of this mould of clientisation and dependency and discover more inclusive forms of practice that reconstruct clients as equal citizens. The UN Commissioner for Human Rights, Mary Robinson has observed that equality and participation are synonymous. Robinson (2000: 5–6) asserted:

> The most important tool in tackling inequality is to enable those experiencing it to remedy the power relationship, to take some control. This is a concept of rights that requires that those who are furthest from the cabinet table own the rights that inhere to them by virtue solely of their humanity. Ownership of this kind enables them to describe their condition, then to challenge it, and then to ensure that any decisions taken in the organisation and the ordering of their lives are made 'by and with' them, not 'about and for' them....
>
> So what links the concept of equality to the practice of rights? I would suggest that the concept, practice and understanding of participation is a basic right. This is core to an understanding of active citizenship, and an understanding of how the relationship between the public body and the individual enables the individual or group to dialogue with the powerful on some basis of equality. This is at the core of this issue.

It is the basic contention of this study that the reconstruction of the client as citizen provides the basis for a civic approach to social work designed to empower service users. Social work in postmodern society needs to be informed by civic values. It replaces traditional professional codes of practice based upon clientisation and dependency by civic values based upon principles that are democratic, inclusive and communitarian. It is designed to respond reflexively to postmodern realities. This involves changes in attitudes, working methods and training approaches adapted to the requirements of civic engagement.

Postmodernists have sought to deconstruct our understanding of what it means to be human. We have noted that various strands within postmodernism, such as feminism and queer theory, have challenged the precepts of liberalism and social democracy, by arguing that the 'personal is political'. The private spaces of social life, first opened to public scrutiny by pioneer social workers in the Victorian era, have become the battleground of cultural politics. Radical democrats espousing the fragmented causes of identity politics have been joined by neo-conservatives in challenging the hegemonic influences of liberalism, social democracy and the nation state. The great metanarratives of the pursuit of human emancipation through social politics and pluralism through diversity and individual choice have lost their persuasive force in postmodern discourse. The politics of postmodernity has reshaped political discourse into an interplay between human subjectivities and the state. This reflexive process is continuously reinventing political issues in new forms, new debates and new subjectivities. Postmodern consciousness has transformed established meanings and relationships between the family, civil society and the state into an anti-bureaucratic and anti-clientist form, based upon the democratic value of the citizen's right to participate.

Vaclav Havel (1999: 54) has powerfully captured the challenges to both civic life and the concept of citizenship posed by postmodern society:

> The dictatorship of money, of profit, of constant economic growth, and the necessity, flowing from all that, of plundering the earth without regard for what will be left in a few decades, along with everything else related to the materialistic obsessions of this world, from the flourishing of selfishness to the need to evade personal responsibility by becoming part of the herd, and the general inability of human conscience to keep pace with the inventions of reason, right up to the alienation created by the sheer size of modern institutions – all of these are phenomena that cannot effectively be confronted except through a new moral effort, that is, through a transformation of the spirit and the human relationship to life and the world.

This observation underlines the importance of civic life in formulating a future in which 'the only kind of politics that makes sense is a politics that grows out of the imperative, and the need to live as everyone ought to live and therefore – to put it somewhat dramatically – to bear responsibility for the entire world' (Havel, 1999: 54)

Social work has defined itself in two ways over time. First, those who advocate a social contract vision promote the state and traditional voluntary organisations as providing an enabling relationship in which the needy are helped. Second, those who seek to promote human emancipation believe that only by changing the social structure can the political and economic basis of inequality and injustice be successfully tackled. Postmodernism challenges the basis of both these visions of social work, inviting its reinvention in new reflexive forms of citizenship. The survival of social work in postmodern society is about a search for new paradigms, designed to empower the socially excluded, in a discursive shift that reconstructs practice as civic engagement and the client as citizen.

Mouffe (1993: 20) observes:

> Our societies are confronted with a proliferation of political spaces which are radically new and different and which demand that we abandon the idea of a unique constitutive space of the constitution of the political, which is particular to both liberalism and civic republicanism.

Spatial discourses, encompassing both material and metaphorical meanings, have become commonplace in the social sciences and cultural studies in recent years. Yet, as noted in Chapter 2, social work originated in the construction of 'new spaces' or sites of social intervention in Victorian society. These spaces had geographical, sociological and political dimensions. They devolved upon the spheres of the state, civil society and the family that constitute the basis of political discourse in liberal democracies. The focus was on the city as the fulcrum of urban industrial society. It became the site of civic life that interacted with social life, producing modern society with its town halls, social services and public amenities. The city became the localised expression of the nation state. Within these spaces social democracy was constituted. The nationalisation of social work by the welfare state largely depended on the local state to deliver the personal social services. The hollowing out of the welfare state has produced a cultural shift, leading to a renaissance of civil society as a discursive site and space for social action in an increasingly globalised world.

Social citizenship required that society expand its horizons of recognition and treat people, who had previously been disregarded, as equals. This has been one of the primary cultural influences upon welfare and explains why modern social work has always partly been an inclusionary project. However, the effect of citizenship has been ambivalent as the welfare state is designed not only to include the marginalised, but also to define their 'conditional' status as citizens: hence the persistence of discrimination. Marxist states in Eastern Europe were characterised by their exclusionary treatment of vulnerable groups (orphaned children, the disabled, gypsies, etc.).

Postmodernity has witnessed a cultural shift in attitudes towards the poor and oppressed that has been evident since the 1970s. Social policy, under the influence of the New Right, is increasingly being used, not for the benefit of those who are thought to be conditional citizens, with a view to their rehabilitation and inclusion, but against those who are increasingly regarded as non-citizens, to punish and exclude them. Vaughan (2000: 35) notes:

> Traditional ideas of citizenship are challenged by such developments and currently punishment is being deployed to shore up citizenship through the exclusion of marginalised members and immigrants. If we look at the use of custody in England and Wales in 1997, there was an increase in the use of custody of 19 per cent for female prisoners and 16 per cent for young male prisoners. Furthermore, 85 per cent of non-criminal prisoners were held under the 1971 Immigration Act.

Punishment has replaced welfare for the marginalised in this world of exclusion and disenfranchisement.

The concept of citizenship opens up a new site for social work practice. In this context the traditional conflict between capitalism and socialism is moved on to new ground. In essence, the struggle of the poor and oppressed is against social exclusion, which can be defined as the absence of social, cultural and political rights. Civic social work is defined by a concern for the rights and needs of citizens. Ten core principles can be distilled from civic social work practice that promote citizenship as a site for practice:

1 **Social inclusion:** There needs to be a clear focus on social inclusion in social work practice that makes it the stated aim of the profession. Professional associations ought to place social inclusion at the heart of their agenda in a reconstructed value base grounded in the concept of civic engagement and citizen empowerment.

2 **Redefining risk:** Social work must reconstruct the language of risk from its current focus on danger and risk management into a vocabulary geared to the promotion of equal citizenship rights that balances rights and risks. This involves placing risk in its social and cultural context, challenging society's limited concept of victimhood.

3 **Trust as symbolic practice:** Social work should promote trust as a symbolic practice through the construction of relationships with service users based upon social inclusion. Trust is constructed through talk and action based upon the principle of equality. This means taking risks for trust. Casualties of misplaced trust will typically be referred to as 'innocent victims' of social work incompetence by the media.

4 **Dialogical relationship:** Social workers committed to promoting trust as symbolic practice need to engage in a dialogical relationship with service users. Problem-solving is replaced by problem-posing in a reflective process, where critical reflection and action are unified in democratic praxis between equal citizens.

5 **Justice, decency and social obligation:** Social work represents a response to society's obligation to respond to the needs of its most vulnerable citizens. It can take both voluntary and professional forms and be pursued within a welfare pluralist context involving the state and civil society.

6 **Promotion of civil society:** Social work in postmodern society ought to be practised in a manner that harnesses community and voluntary initiative, with a view to promoting partnership and sustainable social development. Practitioners, managers and educators need to recognise and appreciate the scale and challenge of the task involved. It implies a discursive shift from individualisation (the basis of clientisation) towards communitarian approaches to practice that promote citizenship.

7 **User participation and empowerment:** The process of users participating as active citizens in shaping community-based initiatives and solutions is vitally important in an empowerment strategy that aims to help the poor and oppressed. This is the essence of the historic mission of social work as civic engagement in a democratic society. It is the antithesis of the competency movement, which removes professional discretion in hierarchical management regimes detached from civic life.

8 **Multiculturalism:** New social movements have had a profound impact on society as a whole and social work in particular. The politics of recognition that lies at the core of a multicultural vision is essential to social work practice that is genuinely transformative.

9 **Poverty proofing and social audits:** Service providers need to continuously assess their policies and procedures to ensure that resources are employed in the most effective manner to benefit citizens and prevent social exclusion.

They need to directly involve practitioners and service users in exercises that go to the heart of democratic accountability and civic engagement.

10 **Public mandate:** The onus is on the government and society to ensure that social work is supported with the necessary resources and given the legitimacy to carry out its public mandate: the civic nature of social work must be recognised. Without this endorsement social work does not have a future. Similarly, if social work is perceived by service users as disempowering, its public mandate will be undermined, since it will have no legitimacy on the ground because its purpose and activities lack trust and community support. Social work requires not only top-down legitimacy but also bottom-up legitimacy.

These are the core principles required by civic social work. It is an invitation to reinvent the historic mission of social work in the vernacular of the times. Hugman (1998: 77) observes:

> Professionalism in this sense can be seen as 'ideas in conversation with context'. Values are the language of this conversation and fluency requires that such language is capable of grasping the complexities faced in practice. It is for this reason that decontextualised formal ethical codes are no longer seen as sufficient.

Conclusion

The challenges faced by social work at the beginning of the twenty-first century are real and formidable. Social work is being impelled into a new orbit defined by an economic imperative or civic mandate. Social work must choose not simply between positivism and humanism but between marketisation, radical resistance or reconstruction if it is to become a vibrant civic force in postmodern society. The marketised option suggests the end of social work as a manifestation of voluntarism or social reform through social citizenship and statutory responsibility. Radical resistance involves tapping into a long tradition of radical social work and applying it in a global context. Social inclusion involves a reassertion of social work's mandate in the conditions and vernacular of postmodernity.

References

Abel-Smith, B. and Townsend, P. (1965) *The Poor and the Poorest*, Bell, London.

Albrow, M. (1996) *The Global Age*, Polity, Cambridge.

Alden, P. (1928) *Proceedings of the First International Conference of Social Work*, Vol. 1. Paris.

Alinsky, S. (1971) *Rules for Radicals*, Random House, New York.

Allan, G. (1997) Family, in M. Davies (ed.) *The Blackwell Companion to Social Work*, Blackwell, Oxford.

Arendt, H. (1958) *Origins of Totalitarianism*, 2nd edn, Meridan Books, New York.

Bailey, R. and Brake, M. (eds) (1975) *Radical Social Work*, Edward Arnold, London.

Barber, B.J. (1998) More Democracy! More Revolution! *The Nation*, 26 October.

Barclay, P. (1982) *Social Workers: Their Role and Tasks*, Bedford Square Press, London.

Barnes, M. (1998) Whose Needs, Whose Resources? Accessing Social Care, in Mary Langan (ed.) *Welfare: Needs, Rights and Risks*, Routledge, London.

Barnett, S. (1895) A Friendly Criticism of the Charity Organisation Society, *The Charity Organisation Review*, 127, August.

Barnett, S. (1898) On University Settlements, in W.H. Reason (ed.) *University and Social Settlements*, Methuen, London.

Bauman, Z. (1992) *Intimations of Postmodernity*, Routledge, London.

Bauman, Z. (2000) Am I my Brother's Keeper?, *European Journal of Social Work*, 3(1), 5–11.

Beck, U. (1992) *Risk Society*, Sage, London.

Beck, U. (1997) *The Reinvention of Politics*, Polity, Cambridge.

Beck, U., Giddens, A. and Lash, S. (1994) *Reflexive Modernisation*, Polity, Cambridge.

Bell, L. and Wilder, G. (1969) *Area Development Project*, ADC Research Minograph III, Vancouver.

Bentham, J. (1797) *Pauper Management Improved*, London.

Berking, H. (1996) Solidary Individualism, in Lash, S., Szerszynski, B. and Wynne, B. (eds) *Risk, Environment and Modernity*, Sage, London.

Beveridge, W.H. (1942) *Social Insurance and Allied Services*, HMSO Cmnd. 6404, London.

Bicheno, J.E. (1830) *Ireland and Its Economy*, London.

Billis, D. and Harris, M. (1996) *Voluntary Agencies: Challenges of Organisation and Management*, Macmillan, London.

Blum, L. (1998) Recognition, Value and Equality, in C. Willet (ed.) *Theorising Multi-culturalism*, Blackwell, Oxford.

Bobbio, N. (1996) *Left and Right: The Significance of a Political Distinction*, Polity, Cambridge.

Booth, C. (1904) *Life and Labour of the People of London*, Macmillan, London. •

Booth, T. (1997) Language Difficulties, in M. Davies (ed.) *The Blackwell Companion to Social Work*, Blackwell, Oxford.

Booth, W. (1890) *In Darkest England and the Way Out*, London International Headquarters of the Salvation Army.

Borrie Report (1994) *Commission on Social Justice*, Vintage, London.

Bourdieu, P. (1998) *Acts of Resistance*, Polity, Cambridge.

Bowlby, J. (1952) *Maternal Care and Mental Health*, WHO, Geneva.

Bradley, H. (1996) *Fractured Identities: Changing Patterns of Inequality*, Polity, New York.

Brewer, C. and Lait, J. (1980) *Can Social Work Survive*? Temple Smith, London.

Brock Report (1934) *Report of the Committee on Sterilisation*, HMSO, Cmnd. 4485, London.

Brown, M. (1997) *Replacing Citizenship*, Guildford Press, New York.

Bruce, M. (1968) *The Coming of the Welfare State*, Batsford, London.

Burden, T. (1998) *Social Policy and Welfare: A Clear Guide*, Pluto Press, London.

Burke, B. and Harrison, P. (1998) Anti-oppressive practice, in R. Adams, L. Dominelli and M. Payne (eds) *Social Work: Themes, Issues and Critical Debates,* Macmillan, London.

Burke, E. (1790) *Reflections on the French Revolution*, London.

Butrym, Z. (1976) *The Nature of Social Work*, Macmillan, London.

Byrne, P. (1997) *Social Movements in Britain*, Routledge, London.

Cabinet Office (1998) *Service First: The New Charter Programme, http://www.open.cabinet-office.gov.uk/charter/list.htm*

Campbell, B. (1993) *Goliath: Britain's Dangerous Places*, Lime Tree, London.

Carmen, R. (1990) *Communication, Education and Empowerment*, University of Manchester Press, Manchester.

CCETSW (1989) *Rules and Requirements for Diploma in Social Work* (Paper 30), CCETSW, London.

CCETSW (1995) *Rules and Requirements for Diploma in Social Work* (Paper 30 revised), CCETSW, London.

Chomsky, N. (1996) *Class Warfare*, Pluto Press, London.

Clarke, J. (1996) After Social Work, in N. Parton (ed.) *Social Theory, Social Change and Social Work*, Routledge, London.

Clarke, J. (1998) Consumerism, in G. Hughes (ed.) *Imagining Welfare Futures*, Routledge, London.

Clough, M. (1999) *Reflections on Civil Society, The Nation*, 22 February.

Cloward, R. and Ohlin, L. (1960) *Delinquency and Opportunity*, Free Press, New York.

Cloward, R. and Piven, F.F. (1982) *The New Class War*, Random House, New York.

Cloward, R. and Piven, F.F. (1990) Introduction to D. Wagner, *The Quest for a Radical Profession*, University Press of America, Lanham.

Cohen, R. (1995) Capitalism Brings Rich Pickings, *Washington Post/Guardian Weekly*, 30 April.

Cohen, S. (1985) *Visions of Social Control*, Polity, Cambridge.

Cohen, J. and Arato, A. (1992) *Civil Society and Political Theory*, MIT Press, Cambridge, MA.

Cole, G.D. and Postgate, R. (1961) *The Common People*, London, Methuen.

Combat Poverty (1995) *Working Together against Poverty: an Information Pack on the Community Development Programme*, Combat Poverty/Dept of Social Welfare, Dublin.

Cooper, D. (1970) *Psychiatry and Anti-Psychiatry*, Paladin, St Albans.

Cooper, D. (ed.) (1986) *The Dialectics of Liberation*, Penguin, Harmondsworth.

Cork Northside Education Initiative (1995) *Making Education Work on Cork's Northside: A Strategy Statement*, Northside Education Initiative, Cork.

Corrigan, P. and Leonard, P. (1978) *Social Work Practice under Capitalism: A Marxist Approach*, Macmillan, London.

Costin, L.B. (1979) *Child Welfare*, 2nd edn, McGraw Hill, New York.

Coughlin, R. (1980) *Ideology, Public Opinion and Welfare Policy*, Berkeley, University of California Press.

Croft, S. and Beresford, P. (1997) *Service Users' Perspective*, in M. Davies, *The Blackwell Companion to Social Work*, Blackwell, Oxford.

Crook, S., Pakulski, J.G. and Waters, M. (1992) *Postmodernisation: Change in Advanced Society*, Sage, London.

Culpitt, I. (1992) *Welfare and Citizenship*. Sage, London.

Dahrendorf, R. (1994) The Changing Quality of Citizenship, in B. Van Steenbergen (ed.) *The Condition of Citizenship*, Sage, London.

Dahrendorf, R. (1995) *Report on Wealth, Creation and Social Cohesion in a Free Society*, Commission on Wealth and Social Cohesion, London.

Dalley, G. (1996) *Ideologies of Caring*, Macmillan, London.

Davies, M. (1981) *The Essential Social Worker: A Guide to Positive Practice*, Heinemann, London.

Delahaye, V. (1994) *Politiques de lutte contre de chomage et l'exclusion et mutation de l'action sociale*, Ecole Nationale d'Administration, Paris.

Demos (1997) *The Wealth and Poverty of Networks*, Demos Collection 12, London.

Department of Health (1995) *Child Protection: Messages from Research*, Department of Health, London.

Department of Social Welfare (1997) *Green Paper on the Community and Voluntary Sector and its relationship with the state*, Department of Social Welfare, Dublin.

De Tocqueville, A. (1956) Democracy in America, ed. R.D. Heffner, Mentor, New York.

Dominelli, L. (1988) *Anti-Racist Social Work*, Macmillan, London.

Dominelli, L. (1997) *Sociology for Social Work*, Macmillan, London.

Dominelli, L. and McLeod, E. (1989) *Feminist Social Work*, Macmillan, London.

Donzelot, J. (1979) *The Policing of Families*, Hutchinson, London.

Dworkin, R. (1982) *Taking Rights Seriously*, Duckworth, London.

Elsen, S. and Wallimann, I. (1998) Social Economy: Community Action towards Social Integration and the Prevention of Unemployment and Poverty, *European Journal of Social Work*, 1(2), 151–164.

Engels, F. (1845) *The Condition of the Working Class in England*, reprinted 1987, Penguin, Harmondsworth.

Esping-Andersen, G. (1990) *The Three Worlds of Welfare Capitalism*, Polity, Cambridge.

Etzioni, A. (1994) *The Spirit of the Community*, Touchstone, New York.

Etzioni, A. (1997) *The New Golden Rule: Community and Morality in a Democratic Society*, Profile Books, London.

European Union (1993) *Green Paper: European Social Policy – Options for Union*, EU, Com. (93) 55, 1, Brussels/Luxembourg.

European Union (1996) *Report by the Comité des Sages for a Europe of Civil and Social Rights*, European Commission, Luxembourg.

Evans, D. (1997) Demonstrating Competence in Social Work, in M. Davies (ed.) *The Blackwell Companion to Social Work*, Blackwell, Oxford.

Ferguson, H. (1996) The Protection of Children in Time, *Child and Family Social Work*, 1(4), 205–217.

Ferguson, H. (1997) Protecting Children in New Times: Child Protection and Risk Society, *Child and Family Social Work*, 2, 221–234.

Fong, R., Spickard, P. and Ewalt, P. (1996) A Multicultural Reality: Issues for Social Work, in P. Ewalt, E. Freeman, S. Kirk and D. Poole (eds) *Multicultural Issues in Social Work*, NASW Press, Washington.

Fook, J. (1993) *Radical Casework: A Theory of Practice*, Allen and Unwin, Sydney.

Foucault, M. (1967) *Madness and Civilisation*, Tavistock, London.

Foucault, M. (1977) *Discipline and Punish*, Penguin Books, London.

Foucault, M. (1980) *Power/Knowledge*, Harvester, Sussex.

Fraser, D. (1973) *The Evolution of the British Welfare State*, Macmillan, London.

Fraser, N. (1997) *Justice Interruptus*, Routledge, London.

Friedan, B. (1965) *The Feminine Mystique*, Penguin, Harmondsworth.

Friedlander, W. and Apte, R. (1980) *Introduction to Social Welfare*, Prentice Hall, Englewood Cliffs, NJ.

Friere, P. (1972) *Pedagogy of the Oppressed*, Penguin, Harmondsworth.

Friere, P. (1973) *Cultural Action for Freedom*, Penguin, Harmondsworth.

Fromm, E. (1961) *Marx's Concept of Man*, Frederick Ungar, New York.

Fuentes, A. (1998) The Crackdown on Kids, *The Nation*, 15 June.

Fukuyama, F. (1995) *Trust: The Social Virtues and the Creation of Prosperity*, Hamish Hamilton, London.

Galjart, B. (1995) Counter-Development: Possibilities and Constraints, in G. Craig and M. Mayo (eds). *Community Empowerment*, Zed Books, London.

Galper, J. (1975) *The Politics of Social Services*, Prentice Hall, Englewood Cliffs, New Jersey.

Galper, J. (1980) *Social Work Practice: A Radical Perspective*, Englewood Cliffs, NJ, Prentice-Hall.

Gans, H. (1996) From 'Underclass' to 'Undercaste', in E. Mingione (ed.), *Urban Poverty and the Underclass*, Blackwell, Oxford.

Geismar, L. and Kriesberg, J. (1969) *The Forgotten Neighbourhood*, Scarecrow Press, Metuchen, NJ.

Gellner, E. (1994) *Conditions of Liberty: Civil Society and its Rivals*, Hamish Hamilton, London.

Giarchi, G. and Lankshear, G. (1998) The Eclipse of Social Work in Europe, *Social Work in Europe*, 5(3), 25–36.

Giddens, A. (1989) *Sociology*, Polity, Cambridge.

Giddens, A. (1991) *Modernity and Self-Identity*, Polity, Cambridge.

Giddens, A. (1998) *The Third Way*, Polity, Cambridge.

Giddens, A. (1999) *Runaway World*, BBC Reith Lecture Series, BBC, London.

Gilder, G. (1981) *Wealth and Poverty*, Bantam Books, London.

Gingrich, N. (1994) *Contract with America*, Random House, New York.

Ginsberg, N. (1979) *Class, Capital and Social Policy*, Macmillan, London.

Goffman, E. (1968) *Asylums*, Penguin, Harmondsworth.

Goldberg, D. (1994) *Multiculturalism: A Critical Reader*, Blackwell, Oxford.

Goodlad, R. (1993) *The Housing Authority as Enabler*, Institute of Housing, Coventry.

Gough, I. (1979) *The Political Economy of the Welfare State*, Macmillan, London.

Gould, K. (1996) The Misconstruing of Multiculturalism: the Stanford Debate and Social Work, in P. Ewalt, E. Freeman, S. Kirk and D. Poole (eds) *Multicultural Issues in Social Work*, NASW Press, Washington.

Gray, J. (1998) Medicine or Symptom, *Times Literary Supplement*, 10 July.

Green, D.G. (1993) *Reinventing Civil Society*, Institute of Economic Affairs, London.

Greer, G. (1971) *The Female Eunuch*, Paladin, London.

Habermas, J. (1984) *Theory of Communicative Competence*, Beacon Press, Boston.

Habermas, J. (1987) *The Theory of Communicative Action*, Vol. 2, Polity, Cambridge.

Habermas, J. (1989) *The New Conservatism*, Polity, Cambridge.

Habermas, J. (1996) *The Habermas Reader* (ed. W. Outhwaite), Polity, Cambridge.

Hadley, R. and McGrath, M. (1980) *Patch Based Social Services*, Lancaster University Press, Lancaster.

Hall, P. (1952) *The Social Services in Modern England*, Routledge and Kegan Paul, London.

Hall, S. (1998) The Great Moving Nowhere Show, *Marxism Today*, November/December.

Hann, C. and Dunne, E. (1996) *Civil Society: Challenging Western Models*, Routledge, London.

Hardcastle, D., Wenocur, S. and Powers, P. (1997) *Community Practice: Theories and Skills for Social Workers*, Oxford University Press, New York.

Harrington, M. (1962) *The Other America*, Macmillan, New York.

Harris, J. (1993) *Private Lives, Public Spirit: A Social History of Britain 1870–1914*, Oxford University Press, Oxford.

Harris, J. (1999) Social Work Sent to Market, in B. Lesnik (ed.), *Social Work and the State*, Pavilion Publishing, Brighton.

Havel, V. (1999) Paying Back the West, *The New York Review*, 23 September.

Haveman, R. and Schwabish, J. (1999) Economic Growth and Poverty: A Return to Normalcy? *Focus*, 20(2), Spring, 1–7.

Hayek, F. (1976) *The Mirage of Social Justice*, Routledge and Kegan Paul, London.

Healy, K. (2000) *Social Work Practices*, Sage, London.

Healy, S. (1990) *Must the Poor Always Wait?*, CORI, Dublin.

Heywood, J. (1978) *Children in Care* (3rd edition), Routledge and Kegan Paul, London.

Hill, O. (1901) The Relations between Rich and Poor as Bearing on Pauperism, *Charity Organisation Review*, 54 June.

Hoggett, P. (1994) The Future of Civic Forms of Organisation, Working Paper No. 4, Demos, London.

Holman, R. (1992) *Family Centres*, Highlight, National Children's Bureau, London.

Holmes, S. (1993) *The Anatomy of Antiliberalism*, Harvard University Press, Cambridge, Mass.

Home Office (1980) *Young Offenders*, Cmnd. 3045, HMSO, London.

Home Office (1990) *Efficiency Scrutiny of Government Funding of Voluntary Sector: Profiting from Partnership*, Home Office, London.

Home Office (1998) *Compact on Relations between Government and the Voluntary and Community Sector in England*, Cmnd. 4100, Stationery Office, London.

Howe, D. (1994) Modernity, Postmodernity and Social Work, *British Journal of Social Work*, 24(5), 513–532.

Hughes, G. (ed.) (1998) *Imagining Welfare Futures*, Routledge, London.

Hughes, G., Clarke, J., Lewis, G. and Mooney, G. (1998) Reinventing the Public?, in G. Hughes (ed.) *Imagining Welfare Futures*, Routledge, London.

Hughes, G. and Mooney, G. (1998) Community, in G. Hughes (ed.) *Imagining Welfare Futures*, Routledge, London.

Hugman, R. (1998) *Social Welfare and Social Value*, Macmillan, London.

Humphreys, P.C. (1998) *Improving Public Service Delivery*, IPA, Dublin.

Ife, J. (1997) *Rethinking Social Work*, Longman, Melbourne.

Ignatieff, M. (1999) Human Rights: the Midlife Crisis, *The New York Review*, 20 May.

Illich, I. (1973) *Deschooling Society*, Penguin, Harmondsworth.

Illich, I., Zola, L., McKnight, J., Laplam, J. and Harley, S. (1970) *Disabling Professions*, Boyars, London.

Jones, C. (1983) *State Social Work and the Working Class*, Macmillan, London.

Jones, C. (1997) Poverty, in M. Davies (ed.) *The Blackwell Companion to Social Work*, Blackwell, Oxford.

Jones, C. (1998) Social Work and Society, in R. Adams, L. Dominelli and M. Payne, *Social Work: Themes, Issues and Critical Debates*. Macmillan, London.

Jones, C. and Novak, T. (1999) *Poverty, Welfare and the Disciplinary State*, Routledge, London.

Jordan, B. (1984) *Invitation to Social Work*, Martin Robertson, Oxford.

Jordan, B. (1990) Social Work in an Unjust Society, Harvester, Hemel Hempstead.

Jordan, B. (1996) *A Theory of Poverty and Social Exclusion*, Polity, Cambridge.

Jordan, B. (1997) Social Work and Society, in M. Davies (ed.) *The Blackwell Companion to Social Work*, Blackwell, Oxford.

Keane, J. (1988) *Democracy and Civil Society*, Verso, London.

Keane, J. (1998) *Civil Society: Old Images, New Visions*, Polity, Cambridge.

Kilbrandon Report (1964) Committee on Children and Young Persons (Scotland), HMSO Cmnd. 2306.

Knight, B. (1993) *Voluntary Action,* Home Office, London.

Kramer, R. (1981) *Voluntary Agencies in the Welfare State*, University of California Press, Berkeley.

Lagey, J. and Ayres, B. (1962) *Community Treatment Programmes for Multi-Problem Families*, Community Chest and Council, Vancouver.

Laing, R.D. (1965) *The Divided Self*, Penguin, Harmondsworth.

Laing, R.D. (1969) *Self and Others*, Penguin, Harmondsworth.

Landry, C. and Mulgan, G. (1995) *The Other Invisible Hand: Remaking Charity for the 21st Century*, DEMOS, London.

Lane, M. (1999) Community Development and a Postmodern Resistance, in B. Pearse and J. Fook, *Transforming Social Work Practice*, Routledge, London.

Langan, M.G. and Lee, P. (eds) (1989) *Radical Social Work Today*, Routledge, London.

Laxton, M. (1976) *Time to Consider*, Family Service Units Occasional Paper, London.

Layburn, K. (1995) *The Evolution of British Social Policy and the Welfare State*, Keele University Press, Keele.

Lee, P. and Raban, C. (1988) *Welfare Theory and Social Policy*, Sage, London.

Lees, R. (1970) Social Work, 1925–50: the Case for a Reappraisal, *British Journal of Social Work*, 1(4), 371–379.

Leissner, A. (1967) *Family Advice Centres*, Longman/National Children's Bureau, London.

Leissner, A. et al. (1971) *Advice, Guidance and Assistance*, Longman, London.

Lemann, N. (1986) The Origins of the Underclass, *The Atlantic Monthly*, June.

Lenroot, K. (1936) *Proceedings of Third International Conference of Social Work*, London.

Leonard, P. (1975) Towards a Paradigm for Radical Practice, in R. Bailey and M. Brake (eds) *Radical Social Work*, Pantheon, New York.

Leonard, P. (1997) *Postmodern Welfare: Reconstructing an Emancipation Project*, Sage, London.

Lesnik, B. (ed.) (1999) *Social Work and the State*, Pavilion Publishing, Brighton.

Levi, P. *If this is a Man*, Touchstone, New York.

Levitas, R. (1998) *The Inclusive Society?*, Macmillan, London.

Lewis, G. (1998a) *Forming Nation, Framing Welfare*, Routledge, London.

Lewis, G. (1998b) Citizenship, in M. Hughes (ed.) *Imagining Welfare Futures*, London, Routledge.

Lewis, J. (1996) What Does Contracting Do to Voluntary Organisations? in D. Billis and M. Harris, *Voluntary Agencies*, Macmillan, London.

Lewis, J. (1998) Feminist Perspectives, in *The Student's Companion to Social Policy*, ed. P. Alcock, A. Erskine and M. May, Blackwell, Oxford.

Lewis, J. (1999) Reviewing the Relationship between the Voluntary Sector and the State in Britain in the 1990s, *Voluntas*, 10(3), 225–270.

Liffman, M. (1978) *Power for the People*, Allen and Unwin, Sydney.

Lis, C. and Soly, H. (1979) *Poverty and Capitalism in Pre-Industrial Europe*, Harvester, Sussex.

Lishman, J. (1998) Personal and Professional Development, in R. Adams, L. Dominelli and M. Payne (eds) *Social Work: Themes, Issues and Critical Debates*, Macmillan, London.

Lister, R. (1997) *Citizenship: Feminist Perspectives*, Macmillan, London.

Lister, R. (1998) Citizenship on the Margins: Citizenship, Social Work and Social Action, *European Journal of Social Work*, 1(1), 5–18.

Loney, M. (1980) Community Action and Anti-Poverty Strategies, *Community Development Journal*, 15(2), 91–103.

Longford Committee, *The Child, the Family, and the Young Offender*, CMND 2742, HMSO, London.

Lorenz, W. (1994) *Social Work in a Changing Europe*, Routledge, London.

Lorenz, W. (1999) Introduction to B. Lesnik (ed.) *Social Work and the State*, Pavilion Publishing, Brighton.

Malthus, T. (1796) *Essay on the Principle of Population*, London.

Marcuse, H. (1968) Liberation from the Affluent Society, in D. Cooper (ed.) *Dialectics of Liberation*, Penguin, Harmondsworth.

Marris, P. and Rein, M. (1972) *Dilemmas in Social Reform*, Penguin, London.

Marshall, T.H. (1950) *Citizenship and Social Class*, Cambridge University Press, Cambridge.

Marshall, T.H. (1973) *Class, Citizenship and Social Development*, Greenwood, Westport, CT.

Marsland, D. (1995) *Self-Reliance*, Transaction Books, New Brunswick, NJ.

Marsland, D. (1996) *Welfare or Welfare State?* Macmillan, London.

Martin, B. (1998) Multiculturalism: Consumerist or Transformational? in C. Willet (ed.) *Theorising Multiculturalism*, Blackwell, Oxford.

Martin, F. (1981) *Children out of Care*, Scottish Academic Press, Edinburgh.

Marx, K. (1994) *Selected Writings* (ed. L.H. Simon), Hackett Publishing Company, Indianapolis.

McLaren, P. (1994) White Terror and Oppositional Agency, in D. Goldberg (ed.) *Multiculturalism: A Critical Reader*, Blackwell, Oxford.

McLintock, A. (1995) *Imperial Leather*, Routledge, London.

Mezirow, J. (1991) *Transformative Dimensions of Adult Learning*, Jossey-Bass, San Francisco.

Midgley, J. (1997) *Social Welfare in a Global Context*, Sage, London.

Millett, K. (1971) *Sexual Politics*, Sphere, London.

Mishra, R. (1997) *Society and Social Policy*, Macmillan, London.

Mishra, R. (1999) *Globalisation and the Welfare State*, Edward Elgar, Cheltenham.

Monediaire, G. (1998) The Social Status of Social Services Occupations, *Social Work in Europe*, 5(3), 19–24.

Mooney, G. (1998) 'Remoralising' the Poor? in G. Lewis, *Forming Nation, Framing Welfare*, Routledge, London.

Moore, S. (1998) The Cultural Revolution, *Marxism Today*, November/December.

Morrison, S.M. et al. (1969) *The Growth of the American Republic*, Vol. 2 (6th edition) Oxford University Press, Oxford.

Mouffe, C. (1993) *The Return of the Political*, Verso, London.

Mowat, C.L. (1961) *The Charity Organisation Society*, Methuen, London.

Mullaly, B. (1997) *Structural Social Work*, Oxford University Press, Oxford.

Mullender, A. (1997) Gender, in M. Davies (ed.) *The Blackwell Companion to Social Work*, Blackwell, Oxford.

Mullender, A. and Perrot, S. (1998) Social Work and Organisations, in R. Adams, L. Dominelli and M. Payne (eds) *Social Work: Themes, Issues and Critical Debates*, Macmillan, London.

Murray, C. (1984) *Losing Ground: American Social Policy 1950–1980*, Basic Books, New York.

Murray, C. (1990) *The Emerging British Underclass*, Institute of Economic Affairs, London.

National Anti-Poverty Strategy (1999) *Social Inclusion Strategy: Annual Report of the Inter-Departmental Policy Committee*, Stationery Office, Dublin.

National Health Service (1971) *Report of the Farleigh Hospital Committee of Inquiry*, CMND 4557, HMSO, London.

Novak, T. (1988) *Poverty and the State*, Open University Press, Milton Keynes.

O'Connor, J. (1973) *The Fiscal Crisis in the Welfare State*, St James, New York.

O'Gorman, I. (1995) Brazilian Community Development: Challenge and Changes, in G. Craig and M. Mayo (eds) *Community Empowerment*, Zed Books, London.

O'Sullivan, D. (1993) *Commitment, Educative Action and Adults*, Avebury, Aldershot.

Offe, C. (1984) *Contradictions of the Welfare State*, Hutchinson, London.

Oliver, M. (1990) *The Politics of Disablement*, Macmillan, London.

Oliver, M. (1996) User Involvement in the Voluntary Sector, in *Summary of Evidence and Selected Papers for the Report of the Commission in the Future of the Voluntary Sector*, NCVO, London.

Onyx, J. and Benton, P. (1995) Empowerment and Agency, in G. Craig and M. Mayo (eds) *Community Empowerment*, Zed Books, London.

Oxford English Dictionary (1989) Vol. XV, Clarendon Press, Oxford.

Oxhorn, P. (1995) From Controlled Inclusion to Marginalisation, in John A. Hall, *Civil Society: Theory, History and Comparison*, Polity, Cambridge.

Parton, N. (1991) *Governing the Family: Child Care, Child Protection and the State*, Macmillan, London.

Parton, N. (1994) Problematics of Government: (Post)modernity and Social Work, *British Journal of Social Work*, 24, 9–32.

Parton, N. (1995) *The Politics of Child Abuse*, Macmillan, London.

Payne, M. (1997) *Modern Social Work Theory* (2nd edition), Macmillan, London.

Pease, B. and Fook, J. (1999) *Transforming Social Work Practice*, Routledge, London.

Phillips, M. (1993) Oppressive Urge to End Oppression, *Observer*, 1 August.

Pierson, C. (1997) *Beyond the Welfare State?*, Polity, Cambridge.

Pithouse, A. (2000) Family Centres, in M. Davies (ed.) *The Blackwell Encyclopaedia of Social Work*, Blackwell, Oxford.

Piven, F.F. and Cloward, R. (1971) *Regulating the Poor*, Vintage, New York.

Platt, T. (1969) *The Child Savers: the Invention of Delinquency*, University of Chicago Press, Chicago.

Poor Law Report (1834) *First Report from His Majesty's Commissioners on the Administration and Practical Operation of the Poor Laws in England and Wales*, Vol. 27, London.

Popple, K. (1995) *Analysing Community Work: Its Theory and Practice*, Open University Press, Buckingham.

Powell, F. (1998) Postcommunist Politics in the New Poland in R. Dingwall and A. Kwak (eds) *Social Change, Social Policy and Social Work in the New Europe*, Ashgate, Aldershot.

Pritchard, C. and Taylor, R. (1978) *Social Work: Reform or Revolution*, Routledge and Kegan Paul, London.

Putnam, R. (1993) *Making Democracy Work: Civic Traditions in Modern Italy*, Princeton University Press, Princeton, NJ.

Putnam, R. (1995) Bowling Alone: America's Declining Social Capital, *Journal of Democracy*, 96, 65–78.

Raffoul, P. (1996) Social Work and the Future, in P. Raffoul and C. McNeece, *Future Issues for Social Practice*, Alleyn and Bacon, Boston.

Raffoul, P. and McNeece, C. (1996) *Future Issues for Social Work Practice*, Alleyn and Bacon, Boston.

Rawls, J. (1971) *A Theory of Justice*, Harvard University Press, Cambridge, Mass.

Rieff, D. (1999) The False Dawn of Civil Society, *The Nation*, 22 February, 11–16.

Rein, M. (1970) Social Work in Search of a Radical Profession, *Social Work*, 15(2), 13–28.

Reisser, L. (1996) The Future of Professionalism and Activism in Social Work, in P. Raffoul and C. McNeece, *Future Issues for Social Work Practice*, Alleyn and Bacon, Boston.

Report of the Commission on the Future of the Voluntary Sector (1996) *Voluntary Action into the 21st Century*, National Council for Voluntary Organisations, London.

Ricardo, D. (1819) *Principles of Political Economy and Taxation*, London.

Richmond, M. (1917) *Social Diagnosis*, Russell Sage, New York.

Richmond, M. (1922) *What is Social Casework?*, Russell Sage, New York.

Ritzer, G. (1993) *The McDonaldization of Society*, Pine Forge Press, Thousand Oaks, CA.

Robinson, M. (2000) Equality and Rights, *Equality News*, Summer, 5–6.

Roche, J. and Tucker, S. (1997) Welfare, in *Introduction and Study Guide* K201, Open University, Milton Keynes.

Rowntree Foundation (1995) *Inquiry into Income and Wealth*, Vol. 1. Joseph Rowntree Foundation, York.

Rusche, G. and Kirchheimer, O. (1939) Punishment and Social Structure, Columbia University Press, New York.

Sainsbury, E. (1977) *The Personal Social Services*, Pitman, London.

Salamon, L. (1994) *The Global Association Revolution*, DEMOS, London.

Saleeby, D. (1990) Philosophical Disputes in Social Work, *Journal of Sociology and Social Welfare*, 17(2), 29–40.

Scull, A. (1984) *Decarceration* (2nd ed), Rutgers University Press. New Brunswick, NJ.

Scull, A. (1998) The End of Freud?, *Times Literary Supplement*, 30 October, 9–10.

Sedgwick, P. (1972) *Laing and Anti-Psychiatry*, Penguin, Harmondsworth.

Seebohm Report (1968) *Report of the Committee on Local Authority and Allied Personal Social Services*, HMSO, Cmnd. 3703.

Seed, P. (1973) *The Expansion of Social Work in Britain*, Routledge and Kegan Paul, London.

Seligman, A. (1998) *The Problem of Trust*, Princeton University Press, Princeton, NJ.

Sen, A. (1985) *Commodities and Capabilities*, New Holland, Amsterdam.

Shanahan, P. and Ward, J. (1995) The University and Empowerment, in G. Craig and M. Mayo (eds) *Community Empowerment*, Zed Books, London.

Shaw, G.B. (1896) *Report on Fabian Theory*, Fabian Tract no. 70, Fabian Society, London.

Sheridan, A. (1980) *Michel Foucault: The Will to Truth*, Tavistock, London.

Silver, H. (1996) National Discourses of the New Urban Poverty, in Enzo Mingione (ed.) *Urban Poverty and the Underclass*, Blackwell, Oxford.

Simpkin, M. (1979) *Trapped Within Welfare*, Macmillan, London.

Skidelsky, R. (1999) Doing Good and Being Good, *Times Literary Supplement*, 26 March.

Smith, A. (1776) *The Wealth of Nations*, London.

Social Exclusion Unit (1999) *Report on Rough Sleeping in England*, Cabinet Office, London.

Specht, H. and Courtney, M. (1994) *Unfaithful Angels: How social work has abandoned its mission*, Free Press, New York.

Spicker, P. (1993) *Poverty and Social Security*, Routledge, London.

Squires, P. (1990) *Anti-Social Policy*, Harvester Wheatsheaf, London.

Starkey, T. (1533) *A Dialogue*, London.

Statham, D. (1978) *Radicals in Social Work*, Routledge and Kegan Paul, London.

Stokes, P. and Knight, B. (1997) A Citizen's Charter to Save our Cities, *Independent*, 1 January.

Stubbs, P. (1999) Social Work and Civil Society in Bosnia-Herzegovina, in B. Lesnik, *Social Work and the State*, Pavilion Publishing, Brighton.

Szasz, T.S. (1962) *The Myth of Mental Illness*, Secker and Warburg, London.

Tam, H. (1998) *Communitarianism: A New Agenda for Politics and Citizenship*. Macmillan, London.

Tarugi, P. (1928) *Proceedings of the First International Conference on Social Work*, Vol. 1 Paris.

Taylor, C. (1994) The Politics of Recognition, in D.T. Goldberg (ed.) *Multiculturalism: A Reader*, Blackwell, Oxford.

Taylor, D. (1991) A Big Idea for the Nineties? *Critical Social Policy*, 11(3), 87–94.

Taylor, I. et al. (1973) *The New Criminology*, Routledge and Kegan Paul, London.

Taylor, M. (1995) Community Work and the State: The Changing Context of UK Practice, in G. Craig and M. Mayo (eds) *Community Empowerment: A Reader in Participation and Development*, Zed Books.

Taylor, M. (1996) The Future of User Involvement, in Summary of Evidence and Selected Papers for the *Report of the Commission on the Voluntary Sector* (Deakin Report), NCVO, London.

Taylor Gooby, P. (1985) *Public Opinion, Ideology and Welfare Policy*, Routledge and Kegan Paul, London.

Teeple, G. (1995) *Globalisation and the Decline of Social Reform*, Garamond Press, Toronto.

Thomas, M. and Pierson, J. (1995) *Dictionary of Social Work*, Collins Educational, London.

Thompson, N. (1997) Anti-Discriminatory Practice, in M. Davies (ed.) *The Blackwell Companion to Social Work*, Blackwell, Oxford.

Thompson, N. (1998) Social Work with Adults, in R. Adams et al. *Social Work: Themes, Issues and Critical Debates*, Macmillan, London.

Thorpe, D. (1994) *Evaluating Child Protection*, Open University Press, Buckingham.

Thorpe, D. (1997) Regulating Late-modern Child Rearing in Ireland, *Economic and Social Review*, 28, 63–84.

Titmuss, R. (1970) *The Gift Relationship*, Allen and Unwin, London.

Tonge, W.L. (1973) *Families without Hope*, Hedley Bros, Ashford, Kent.

Tonkiss, F. (1998) Civil/Political, in C. Jenks (ed.) *Core Sociological Dichotomies*, Sage, London.

Twelvetrees, A. (1973) *North Braunstone Neighbourhood Project*, FSU, London.

Towle, C. (1939) The Individual in Relation to Social Change, *Social Services Review*, 13(1).

Vaughan, B. (2000) Punishment and Conditional Citizenship, *Punishment and Society*, 2(1), 23–38.

Wadden, A. (1997) *The Politics of Social Welfare*, Edward Elgar, Cheltenham.

Wagner, D. (1990) *The Quest for a Radical Profession*, University Press of America, Lanham.

Walker, A. and Walker, C. (1998) Social Policy and Social Work, in R. Adams, et al. (eds) *Social Work: Themes, Issues and Critical Debates*, Macmillan, London.

Walzer, M. (1983) *Spheres of Justice: A Defence of Pluralism*, Martin Robertson, Oxford.

Waterhouse, L. and McGhee, J. (1998) Social Work with Children and Families, in R. Adams et al. (eds) *Social Work: Themes, Issues and Critical Debates*, Macmillan, London.

Wellington City Council (1999) Consultation Policy, *http://www/wwc/govt.nz.wcc. commissioning/consultation/council.shtml*.

White, V. (1999) Feminist Social Work and the State, in B. Lesnik (ed.), *Social Work and the State*, Pavilion Publishing, Brighton.

Wievel, W. and Gills, D. (1995) Community Development Organisational Capacity and US Urban Policy, in G. Craig and M. Mayo (eds), *Community Empowerment*, Zed Books, London.

Williams, F. (1989) *Social Policy: A Critical Introduction*, Polity, Cambridge.

Williams, R. (1965) *The Long Revolution*, Penguin, Harmondsworth.

Williams, R. (1974) *Proceedings of the 17th International Conference on Social Welfare*, Nairobi.

Wilson, E. (1977) *Women and the Welfare State*, Tavistock, London.

Winerip, M. (1999) Bedlam on the Streets, *New York Times Magazine*, 23 May.

Wistow, G. et al. (1994) *Social Care in a Mixed Economy*, Open University Press, Buckingham.

Wood Report (1929) *Report of the Joint Committee on Mental Deficiency*, HMSO, London.

Woodroofe, K. (1962) *From Charity to Social Work*, Routledge and Kegan Paul, London.

Workfare Watch (1996) Workfare and the Voluntary Section. *http://www.eagle.ca/-nccoa/workfare* watch/wrkvol.htm.

Zavirsek, D. (1999) Civil Society, Memory and Social Work, in B. Lesnik (ed.) *Social Work and the State*, Pavilion Publishing, Brighton.

Index

Urwick, E.J. 37
utilitarianism, and
     individualism 15
utopianism
     and mutualism 46
     socialist 28

values
     classical 6, 93
     humanist 18, 21, 66–8,
          80, 161
     market 16, 18, 68, 93,
          124, 126, 159
Vaughan, B. 163
virtue, civic 4, 6, 16, 67, 95–7,
     118, 123, 127
     and capitalism 73
     and Fabianism 45, 46, 67–8
Voice of the Child in Care
     (UK) 131
voluntary sector
     and Charity Organisation
          Society 32–5
     and civil society 32, 43, 66,
          88, 117–23, 124, 128,
          131, 141
     and community care 19, 20
     and community
          development 111
     and family centres 63
     global 118–19
     and Guild of Help 36
     and holistic approach 61, 63
     and managerialism 19, 24
     and marketisation 159
     in nineteenth century
          25, 36
     and poverty 25, 31–2
     and renaissance of
          voluntarism 123–5
     and the state 46, 50, 88,
          97–8, 121, 123–6, 141
     and therapeutic
          approach 47
     and welfare state 51, 98,
          117–21, 123, 130–1
     and workfare 12
     see also non-governmental
          organisations

Wadden, A. 58
wages
     in political theory
          29, 30, 72–3
     and poverty 36
     and the state 121
Wagner, D. 50
Walker, A. and Walker, C. 104
Walzer, M. 16, 17
War on Poverty (US) 58,
     59, 60, 62
Waterhouse, L. and McGhee, J.
     100–1
wealth
     inequalities 94–5
     redistribution 18, 50, 58, 59
Webb, Beatrice 25, 35,
     43, 45
Webb, Sidney 45
Weber, M. 21
welfare state
     and Beveridge 51
     and civil society 123
     contradictions of 5, 6,
          71, 73, 79
     crisis of 4, 5, 126–7
     and dependency culture
          4, 10, 11, 16, 94, 105
     early 43–4
     effectiveness 54
     Fabian 5, 6, 23, 45,
          51–2, 54, 62
     and gender 150, 152
     and globalisation 4
     McDonaldisation 21
     in Marxist theory 5, 6,
          71–2, 79, 80
     and nationalisation of
          social work 2, 4, 5
     and 'new consensus' 10
     and new Poor Law 17
     and New Right 4, 5, 6, 10,
          24, 58–9, 105
     and political consensus 5, 7,
          58–9
     and postmodernity 4, 9, 10,
          13, 14, 17, 21–2
     reform of 10, 12, 17, 18, 58,
          84, 93, 103

welfare state, *cont.*
     and social citizenship 52–4,
          117–21
     and social control 54–5, 57,
          65, 70–1, 77–8, 93, 106,
          114, 129–31
     and social market 9
     and voluntarism 51, 98,
          117–21, 123, 130–1
     see also reformism
welfare to work *see* workfare
Wells, H.G. 45
White, V. 19, 151–2
Wievel, W. and Gills, D. 50, 111
Williams, F. 74, 150
Wilson, E. 150
Winerip, M. 103
Wistow, G. et al. 139
women
     as carers 66, 150–1
     and economic dependency 70
     in labour market 90
Wood Report (1929) 55
Woodroofe, K. 32–3, 35, 47
workfare 10, 12, 17, 98
workhouse 31, 66
working class
     and nineteenth-century
          social work 26–7
     proletarianisation 7, 9,
          16, 72, 160
     and radical social work 86
     and remoralisation of the
          poor 26, 33–5, 38, 42, 146
     and solidarity 93
     and utility of poverty 29, 79
     and welfare state 47, 53,
          54, 75
working hours, for women 39
World Summit for Social
     Development (1995) 95

xenophobia 143

young offenders, and risk
     management 101–2
Young Offenders (1980) 102
youth workers 61

Zavirsek, D. 27, 129